Uncompromising Integrity:

Motorola's Global Challenge

Uncompromising Integrity:
Motorola's Global Challenge

RS Moorthy, Richard T. De George,
Thomas Donaldson, William J. Ellos, S.J.,
Robert C. Solomon and Robert B. Textor

For catalog and additional copies
of this publication contact:

Motorola University Press
1295 E. Algonquin Road,
Schaumburg, IL 60196.1097
Tel: 847 576 3142
Fax: 847 576 7507

 **MOTOROLA**

Copyright © 1998 by Motorola, Inc.
Second Printing, 1998
Printed in the USA by Universal Press 3/98

ISBN 1-56946-025-6 (cl)
ISBN 1-56946-026-4 (p)

Uncompromising Integrity:

Motorola's Global Challenge

RS Moorthy
Richard T. De George
Thomas Donaldson
William J. Ellos, S.J.
Robert C. Solomon
Robert B. Textor

Foreword by Robert W. Galvin
Afterword by Glenn A. Gienko

Global Leadership and
Organizational Development
Motorola
1998

Dedication

We dedicate this book to

all those countless Motorolans,

living and dead,

sung and unsung,

who through the years

have placed ethical values first

and done the right thing

for the right reasons.

Contents

Foreword

Robert W. Galvin
*Chairman of the Executive
Committee of the Board,
Motorola, Inc.*

Motorola's ethical values and standards are an indispensable
foundation for our work, our relationships and our business success.
Our ethical tradition is an ongoing source of strength. Its sustenance
demands constant commitment and renewal.

We think of renewal, our driving thrust, as key to technology and
competitiveness. Renewal is essential for ethics also; especially as
Motorola expands its operations around the world.

This book will help us to develop our ethical skills by facilitating
dialogue about ethical issues in informal business conversations, in
formal discussions at scheduled meetings, or in stand-alone special
conferences. The carefully prepared cases and commentaries are
excellent stimulators and guides.

Motorola's leadership is committed to ensuring that we live by
Motorola's ethical values throughout the world. You will find this
book useful in achieving that goal.

Schaumburg, Illinois
January 1998

Preface

The Challenge We Face

This book addresses the ethical challenge that Motorola faces as it becomes an important player in the new global economy. For the first four decades of our nearly 70-year-old history, all of our manufacturing facilities were located in the United States. Not until the 1960s did we begin significant manufacturing overseas in Korea, Taiwan and France. Since then we have been growing steadily more global, and in the past several years the pace of our international involvement has accelerated steeply. We now manufacture in more than 20 countries, and market our products in virtually every country in the world. Almost half of our 150,000 employees are now non-American, and more than half of our revenues come from non-American markets — and both of these proportions are likely to grow substantially in years to come. We have indeed become a corporation of global reach.

To be truly effective in our new global context, Motorola employees must be able to relate well with people who have grown up in different host cultures. These people might be fellow Motorolans, or they might be our agents, distributors, suppliers or ultimate consumers.

To relate well with people from other cultures means, among other things, to deal well with them in an **ethical** sense. This in turn means developing an understanding of their ethical standards, which are typically embedded in their home culture. It means

actively and creatively seeking "overlaps," or "common ground," in which local ethical standards and Motorola ethical standards are similar.

An essential part of making sound ethical decisions involves obeying the laws of the United States and the host country, as well as adhering to the Motorola Code of Conduct (Appendix One). However, as important as these laws and this code are, they do not cover the entire range of ethical behavior. For example, lying is usually unethical, but it cannot be fully covered by any law or code. We must often supplement our obedience by determining to follow the ethical path rather than the unethical, even when these laws and codes would allow us to do either. We must, in short, be value-driven rather than compliance-driven.

Being value-driven means that we must look not only to laws, but also to the ethical values and standards of the Motorola Culture — as partially stated on the wallet-sized "Total Customer Satisfaction" Card that all Motorolans are encouraged to carry. For example, in the matter of lying, a Motorolan can refer to the TCS Card's Key Belief in Uncompromising Integrity.

But even the TCS Card lists only a part of the total range of ethical values and standards found in the Motorola Culture. Most Motorola employees can think of other standards that are part of the Motorola tradition, even though they have never been listed on the TCS Card. The Motorola value of "good corporate citizenship," for example, is not listed on the Card, but is certainly well established in the corporate culture.

The Motorola Culture is similar to all cultures in that it is partly codified and partly implicit. The mere fact that a standard is implicit does not mean that it is unimportant. Sometimes it can provide as much guidance for ethical behavior as explicit standards can.

Every organization has "tacit knowledge" about such implicit matters. One of this book's goals is to share key elements of our tacit knowledge — both successes and failures — explicitly and widely within the corporation, as part of a knowledge management and cyclical learning process that will move us all continuously toward being more value-driven. A learning corporation must courageously face up to this task. As Bob Galvin once said to me, "We must not be embarrassed by embarrassment."

Even assuming that we have a good understanding of both the explicit and implicit ethical values of our corporate culture, however, there still remains a vital question: How are we to remain faithful to Motorola's core ethical values, while at the same time respecting the values of the host cultures where we manufacture and market our products?

This book is intended to help answer this question, by raising and discussing typical ethical issues that Motorolans face in the global business context. While the book does not and should not attempt to provide "correct" Motorola responses to the issues, it does attempt to stimulate independent, rigorous and creative thinking about them.

The Genesis of This Book

In 1994, the President of Motorola University, A. William Wiggenhorn, asked MU's Center for Culture and Technology to prepare a set of case studies for discussion by senior Human Resources officers during their meeting in Yokohama. The cases were all transcultural and each presented an ethical dilemma from real life. The participants at Yokohama found the discussions stimulating, learned a great deal about how much they had in common, and learned where some possible differences lay. They became more aware of the need for **clarity** in stating Motorola's core ethical values, and for **skill** in applying these values to complex and challenging new global business situations.

From the Yokohama experience arose many questions as to how we can better integrate our core ethical values into our everyday operations, and how we can transmit these values effectively to all members of the Motorola family. How, in short, do we achieve a "Six Sigma" level of excellence in ethical behavior?

I believe that part of the answer lies in systematic education and training in ethical decision-making. As a follow-up to Yokohama, I assembled a team of five outstanding consultants to work with me as a highly participatory team, to produce this book. Four of the five are philosophers of ethics who have devoted serious attention to global business ethics: De George,

Donaldson, Ellos and Solomon. The fifth, Textor (who worked with me on case development and accepted responsibility for providing day-to-day editorial coordination), is a cultural anthropologist who has done intensive fieldwork in a variety of cultures and has consulted extensively for Motorola University.

The Scope of This Book

This book is organized as follows:

Chapter One, Introduction, presents the core ethical values of the Motorola Culture and puts them into historical perspective.

Chapter Two, Approaches from the Cultural Sciences, presents key cultural approaches used by anthropologists and other cultural scientists, which I believe will help Motorolans think in cultural terms as they make ethical decisions in transcultural situations.

Chapter Three, Approaches from the Field of Ethics, introduces key ethical approaches used by professional ethicists. Some are recent, others trace back to Plato and Aristotle. These approaches provide practical guidelines that Motorolans can use, singly or in combination, in making sound and effective ethical decisions.

Chapter Four, Twenty-Four Cases with Commentaries, provides a wide variety of cases illustrative of the ethical problems that Motorolans might encounter in the global economy. Discussion about these cases will help clarify ethical issues. Each case is based on actual experience — either that of a Motorolan, or that of someone in a similar company of which a Motorolan had knowledge.

Each case is followed by **"discussion questions,"** which I urge you to answer for yourself, independently, before reading the two expert **commentaries** that follow that case. Each commentary is written by one of the four ethicists on our team of coauthors. They discuss the particular issues of the case, the broader concerns that it raises, and the possible actions or policy decisions that it suggests. You can compare these opinions with your own answers to the discussion questions.

Chapter Five, Key Conclusions, offers seven key conclusions to help you integrate and use the ideas in this book.

Recommended Readings in Business Ethics are next provided for readers who wish to do further study.

Appendix One reproduces the full text of the Motorola Code of Conduct.

Appendix Two provides excerpts from Motorola/Japan's policy on the giving and receiving of gifts as an example of ethics in action.

Appendix Three, finally, provides a preliminary case guide to help the facilitator or instructor choose which cases to assign to a particular learning group.

All together, the book forms a mini-course in transcultural approaches to business ethics. Readers or facilitators can build on this basis, deepening their investigations into techniques of ethical analysis, or developing additional cases for discussion by Motorolans working in different locations or functions.

How to Use This Book

This book is designed to be useful both to:

- the individual reader who simply wishes to learn more about the subject; and

- the facilitator of, or participant in, an organized seminar on ethics.

Use by the Individual Reader

If you are an individual reader, I recommend that you read the chapters in order. When you get to Chapter Four, I recommend that you first answer the discussion questions that follow each case, using your **independent** judgment. After this, you will find it helpful to compare your judgment with that of the commentators.

Use by Seminars

If you are a facilitator preparing for a seminar, I recommend the following steps:

1. Read all the chapters of the book.

2. Using Appendix Three as a preliminary guide, select cases to assign to the seminar's participants on the basis of what you know about their interests and needs. Each case is independent; none is prerequisite to any other case.

3. Decide whether to assign the entire book as an advance reading assignment, or whether to distribute copies of the selected cases and discussion questions in advance.

4. Participants should leave the seminar with their own copy of the book for further reference and study.

The six coauthors wish to emphasize that this book is designed to stimulate, not pontificate. There is no "official" Motorola solution to the cases in this book, nor does Motorola necessarily endorse the position taken by any of the commentators. This book is not intended to be the last word on any issue. Its purpose is to start dialogue, not end it.

As far as I know, this book is the first ever written, based on numerous cases, each with expert commentaries, that examines issues of ethical decision making in an explicitly **transcultural** business context. I welcome reactions, criticism and advice from Motorolans, ethicists and other readers of varying cultural and professional backgrounds.

RS Moorthy
Internet: aahr15@email.mot.com
Schaumburg, Illinois
January 1998

Disclaimer

The 24 cases appearing in Chapter Four of this book are based on ethical issues that have been experienced by Motorola employees, or those of similar companies, in real transcultural interaction situations. To protect the privacy of individuals and organizations presented in these cases, we have given them fictional names and identities, and also fictionalized many locations, products, etc. The first time a new fictional name is used, it appears in *italics* to emphasize its fictional nature. Any resemblance of these fictionalized identities to real persons, organizations or products is totally unintended and purely coincidental.

The 24 cases involve various actions of which Motorola disapproves. The cases do not at all imply that Motorolans, typically or in any numbers, actually act in these ways. The contrary is true.

Fictionalization also makes possible the sharpening of ethical issues, and for this purpose some of the ethical infractions in the cases have been magnified beyond what actually occurred.

This wide array of cases is presented to stimulate awareness of ethical issues, and dialogue about them, on the part of Motorola employees, and also on the part of interested readers and business people around the world.

Acknowledgments

We six coauthors wish to thank the following people who helped us produce this book.

To begin with, we owe a crucial debt to A. William Wiggenhorn, senior vice president, Training and Education, and president of Motorola University, for first conceiving of this project, and providing vision and leadership for our efforts. Our project was then further supported by Ken Hansen, vice president and assistant director of Motorola University.

In addition, we would like to thank Robert W. Galvin, chairman of the Executive Committee of the Motorola Board, and Glenn A. Gienko, executive vice president and Motorola director, Human Resources. Like Mr. Wiggenhorn, both of these Motorola leaders critiqued the manuscript for this book. In addition, they contributed the Foreword and Afterword, respectively.

Our gratitude goes also to Patrick Canavan, senior vice president and director of Global Leadership and Organizational Development, for acting as a sounding board for many of our ideas and giving us numerous wise insights.

A number of other Motorolans also critiqued all or part of this book in manuscript, and we thank them: Nick Azelborn, Carolyn Blauw, Jean Canavan, Tajuddin Carrim, Chan Lai Ngoh, Malcolm Fraser, Don Jerome, Ameet Kotak and Oscar Rebollo.

We also thank Dr. Charles Hampden-Turner, permanent visitor at the Judge Institute of Management Studies, University of Cambridge, England, for his critique. We are also grateful to Steve Priest, president of the Ethical Leadership Group, for his very valuable input.

We are indebted to the following from the Corporate Law Department for checking the manuscript from a legal perspective: A. Peter Lawson, Richard H. Whited and Janice A. Solarz.

We also thank Ruksana Shibly and Stephanie Gordon of Motorola University, who provided numerous administrative support services. We are also indebted to Janice Matsumoto for her editorial services.

Our thanks go also to the participants in several Motorola Ethics Renewal Process working sessions, held during 1997 — in Mexico City, Sao Paulo, Moscow, Beijing, Caracas, Bogota, Dubai, Singapore, Toronto and Athens — for their input on various cases presented in this book.

Last but far from least, we thank those Motorola employees from across the globe who kindly granted us the confidential interviews on which are based the cases presented in Chapter Four, "Twenty-Four Cases with Commentaries." We regret that we cannot acknowledge them by name, because permanent anonymity was one of the conditions of the interview, so that each of them would feel free to speak with complete frankness. Their anonymity in no way diminishes our gratitude.

We thank all these people sincerely. We, not they, are responsible for any errors or shortcomings in this book.

Chapter One:
Introduction

This chapter summarizes the ethical history of Motorola, and stresses the importance of the concept of culture in understanding how to make sound and effective ethical decisions.

The purpose of this book is to help professionals at Motorola and other companies make sound and effective ethical decisions in situations where the persons or organizations involved are from more than one culture. A "sound and effective" ethical decision is one that is well-reasoned and that stands the test of time.

The Ethical Values of the Motorola Culture

From its beginnings under the leadership of Paul Galvin, Motorola has been concerned about behaving ethically. Three historical examples will illustrate:

• In the corporation's early struggling years, there were times when Paul Galvin nearly went broke to ensure that his regular employees were kept on the payroll.

• Paul and Bob Galvin displayed a steadfast respect for female Motorolans, and protected them against harassment and danger of all sorts — decades before public opinion and legislation made such protection more common.

• During the 1950s Motorola had an opportunity to secure a multimillion dollar contract with a certain South American government. This contract would have been exceptionally profitable because all of the fixed costs for that year had been absorbed. Even so, the operating executives of the relevant division refused the contract, because the officials offering it had structured it in a way that suggested a kickback. The Galvins, Paul and Bob, applauded their associates' action. They also decided that Motorola would not do any business at all with the regime then in control of that government because of its widely known corruption. For Motorola to have done so could have created the **appearance** of participating in corruption.

Other examples could be cited, such as Motorola's strong policies on environmental protection, and on affirmative action for racial and gender equity. From the very founding of the corporation, ethical behavior and management by high principles have been an integral part of the corporation's private image, which has promoted high employee morale — and also an integral part of the corporation's public image, leading to public trust, and unquestionably contributing to Motorola's remarkable business success through the years.

During the 1980s the corporate leadership decided to clarify the key values of the Motorola Culture in the form of a "Total Customer Satisfaction" (TCS) Card. This Card — which employees can carry in their wallets — states the following:

Our Fundamental Objective

(Everyone's Overriding Responsibility)

Total Customer Satisfaction

Key Beliefs — How we will always act

- Constant Respect for People
- Uncompromising Integrity

Key Goals — What we must accomplish

- Best in Class
  People
  Marketing
  Technology
  Product: Software, Hardware and Systems
  Manufacturing
  Service
- Increased Global Market Share
- Superior Financial Results

Key Initiatives — How we will do it

- Six Sigma Quality
- Total Cycle Time Reduction
- Product, Manufacturing and Environmental Leadership
- Profit Improvement
- Empowerment for all, in a Participative, Cooperative and Creative Workplace

Two of the above items have special bearing on a discussion of ethics: Constant Respect for People, and Uncompromising Integrity. Throughout the book we will give close attention to these two Key Beliefs, and to the ways in which adherence to one impacts adherence to the other.

During a briefing session with the authors of this book, Bob Galvin observed that all ethics — including these two Key Beliefs — are grounded in what Westerners call the "Golden Rule": "Do unto others as you would have them do unto you." This understanding of the Golden Rule focuses on the respect that is due each individual, and suggests that the corporation does not use people solely for its own ends, but rather encourages them to live and work with integrity in an environment of mutual respect and trust.

The Motorola Culture's Midwestern American Roots

Motorola's founder, Paul Galvin, was brought up in the small town of Harvard, Illinois. In a broad way, Motorola's ethical values of today stem from this small-town Midwestern culture of the early 20th century.

At the same time, the Motorola Culture is **not** just a simple mirror image of that earlier Midwestern culture. Its priorities are more focused. While small-town Midwestern culture emphasized integrity and respect for people, the Motorola Culture emphasizes **uncompromising** integrity and **constant** respect for people.

No doubt other small-town Midwestern businesses also emphasized the **value** of integrity and respect for people, but Motorola sets unusually high **standards** for measuring and fulfilling these values. The twin values receive such a high priority that they will be honored even at the risk of sacrificing other, primarily non-ethical values, such as the Key Initiative of Profit Improvement.

The term "value" refers to a person's concept of the desirable, and the term "standard" refers to the person's:

• actual mode of **expression** of that value; or

• mode of **assessment** of whether he has lived up to that value.

This distinction is important. It is only when one looks at actual standards — at what an individual or group is prepared to **sacrifice** in order to uphold a value — that true insight can be gained into the depth of that value.

The Motorola Culture in Its New Global Context

One of Motorola's first products was automobile radios made for American consumers. Although many of the corporation's early employees were of Irish, Polish or Italian descent, they all shared a common American cultural membership. Thus, in the early days, the key ethical values and standards of the Motorola Culture were readily understood by everyone involved: shareholders, employees and customers.

Today the situation is far more complex. Motorola has moved from a U.S. to a global context — and from the production of automobile radios for the domestic market, to the provision of a wide variety of products and services for the entire world, in such areas as wireless communications, semiconductors, advanced electronic systems and components. Through the decades, a small Illinois corporation has evolved into a world player, with 150,000 employees, manufacturing facilities in more than 20 countries, and marketing efforts in every corner of the earth. This growth has been so dramatic that by the early 1990s, almost half of the corporation's employees were non-American in their cultural backgrounds, and more than half its revenue came from markets outside the United States.

All of this means that today Motorola faces new **cultural** challenges. Its workforce hails from more than 50 different home cultures and languages, and hundreds of **sub**cultures based on region, dialect, gender, social class, wealth, education, occupation, religion or age-group. A Motorolan will often be from one culture or subculture and his subordinate from another. They might be in electronic interaction with a third, 5,000 miles away, from yet a different culture. Similar gaps will often exist between salespersons and consumers, especially since Motorola is increasingly becoming a producer of consumer goods. This new situation demands that Motorolans understand the unique attributes of particular host cultures around the world.

Further compounding the challenge is the rapidity with which this new cultural complexity has developed:

• In the past five years the corporation has hired about 50,000 new employees.

• The corporation is rapidly developing its managerial talent pool in emerging markets by training and promoting citizens of host countries where Motorola ethical values might not be well understood.

• To manage this growing business, the corporation has been hiring many new employees from other companies, with corporate cultures that might be different from Motorola's.

• Senior Motorolans of various nationalities, deeply familiar with the corporation's ethics, are retiring and no longer available to serve as role models.

These new complexities raise questions of policy and practice:

• How can Motorola translate its ethical values into repeatable business practices around the world?

• How can the corporation convey to new employees, quickly and effectively, the key ethical values of the Motorola Culture — so that they will accept these values and live by them in appropriate situations?

It is worth noting that the Total Customer Satisfaction Card has already been translated into some 20 languages, a useful first step in communicating the content of Motorola's key values. However, it is just a beginning. The greater need is to develop a deeper understanding of what Motorola's ethical values **mean** in various countries — to its employees, of course, but also to its customers, distributors, suppliers and the local general public.

Good Ethics Will Always Be Good Business

As Motorola becomes more global, it faces the challenge of adhering to its cardinal belief that good ethical behavior is also good business behavior. Pursuing this belief is not always easy, but it is always worth the effort. Motorola can take some comfort in the old maxim that ethics are their own reward. And it can take additional comfort in the notion that ethics can provide major **practical** competitive advantages in the global marketplace. In our view, these practical advantages include the following:

- Ethics can help keep employee **morale** high. Working for an ethical corporation produces a feeling of pride among its employees. An atmosphere of integrity in both management and the workplace helps make work satisfying.

- Ethics allow a corporation to grant **dignity,** empowerment and responsibility to all its employees.

- Ethics inspire mutual **trust.** They make it possible for a corporation to encourage and empower its employees to make sound decisions in the interest of the customer and the corporation.

- Ethics encourage **honesty** of communication, and allow all employees to raise and discuss issues with all other employees regardless of level. The right questions can be raised, and the right criticisms can be responded to in a constructive manner.

- Ethics help in handling **crises.** Well-grounded and -integrated ethics allow a corporation to respond effectively when its ethical standards are suddenly challenged, or when an unexpected crisis strikes. Those who live ethically on a continuous basis can respond ethically in times of stress and crisis.

- Ethics help a corporation gain a favorable **reputation.** This makes it attractive to employees, who know it will treat them with dignity and respect; to consumers, who know it will stand behind its products; to suppliers, who know it will honor its commitments; to potential partners, who know it can keep transaction costs low; and to the investing public, who know it will treat them honestly.

Merely following the letter of the law is not enough. Ethics extend far beyond legality. In some instances, such as the former apartheid laws in South Africa, the law might even command people to do what is **unethical.** But even in the vast majority of situations where this is not the case, the law cannot be the only guide to conduct. Not everything that is unethical can be criminalized. Lying, for example, is unethical, but clearly not all instances of lying can or should be criminalized.

Another limitation of the law is that it frequently lags behind what people know to be right. Knowingly disposing of toxic wastes into public water sources was unethical before it became illegal. An ethical corporation will do what is right, even when not required to do so by any law. For example, Motorola is committed to eradicating chlorofluorocarbons at its facilities worldwide, although this action is not always mandated by local law.

Motorola's Willingness to Learn from Other Cultures

So far this discussion has proceeded from a "Motorola-centric" point of view, as though employees were asking:

"How can **we** apply **our** ethical values and remain faithful to our Key Beliefs in different host cultures around the world?"

There is a second important question as well:

"As a learning organization, how can we learn from the various host cultures with which we engage, and weave the best of what we learn into our corporation's culture to make it more robust and socially useful in the new global context?"

Since no culture has a monopoly on wisdom, this second question will yield valuable answers. To illustrate, consider the fact that some host cultures where Motorola operates possess strong group-oriented ethical and social values that result in high levels of employee morale and productivity. Would it not be prudent for Motorola to be open to learning from these other cultures, and to incorporating certain elements of their patterns into the global Motorola Culture?

Such openness does exist. The corporation's "Total Customer Satisfaction" competition, held annually among teams of Motorola employees from throughout the world, is the result of borrowing from Japanese practice. This competition has demonstrated its value from a business standpoint and is now an established part of the global Motorola Culture.

The Motorola Ethics Renewal Process

The rapid expansion and cultural diversification of Motorola businesses worldwide has led to the initiation of the Motorola Ethics Renewal Process. This process seeks:

• to help Motorolans throughout the world to examine and renew their commitment to Motorola ethics;

• to empower local employees to take responsibility and be accountable for ethical issues, by such means as participating in local or regional committees for this purpose;

• to educate and train all new employees in the content of relevant U.S. and local laws, and of Motorola ethical values and standards; and

• to enskill new and old employees, especially managers, in making sound and effective ethical decisions in particular cultural settings.

This book is aimed at supporting the Motorola Ethics Renewal Process.

Chapter Two:
Approaches from the
Cultural Sciences

This chapter discusses the relationship between ethics and culture. We describe how the values and standards of the Motorola Culture overlap to varying degrees with the values and standards of a given host culture, and stress the importance of actively seeking such overlaps. Motorola can express and validate its core ethical values in those host cultures by a number of processes, as well as remain open to learning and benefiting from contact with those cultures. Finally, ways in which the Motorola Culture can impact the local host culture are discussed.

In the previous chapter, the term "culture" appeared in virtually every paragraph. This was no accident. It would be impossible to discuss global issues of business ethics without reference to this crucial concept, for three key reasons:

- All humans are cultural beings, and every human belongs to at least one of the world's thousands of cultures.

- Every culture includes a distinctive set of ethical values and standards.

- To even begin to understand the ethical values and standards of a person who has grown up in another culture, one must understand something of his or her cultural background.

A person's membership in a given culture or subculture is not the only factor shaping his or her ethical standards. Other factors include: personal, educational, situational, historical and "accidental" elements. Nonetheless, the concept of culture is crucial to understanding the subject of this book. This chapter will explain several concepts from the cultural sciences as they are used in the chapters that follow.

Definition of "A Culture"

Social scientists, anthropologists, historians and interculturalists have produced hundreds of definitions of "a culture," but the following general definition will serve our present purpose:

> A culture is a learned, shared and intergenerationally transmitted set of more or less stable, consistent and patterned values and standards of and for behavior, characteristic of a particular population, which standards usually affect actual behavior.

Concepts Related to Culture

In addition to the master concept of culture, there are several related concepts that require brief introduction:

- Home culture
- National culture
- Motorola Culture
- Subculture
- Enculturation•
- Transcultural
- Host culture

Throughout this book, two basic types of culture are often referred to: the **"home"** culture and the **"Motorola Culture."** A "home" culture is the culture in which one is brought up from childhood. One is **"enculturated"** into one's home culture — meaning that one internalizes its values and is guided by its standards.

The Motorola Culture is the "organizational culture" of Motorola worldwide. A given Motorolan, whether Russian, Brazilian, Japanese or American, is obligated to follow the relevant ethical standards of the Motorola Culture while on the job.

A home culture is often the same as a **"national"** culture — but not always. Switzerland has German, French, Italian and Romansh home cultures, each with its own language — in addition to an overarching national Swiss culture. Malaysia has Malay, Chinese, Indian and other home cultures — in addition to an overarching national Malaysian culture.

A **"host"** culture is that of the host society or community within which a given Motorola unit manufactures, markets or otherwise operates. Thus, the host culture of Motorola/Sendai is the Japanese culture, or the home culture of the Japanese people. The host culture of Motorola/Tel Aviv is Israeli in one sense, but might additionally be German, Russian, American, Polish, Moroccan or Ethiopian, reflecting the multicultural origins of the population of Israel.

There will also usually be a number of distinct host **"subcultures."** A Brazilian Motorolan assigned to Motorola/Dublin might find himself dealing not just with the general Irish home culture, but also with an "Irish business subculture." The Brazilian will probably find that an Irish colleague's or customer's behavior will be understandable partly in terms of the Irish home culture, but also partly in terms of the Irish business subculture.

Finally, when an individual or group communicates, cooperates, competes, manages, leads or otherwise interacts with an individual or group from another culture, we refer to this as **"transcultural"** interaction.

Finding Ethical Overlaps Between Cultures

So far our presentation has emphasized **differences** between cultures. This is appropriate, but must not deflect attention from the fact that there are also many similarities or "overlaps" between the ethical systems of any two cultures. Generally speaking, the greater the amount of ethical overlap, the fewer the difficulties that will arise in transcultural dealings.

These overlaps can occur in varying degrees:

• To begin with, there are many ethical standards that are universal or nearly so. For example, there is no culture where it is considered ethical to take the life of a member of one's society arbitrarily. Similarly, in matters such as theft and various types of violent crime, the overlap is almost total; few, if any, of the world's cultures regard such crimes as ethical.

• There are other ethical standards that might not be found in all cultures, but are nearly universal among the world's more industrially developed cultures where Motorola is most deeply involved. For example, these cultures generally have instituted extensive government programs to assist unemployed workers.

• Beyond this, there are numerous, less obvious overlaps between cultures. Where these overlaps are substantial, transcultural ethical decisions pose few difficulties, but where they are minimal, problems might arise. For example, some host cultures where Motorola operates implicitly favor limiting female employees to subordinate positions, regardless of their ability.

A key theme throughout this book is that as business professionals make decisions in their interactions with people from other cultural backgrounds, they should be encouraged to seek these ethical overlaps. Those who can find and creatively utilize such overlaps will be adding value to their company and to society at large.

Ethics, Culture and the Individual

Although a person may have been enculturated in a given home culture, other factors are also involved in determining his personal standards for ethical decision making. The late Dr. Martin Luther King, Jr. was enculturated in the American South, but deliberately undertook a study of the nonviolent values of the Indian tradition as articulated by Mahatma Ghandi. He incorporated some of those values into the African-American civil rights movement he led in the 1960s. The results were historic.

Transcultural learning and sharing can also occur inside a company. A Motorolan from one home culture assigned to a facility in a different host culture will often develop many ideas and values through contact with that culture. And persons who join Motorola, from whatever home culture, might develop new ethical perspectives through their contact with the corporate culture itself. We will return to this important phenomenon on page 25.

The Special Nature of the Motorola Culture

The Motorola Culture, like any corporate culture, is best regarded as a "quasi"-culture because its impact on the individual is more limited than that of a home culture on several dimensions, including the following:

- **Scope of guidance offered:** First of all, a home culture provides guidance to its members for making decisions in virtually every aspect of life, from food tastes to humor, from courtship to kinship, from the after-life to ethics. By contrast, the Motorola Culture provides members with guidance for a more limited, and largely job-related, range of decisions. The guidance that a home culture provides to its members applies throughout each day of the members' lives. By contrast, the guidance that the Motorola Culture provides applies largely to the working hours of the day.

- **Point in life at which cultural membership begins:** An individual begins to learn and internalize the content of his home culture virtually from the day of birth — typically through interacting with members of a senior generation, such as parents, grandparents or teachers. By contrast, a Motorola employee typically begins to learn the content of the corporate culture as an adult, on her first day of employment — mainly through interacting with Motorolans who are senior to her in service, though not necessarily in age.

Some Motorolans, however, will know about the company culture long before their first day of employment. These are the second- and subsequent-generation Motorolans, who have learned about Motorola as children, "at the dinner table," from their parents or relatives. There are thousands of these second- and subsequent-generation employees, due to a corporate policy that encourages a "family" approach to recruitment. In this respect, Motorola is unusual among large multinational companies — a fact that has powerful implications for the long-run stability of the Motorola Culture.

- **Point in life at which cultural membership ceases:** In general, an individual's membership in his home culture is lifelong. One is born a Japanese, grows up a Japanese, lives one's life as a Japanese, and dies a Japanese. Consider Watanabe Taro, a Japanese Motorolan who leaves his job at Motorola/Sendai and moves to Australia. Although Watanabe will make various adjustments to his new Australian surroundings, he will essentially "remain Japanese." He will tend to speak Japanese whenever possible, view the world through Japanese perceptual lenses, and make decisions according to Japanese cultural standards. By contrast, Watanabe's adherence to Motorola Culture standards could end on the day of his termination. After leaving the company, he has no legal or social obligation to continue to abide by Motorola values.

On the other hand, it is also possible that Watanabe will have internalized Motorola standards to the point where, in certain situations, he will feel a **personal** obligation and preference to continue to follow them more closely than the corresponding standards of the Japanese business subculture. For instance, Watanabe might have had positive experiences with Motorola's Key Initiative of "Empowerment for All, in a Participative, Cooperative and Creative Workplace." In his subsequent jobs he might insist on more emphasis upon empowerment and creativity than is found in a typical Japanese company.

How the Motorola Culture Changes Through Time

All cultures change, even those that appear very stable to the outsider. They might change rapidly in some aspects, such as technology, but slowly in others, such as religious belief or ethical values.

Changes occur differently in a large national home culture than in the Motorola Culture. A home culture, being much broader and more complex, does not ordinarily change because one or a few persons decide that it should — except in rare historical instances, such as those of Napoleon Bonaparte with his "Code Napoleon" for France; or Mustapha Kemal Ataturk with his modernization edicts for Turkey. Usually, changes in home cultures are the result of highly complex forces: demographic, ecological, political, economic, social, media and religious — and involve decisions by thousands or millions of people.

The beginnings of change are often signaled by the emergence of a new subculture. Sooner or later, some of these subcultures will impact the overall culture. For example, in the United States:

• The "civil rights" subculture has helped cause many more American companies to practice effective affirmative action than was true 40 years ago.

• The subculture of people who were once ridiculed as "computer nerds" has produced new ways of using information that have now been adopted by the general U.S. populace.

Corporate cultures, by contrast, are more easily changed by a small group of leaders, often quite quickly. Motorola's "Total Customer Satisfaction" Card is revised occasionally, reflecting adjustments that the leadership believes should be in place. Thus, in August 1992, the Card was updated to include the new Key Initiative of "Empowerment for All, in a Participative, Cooperative and Creative Workplace."

The process for adding a new standard to the Card appears to consist of these steps:

• The leadership obtains data and input from many parts of the corporation.

• They develop the belief that adding this explicit new standard would be a wise and ethical thing to do.

• They note that many Motorolans are already behaving more or less in accordance with this standard.

• They are confident that if the standard were spelled out on the Card, it would be backed by key corporate leaders.

• They judge that the explicit listing of this standard would strengthen this behavior throughout Motorola worldwide.

In short, changes in the Motorola Culture can, to a considerable extent, be "managed." Indeed, without support from corporate and business leadership, important adaptive changes in the Motorola Culture are much less likely to occur.

Up to this point, it may seem as if Motorola were managed by leaders who steer changes in the corporation's culture exclusively according to Anglo-American values. In fact, a certain percentage of the corporation's top leadership come from non-American home cultures. This percentage will almost certainly increase through time. These non-American leaders bring to Motorola important values from their own home cultural backgrounds, plus useful ideas from their previous work experiences. In this way, the Motorola Culture has been, and will continue to be, enriched by the presence of highly talented leaders from both the United States and elsewhere.

Modes of Handling Ethical Issues Transculturally

There are numerous modes that Motorola might use in handling ethical issues transculturally, of which we will here briefly introduce four:

- Value Clarification Without Adjustment

- Value Expression Adjusted to Local Standards

- Deeper Substantive Adjustment

- Global Reconciliation

These four modes are arranged in order of increasing complexity. The first two apply principally to dealings with non-Motorolans in the host country, and the second two to dealings with host country Motorolans.

Value Clarification Without Adjustment

The simplest mode is one in which Motorola makes no particular effort to adjust to the local culture, but merely clarifies its policy on a given issue, and implements that policy regardless of whether it overlaps with the values or standards of the host culture. For example, Motorola adheres to the value of Uncompromising Integrity, and expresses this through the standard of refusing to pay or accept bribes. The standard is essentially the same whether Motorola is operating in Chicago, Moscow, Seoul or Sao Paulo. The Total Customer Satisfaction Card and Code of Conduct clearly state that no Motorolan may participate in bribery, or give the appearance of doing so.

In some situations, the overlap between Motorola's standards and certain practices of the host culture might be so limited that the corporation has no choice other than simply to abide by its own standards and attempt to remain viable in that country.

Value Expression Adjusted to Local Standards

Simple clarification shades into this second mode of handling ethical issues, in which Motorola remains essentially true to its core ethical values, but at the same time expresses those values in ways that take into account the standards and sensitivities of the host culture. This adjustment might be strictly symbolic, or might also involve limited amounts of money or items of monetary value.

An excellent example is provided by Nippon Motorola Ltd. (NML), which has squarely faced the fact that gift-giving and -receiving have been deeply imbedded in Japanese culture since long before the advent of modern industry there. Most large Japanese companies traditionally engage in extensive gift giving to organizations or individuals whose goodwill they seek — government officials, company policy makers, purchasing agents, etc. They give some of these gifts on an annual seasonal basis, and others in special situations where congratulations or consolations are culturally appropriate.

It is clear that NML judges this general Japanese tradition as inconsistent with Motorola's Key Belief in Uncompromising Integrity. However, NML **does** make certain carefully limited adjustments to this tradition, and specifies them with admirable thoroughness, as illustrated by the following abridged excerpt from the NML policy on gifts as of this writing. (For an expanded version, see Appendix Two.)

NML-Special Exemptions
The following special exemptions to the Motorola Code of Conduct are provided to NML to accord with Japanese custom:

1. Two gift seasons
In lieu of seasonal gifts (*O-seibo* and *O-chugen*) [the two main annual gift seasons], NML will make an appropriate gift to charity on behalf of our customers [rather than to a customer company itself, or one of its agents].

2. Gifts from vendors
Receiving gifts from vendors or business associates is not permitted, unless to refuse or return the gift would disrupt the business relationship, and provided that the gift, if accepted, is used for the benefit of the corporation and not the individual. In principle, all gifts should be returned to the sender with a copy of Form Letter A [politely informing the giver that the gift is being returned], signed by the recipient. In exceptional cases when the gift must be accepted, the recipient should send a copy of Form Letter B [politely requesting that the giver refrain from such giving in the future].

3. [Gifts of minimal value]
Giving gifts of minimal value, preferably Motorola promotional items, as part of an entertainment expense is normally acceptable on the condition that the entire transaction has been preapproved by the general manager in charge.

Deeper Substantive Adjustment

The above mode merges into a third mode of handling ethical issues transculturally. This third mode is more likely to involve Motorola's own local employees, rather than local non-Motorolans. For example, in the Motorola Culture there is a tradition of rewarding outstanding performance with annual bonuses to **individual** employees. This reflects a basic value placed by Anglo-American culture upon the individual and his performance. One Motorola facility in Malaysia, however, suggested that funds available for annual productivity bonuses be used to reward **teams** of employees. This reflects the less individualistic, more group-oriented Malaysian value system.

The manager of the Malaysian facility was a Malaysian who recommended firmly against the individual reward approach, saying that Malaysian employees cared more deeply about steady annual raises at least sufficient to keep up with inflation, and about life-long job security.

In this case there was clearly an overlap between the Motorola and Malaysian cultures, in that both shared the broad value that deserving employees should be rewarded. What was **not** shared, though, were the **standards** for implementing that value. A real non-overlap became clear between:

- The Anglo-American individualist approach, which carries with it the implied fear that if rewards are distributed by team, some marginally contributing team members will receive unfairly high rewards; and

- The Malaysian group approach, which carries with it the implied fear that if rewards are distributed by individual, unjustified distinctions will be made.

Proponents of both approaches would argue that unless theirs was followed, employee performance would suffer. And they would probably both be right — each with respect to a particular culture. The performance of American Motorolans might indeed suffer if the group approach were used at an American facility; and likewise the performance of Malaysian Motorolans might suffer if the individualist approach were used at a Malaysian facility.

However, the key point here is the obvious one that the Malaysian manager was recommending the group approach for **Malaysians**, not Americans — and in the end the corporation decided to allow the group approach to be used for that facility. In making this decision, the Motorola leadership was to some extent yielding on value grounds — but **only** with respect to compensation for Malaysians, not for Motorolans worldwide.

This case also illustrates how trade-off adjustments are sometimes necessary between the two basic Motorola values of Uncompromising Integrity and Constant Respect for People:

- In the eyes of many Anglo-American Motorolans, individual bonuses reinforce Uncompromising Integrity in the sense that they are intended to reward the contribution of each Motorolan with exact **fairness.** This position assumes that individual contributions can be precisely measured — which some would say is impossible in many situations.

• In the eyes of many Malaysian Motorolans, by contrast, group bonuses reinforce Constant Respect for People because such bonuses reward Malaysian Motorolans the way **they** prefer to be rewarded. A Malaysian might feel strongly that true "respect" for a person or group implies that Motorola should, within limits, respect the (culturally shaped) **preferences** of that person or group.

Global Reconciliation

The fourth mode is the most complex because it involves actual or potential changes in values and standards for the worldwide Motorola Culture as a whole. To illustrate, let us hypothetically carry the above Malaysian example further, to the point where Malaysian cultural input impacts not only Motorola/ Malaysia, but the entire global Motorola Culture. Imagine the following scenario:

• The Motorola leadership embarks on a careful consideration of its ethical values with respect to bonuses.

• This leadership consists of Motorolans from a variety of home cultures.

• The leadership decides to authorize limited pilot projects in the direction of group bonuses.

• The leadership makes it known at selected facilities worldwide that it is amenable to such pilot projects **if** employees and managers at a given facility show an informed desire for it.

• Several facilities express such a desire.

• The pilot projects are then carried out for expressly limited periods of time, and their effects on morale and productivity are carefully monitored.

In this hypothetical example, quite possibly a broad process would ensue over time in which the global Motorola Culture would change in the direction of allowing group-oriented incentives under certain conditions. If this were to occur, it would constitute a genuine reconciliation between the individualist values typical of the current Motorola Culture, and the group-oriented values typical of the Malaysian and certain other cultures.

We here take no position on the rightness or wrongness of this hypothetical scenario. However, we do believe that simply being **receptive** to suggestions from local Motorola managers and employees could be a key factor in the corporation's future evolution as a successful, pace-setting global organization.

The Motorola Culture's Possible Impact on a Host Culture

Our presentation has so far focused mainly on transcultural interaction in which the Motorola Culture **adapts** to a host culture. But could this also be a two-way street, in which the Motorola Culture might have an **impact** upon the host culture? Can the Motorola Culture sometimes be a force for change in Malaysian culture? Russian culture? Brazilian culture?

Our answer is "Yes — sometimes."

Recall the earlier hypothetical example of the Japanese ex-Motorolan Watanabe, who, as a result of his employment in the company, experienced change at the personal level. Let us now go beyond this, and give two additional examples that illustrate possible change at the cultural level:

• The Motorola Culture emphasizes competing on the basis of product and service quality plus price, and rejects the use of corrupt practices. How could this impact contemporary Russia, in which corruption is reliably reported to be widespread? One plausible scenario is that as more and more Russians observe that Motorola/Russia can survive and flourish in a Russian business context, this could have the effect of stimulating positive changes in the business

subculture of that country. Such changes are especially likely if Motorola works in cooperation with other multinational companies to secure, for example, bribe-free handling of imports and exports by a host nation's customs inspectors and licensing authorities.

• In a certain Asian nation, Motorola has a large facility whose director, for several years, has been a woman native to that country. The result has been a positive impact on public opinion, for three reasons: (1) Motorola is highly respected; (2) it is widely known that **local** manufacturing companies would rarely appoint a woman to such a responsible post; and (3) the female director has produced excellent results, thus vindicating Motorola's judgment in appointing her.

As reports of precedent-setting events such as this become more widely known in this particular host country, they can become a significant factor in bringing about greater gender equity in that host culture.

Chapter Three:
Approaches from the
Field of Ethics

This chapter briefly summarizes a number of tools from the field of ethics, which can be used in analyzing the 24 cases presented in this book. Three preliminary steps to solving an ethical problem are to: take an objective approach to the facts of each case, consider the total situation and cultural context, and identify the intentions and motives of people involved, if possible. Seven major analytical approaches to the problem are: consequences, justice and fairness, rights, duties, traditions and stories, virtue, and ideals. Before reaching a final conclusion, two useful reflective stances are that you: undertake a creative quest for imaginative, nontraditional solutions; and attempt to develop policies and practices that will prevent the recurrence of similar cases.

Ethics can be defined as the values and rules of behavior that are necessary for a society or community to function. The systematic study of ethical issues is undertaken by ethicists, that is, philosophers of ethics.

Ethics, however, is not a subject only for scholars. All people, regardless of how much or how little they may have studied the subject, possess their own ethical values and standards. In discussing ethical issues, most people proceed intuitively, based on what they have been taught from childhood, and on their personal beliefs that have evolved over time. They generally use such basic rules as: it is wrong to kill, steal or lie; love your neighbor; respect others; and so on. Their reactions to an issue are usually quick, and this is often sufficient.

But, sometimes simple intuitive responses and judgments are **not** enough. Issues can present new problems that the individual has never dealt with or heard about. With complex issues, one intuitive rule may clash with another. Anyone encountering such cases needs to analyze them as carefully and clearly as possible. This is where ethicists can help.

The 24 cases presented in the next chapter are designed to help Motorolans and others analyze carefully and think clearly. The cases are material for group dialogue. Yet, if discussion participants simply stated their opinions without supporting reasons, it would be difficult to reach a conclusion that could be convincingly justified to others.

This chapter will present a number of approaches to ethics that ethicists have found useful through the years — indeed, often through many centuries. As you work through them, keep the following provisos in mind:

• We do not imply that all of these approaches are equally important, or that the four ethicists on our team of authors would necessarily use all of them.

• We do not imply that Motorola necessarily does or should endorse a particular approach.

• The approaches are intended to be a **supplement** to adherence to the ethical values on the Total Customer Satisfaction Card and in the Motorola Code of Conduct, as well as to relevant law.

Preliminary Steps

Before beginning any ethical analysis, there are three preliminary steps that one must take: ascertaining the facts, considering the total situation and cultural context, and identifying the intentions and motives of the persons in the case.

Ascertaining the Facts
The essential first step in any case analysis, collecting the facts, means looking for the pertinent details in an objective manner. It involves describing a case, rather than prejudging it. To call an action "murder," "bribery" or "theft" is to characterize it from the start as ethically wrong — when the REAL issue is **whether** the action should correctly be so characterized. For example, several of the cases involve the accusation of "misusing Motorola funds." Before such charges can be substantiated as ethically wrong, one must determine the nature of the "use," the claims made by the user, and relevant corporate policies.

Considering the Total Situation and Cultural Context
The second preliminary step springs from the fact that when people in any society make ethical judgments, they will usually automatically and uncritically

assume the context of their **own** situation and culture. They tend to take familiar background conditions for granted: the laws, the local expectations, the customs of their society, and so on. For the Motorolan, these "taken-for-granteds" include the Motorola Culture, its key values and its full adherence to the U.S. Foreign Corrupt Practices Act.

While Motorolans can and should honor the core values of the Motorola Culture, they cannot assume that **others** will necessarily do the same. With **trans**cultural cases, where two or more cultures are involved, the relevant background cannot be simply assumed. The local situation and culture will differ from case to case, possibly changing the ethical character of the action in question. For example, some of the cases in this book involve misunderstandings rooted in differing cultural standards as to what is an appropriate business gift, or what is the proper way to treat female employees.

Identifying Intentions and Motives
The third preliminary step concerns intents and actions. In analyzing a case you can consider:

• the action independently of the intent;

• the intent independently of the action, or

• both together.

Good intentions are necessary for good actions, but are not sufficient. Frequently, when doing a case analysis, or judging the actions of individuals or companies, you cannot know the intentions of those involved, and so must judge the actions strictly on their own merits.

However, you do know your **own** motives, and can judge your own actions more fully than those of others, if you choose. By doing so, you accept responsibility for your actions, and can feel pride in acting ethically — or shame in acting unethically. Ethically speaking, it makes a considerable difference whether a manager who causes conflict among his employees in implementing a new bonus system intended to simply follow company policy, or to "settle accounts" with an associate of whom he does not approve.

Analytical Approaches
A variety of analytical approaches have evolved in the field of ethics. Seven are briefly summarized in the following pages:

• Consequences

• Justice and fairness

• Rights

• Duties

• Traditions and stories

• Virtue

• Ideals

When you encounter an ethical case of any complexity, we recommend that you consider, at least briefly, using **all** of these approaches. This will help you quickly decide which are most relevant, and in what combination.

Consequences

This approach, the most commonly used version of which is **utilitarianism,** consists of looking carefully at all the consequences of an action. If more good than bad results from the action, then the action tends to be right. If more bad results, it tends to be wrong. You must be completely objective and impartial in spelling out all the consequences to everyone affected, each of whom counts equally. You cannot justify harming others in order to benefit yourself. They count as much as you do.

Although this approach superficially resembles cost-benefit analysis, it differs for these reasons:

- You consider **all** the people affected, not just one individual or company.

- You weigh the value of both monetary and **non**monetary variables — such as the fear your actions might create, the reputations you might hurt, the morale you could ruin, or the extent to which your actions might undermine important practices that have implications for the long-run well-being of the organization.

- Your action will be right if it produces more **overall** good to compensate for any harm done.

Doing a complete analysis of consequences is not simply a matter of intuition. It requires time and care. One way to proceed is to adopt a so-called "stake-holder's" perspective, which forces you to consider not just those who own stock in a company, but all others who also have a stake in it: employees, customers, suppliers, consumers, the community where the company's facilities are located or where it does business, and any other persons or groups directly affected by the company. For example, a decision that provides a small, short-term benefit for the stockholders, but that will endanger customers or cost many employees their jobs, would not pass even the most casual consequences calculation.

Justice and Fairness

Justice, or fairness, is a concept that people in almost all cultures come to appreciate early in life. Is the action you are performing fair? Are there some who could claim that they are being treated unjustly? Can you satisfactorily answer to their claims? Doing so involves treating similar cases similarly and giving each person his due. What is due a person may be measured in many ways. Standards vary from culture to culture, and frequently disputes about justice are actually disputes about the proper standard to use. For example, the death penalty for property crimes or drug trafficking might be seen as a "fitting punishment" in one society, but wholly unacceptable in another.

Rights

This approach springs from the fact that people frequently state their ethical claims in terms of rights. Whose rights might your actions violate? Generally speaking, you may violate another person's right only if there is a more serious right that you are upholding. Ethicists call this the "logic of rights." Rights carry with them obligations, and can impose obligations on others.

Rights fall into various categories:

- **Human** rights are widely recognized, as for example, those stated in the United Nations Universal Declaration of Human Rights. The right to life is basic, and rights that support the right to life are secondary. For example, to say that an employee has the human right to work in a safe environment is to say that this claim should override simple calculations of cost.

- There are also **civil** rights based on law within a given country (such as the right of American citizens to vote in U.S. elections) and **special** rights (which come with a position or are granted within an organization, for example, seniority rights).

Duties

Duty is another basic analytical approach. A defense of the claim that something is a person's duty involves showing where the duty comes from or how it applies in a given situation. Duties arise from various sources. You have some duties simply because you are a human being and part of the human community. Respect for others can be considered such a duty. Sometimes you have duties because of a promise, contract or debt, or because of your position. Frequently duties come from rules laid down by the holy books of various religions, the laws of various countries, or the policies of various companies. For example, the ethical values of the Motorola corporate culture dictate that you have a duty to refuse to participate in any transaction that involves bribery, regardless of the situation or the culture, and regardless of how profitable. But laws and rules cannot specify every action that is required, and thus are always subject to interpretation and extension.

Duties are often expressed in terms of obligations. Having a duty implies that one has the responsibility to perform as duty commands. Uncompromising Integrity implies in part that you fulfill your responsibilities and obligations, and that you act in accordance with what duty commands.

Traditions and Stories

This approach calls for analyzing a case by seeing it as part of an ongoing tradition or story. Thus, Motorolans might view an ethical issue in terms of the corporation's storied history and tradition, and handle the case accordingly. They could ask how it might develop further, and whether such developments would be consistent with previous tradition and similar cases. In so doing, they might be contributing to the further evolution of that tradition. In short, sometimes it is helpful to look back on company tradition for constructive resolutions and appropriate future actions, such as in the story of the refusal by Motorola's divisional executives, and by Paul and Bob Galvin, to do business with a government that had asked for a kickback (page 10).

Virtue

A sixth and vitally important analytical approach is that of virtue. Virtues are excellences of human activity in various areas. While virtues differ somewhat from one culture or company to another, qualities such as honor, courage, integrity, honesty and respect for others are widely recognized. Virtuous people exercise sound judgment, creativity and wisdom in deciding how to act. They frequently become role models.

When using the virtue approach to ethical issues, you should ask yourself how someone you admire would react in these circumstances. For example, in a given situation, justice might allow you to terminate an employee, but justice tempered with mercy might lead you to apply some lesser sanction.

Ideals

The above six approaches have all dealt with ways of deciding what is ethically right or wrong. But ethics goes beyond simply doing one's duty or avoiding doing what is ethically prohibited. From an ethical point of view we can divide actions into four categories:

- Actions that are ethically forbidden

- Actions that are ethically required

- Actions — a great many — that are **neither** forbidden nor required, and are neither ethically praiseworthy nor blameworthy

- Actions that are not required but that are ethically praiseworthy

The last category is that of ethical ideals. A person or company that performs such actions is worthy of ethical praise and commendation; but failure to perform such actions does not bring with it any ethical blame. Examples:

- In June 1996, Motorola announced an alliance with the World Wildlife Fund that would improve the effectiveness and productivity of wildlife conservation efforts by enhancing communications in remote areas. Motorola would donate two-way radio equipment and systems, and would provide service and support for those systems free of charge, to help that organization protect many diverse ecosystems around the globe (*Corporate Briefing*, June 18, 1996).

- In July 1996, Motorola announced a policy concerning anti-personnel land mines (APMs). Noting that millions of APMs planted in various countries around the world have been killing and maiming innocent people, Motorola decided to step out in advance of a possible global treaty banning the use, production or stockpiling of these brutal weapons. Specifically, Motorola pledged as follows:

> We will do everything reasonably possible to make sure that Motorola does not knowingly sell any part that is intended for use in an anti-personnel mine. Although it is impossible for a manufacturer to trace each component through to its ultimate application, we believe that we have an obligation and a unique opportunity to proactively support the elimination of anti-personnel mines (*Executive/Professional Briefing List*, July 16, 1996).

- In the autumn of 1996, Motorola was recognized by two leading magazines for its "family friendliness." In its September 16 issue, *Business Week* for the first time recognized ten leading American companies for their work and family strategies, based on a random sampling of employees. Motorola was rated No. 2 among these ten, and cited for its "commitment from managers and employees alike," and for being "a culture where the embrace of family balance is pervasive and consistent." In its October issue, *Working Mother* cited Motorola for its heavily subsidized "mildly ill child care program," and termed its investment in on-site child care to be unsurpassed by any other company. Both magazines added the comment that actions of this type are also good business (*Executive/Professional Briefing List*, October 8, 1996).

Reflective Stances

No matter which of these seven analytical approaches you use in analyzing a case, pause and reflect on the situation before reaching a conclusion. Ask yourself:

• Is there an imaginative solution other than the ones investigated?

• Is there any way to prevent similar cases from arising in the future?

Seeking Imaginative Solutions

Every multinational company must constantly confront ethical issues in new cultural contexts. When confronting them, Motorolans should make it a practice to take the initiative in looking for imaginative solutions that preserve integrity. It is not appropriate to assume that there is only one ethically correct answer, or that the choice is necessarily between two obvious courses of action. An ethical analysis will tell us what is clearly **not** ethical behavior. But there might be **alternatives** that are not obvious. Ethical imagination requires looking beyond the obvious, and even engaging in counter-intuitive thinking. In the end, there might turn out to be no acceptable new solution — but often there will.

How do we proceed to seek the nonobvious? There are, of course, no rules for creativity, but two examples might help:

• When one company was faced with the issue of paying bribes in a certain country, it knew it could not ethically do so. At first, the only alternative seemed to be to forgo doing business there. But this company used its ethical imagination. It learned that the bribes went not into individual pockets but into a communal fund for works needed by the local community. Learning of the community's needs, the company offered to help local officials set up a school and a hospital for the townspeople. Contributions were made openly and were considered part of the company's fulfilling its social responsibility. The company was warmly and gracefully received by the community, and there was no longer a question of being asked to pay bribes.

• Another company, when faced with the fact that a supplier used child labor, determined that it could not ethically use this supplier. The alternative seemed to be to search for a new source, even though the quality and record of the existing supplier had been very satisfactory. Instead, the company suggested that the existing supplier pay the wages of the children while they attended a school, which the company helped build. The supplier was happy to agree, the children and their families were delighted, and the company was still able to maintain an acceptable profit margin using the supplier under these conditions.

Seeking to Prevent Recurrences

A primary purpose of analyzing ethical cases is to develop ways to prevent similar situations from arising in the future. To do this, it is vital to establish certain elements of the case, such as the following:

- At what point did the system begin to go wrong?

- Why and how did it go wrong? For instance, did some manager put too much emphasis on certain goals, or put inordinate pressure on an employee to fulfill a quota?

- Were "rules of engagement" provided, and were all the Motorolans involved aware of them?

- Were there signs that things were going wrong, that Motorolans failed to notice?

- Did someone notice these signs, but fail to report them to higher authority? If so, why?

- Did higher authority, upon receiving a report, fail to act? If so, why?

As answers to such questions are found, further questions can be directed toward creating solutions:

- How can employees be sensitized so that they will detect unethical episodes or tendencies earlier rather than later?

- What procedures can be developed so that employees who detect such behavior will report it, and so that those in authority will act?

- At what level can a solution be made to work? Can it be successfully handled at the level of the individual, the corporation, the industry — or does it require international negotiation?

- What changes in the corporation's leadership mode, procedures, rules, reward and recognition systems, or culture could reinforce employees' ethical inclinations and reward ethically appropriate actions?

Chapter Four:
Twenty-Four Cases
with Commentaries

This chapter presents 24 cases that pose ethical issues that have arisen when Motorolans, or persons in similar situations, have interacted with persons from different home cultures. The cases have been fictionalized to preserve anonymity and sharpen ethical issues. Each case is followed by discussion questions, and then by two commentaries, each written independently by an expert on ethics. For each case we ask you to compare these commentaries with your own independent responses to the discussion questions.

This chapter is organized as follows:

- It presents 24 **cases,** selected to cover a wide spectrum of issues, including environmental protection, occupational safety, human and gender rights, freedom from sexual harassment, bribe-free dealings, protection of intellectual property, compensation equity and personal virtue. The order of presentation of the cases is roughly from simpler to more complex.

- At the end of each case are several **discussion questions** for you to answer independently.

- Following the discussion questions are two **commentaries** on the case, written independently by experts in ethical analysis, so that you can compare your analysis with theirs.

The Cases

The 24 cases have all been derived from tape-recorded interviews or informal conversations with knowledgeable Motorolans. Some of the cases describe actual events that have occurred within Motorola; others, events known to have occurred to companies similar to Motorola.

In developing the cases we followed these policies:

- To ensure frankness and completeness, we guaranteed anonymity to each interviewee.

- To sharpen ethical issues, we fictionalized some parts of the "plots," or added new subplots. Fictionalization also disguises the identity of the persons in a case, thus protecting their privacy.

- To ensure accuracy and balance, wherever possible we submitted the draft of each case to the interviewee for editing and approval.

By reporting these cases and raising these issues we hope:

- to sensitize readers to ethical issues that might arise, and illustrate how to analyze and solve them;

- to foster positive thinking that will help enable those faced with temptations to resist them;

- to help those in key positions devise strategies, systems, policies and procedures that will prevent such situations from arising in the future; and

- to reinforce our commitment to constant ethical renewal and management by high principles.

The Discussion Questions

The discussion questions following each case are designed to stimulate independent thinking by individual readers, and productive discussion by seminar groups. These questions are mainly of three kinds:

- **Action**-specific questions ask what you would do in the same or a similar situation.

- **Reflective** questions ask you to consider how the situation came about, how similar situations can be avoided, and how to assess the sensitivity of such situations.

- **Philosophical** questions ask you to think about the nature of business as a social phenomenon, especially in the new global context.

The questions are not exhaustive, but they are intended to be systematic to ensure a reasonable degree of uniform treatment for all the cases.

For some of the discussion questions, the case may not seem to include enough information for an adequate answer. This can be frustrating, but it should come as no surprise. In real life, ethical dilemmas rarely come with a complete set of information. Indeed, in real life an important part of any ethical decision-making process is to decide what further information to look for.

We urge you to consider these discussion questions actively, and to make up your own mind independently, mindful that ethical dilemmas often have no single "right" answer (although they might have a number of clearly **wrong** answers). If you are working with a discussion group, you should discuss your answers with other members, and listen carefully to all ideas expressed, especially those that challenge your own positions. Honest dialogue promotes the formulation of justifiable and sometimes highly creative solutions.

The Commentaries

Each commentator is identified by his initials: Richard T. De George (RTD), Thomas Donaldson (TD), William J. Ellos (WJE), and Robert C. Solomon (RCS). All four are experts with long experience in the area of ethical analysis. A short biographical sketch of each is provided at the end of this volume.

The purpose of having two commentaries on each case is to demonstrate that there is more than one way to approach an issue. They are designed to illustrate what a case analysis looks like, and to deepen the reader's appreciation of relevant ethical issues. Each commentator has approached the cases independently, without knowledge of what the other would say.

Wherever possible, we submitted drafts of the commentaries, unsigned, to the interviewee who provided the case, asking for input. When each commentator received this input, he was free to change his commentary, and equally free not to.

It usually turns out that each pair of commentators is in basic agreement on the central ethical issue of the case. This is not surprising, since one would expect most people to be in agreement on these issues. Equally important, however, is the **way** in which the commentators approach a case, what they see as its most important aspect, and how they justify their position.

The commentators tend to be open in their approach. Sometimes they will deal directly with the discussion questions, but at other times they will not, preferring to allow the reader or discussion group to formulate their own judgments. At the end of each commentary, the writer lists which ethical approach he primarily used — out of the seven explained in the previous chapter: consequences, justice and fairness, rights, duties, traditions and stories, virtue, and ideals. If he used more than one approach, he lists them in order of importance.

The commentaries should not be read as the final word, but as thoughtful analyses of the cases and the issues they raise. If you disagree with any of the analyses, you are challenged to specify:

- Why that analysis is mistaken.

- Why the judgment made is invalid in this instance.

- Why your alternative analysis, judgment or reason is preferable.

If the commentators were present, they would listen carefully to your presentation, which might convince them. But they might give an additional defense of their views, possibly with some modification reflecting your input. What distinguishes such a reasoned dialogue from a casual conversation is that in the latter, each person freely states an opinion and there is no sustained attempt to determine who, if anyone, is right. A reasoned discussion is one that attempts to reach a conclusion that is, at that point, supported by the strongest arguments that have been presented and discussed (even though they might ultimately prove to be unsound).

Each of the commentators has developed a certain style of approaching the cases. Are any of their approaches more compatible with your own way of thinking than others? Do you have a different approach from any of theirs that you can articulate with some consistency?

The aim of this book is to help you develop your own **independent** ability to think clearly about ethical decision making. Challenging the experts is one way to accomplish this. We hope you will accept the challenge as you turn to the 24 cases.

Case 1
"Uncompromising Integrity" and Egregian Justice

This case occurs in a country called *Egregia* and concerns a company called *Cosmotronics, Inc.*, an electronic corporation doing business broadly similar to Motorola's. One day recently at Cosmotronics' Egregian facility, the company detected one of its Egregian employees stealing corporate property valued at less than $100. The circumstances were such that the manager of the facility, a transpatriate American, had little doubt as to the employee's guilt.

The manager reported the incident to the local Egregian police. The police arrived on the scene and arrested the suspect. They took him to the station and interrogated him according to regular Egregian procedures.

The suspect confessed.

The police then took the suspect out and shot him **dead.**

When the American manager heard the news, he was devastated. For months afterwards, he was haunted by the fact that his action, taken in the interest of what he considered to be fairness, had produced a result he felt was tragically unfair.

Discussion Questions...

1. Should Cosmotronics have protested the killing as a violation of the rights of its employee, regardless of the fact that such punishment was locally considered appropriate to the crime?

2. If a **second** Cosmotronics employee were caught stealing property, what should the manager do?

3. Is it acceptable that Cosmotronics have one policy in Egregia regarding such crimes and violations, and another elsewhere? Is it ethical to have such different policies in different cultures, based on the corporation's sense of what is just and what is not?

4. If the corporation were Motorola, would the Key Belief in Uncompromising Integrity imply that it is acceptable for a manager to disregard possible differences between the standards of the local national culture and the standards of the Motorola Culture, with respect to how miscreants should be dealt with when they compromise integrity?

5. If the corporation were Motorola, would turning an employee who has committed a crime against Motorola over to the Egregian police be consistent with Motorola's Key Belief in Constant Respect for People?

Commentaries on Case 1

[TD] This case has a straightforward ethical solution — once one sees murder as the outcome. The trick is knowing what to do **before** the person has been shot dead!

The case illustrates two factors that are often neglected by multinational companies and that are often responsible for their stumbling into difficulties of this sort (although the consequences are usually less severe than the loss of innocent life).

The first factor is cultural ignorance, and a failure to come to grips with relevant details of the host culture's habits and attitudes. The Egregian tradition of justice is greatly at variance with the Roman or English legal traditions that dominate the West. As a part of starting operations in Egregia, Cosmotronics should have sought advice from people well acquainted with Egregian customs. Forewarned is forearmed. Examples:

• In some parts of Russia, businesses can't operate without passing on 20 percent of their profits to Russian gangsters.

• In some parts of Burma, working on cooperative projects with the Burmese government means participating in practices of slave labor, in which villagers are involuntarily conscripted for hard, sometimes dangerous work for long periods of time.

A corporation should not be taken by **surprise** in such situations. Advance preparations for business ventures should include assembling and digesting basic demographic, political and cultural information on the host country — including information about its ethical standards. In some instances, a corporation such as Motorola might simply want to back out of a business possibility instead of placing itself in a situation where its Key Beliefs are subject to compromise. In other instances, business might be possible — but only with special precautions not necessary in other host countries.

The second factor illustrated by this case is a tendency toward ethical "photocopyism," or blind, ethnocentric application of one culture's standards and criteria in another culture. Some companies fail to understand that rules do not always and necessarily need to be implemented the same way regardless of cultural context. True, some basic standards must be rigidly adhered to — for example, the principles in Motorola's Code of Conduct or the Key Beliefs on its Total Customer Satisfaction Card — and this can be accomplished by carefully constructing them in ways that allow them to remain uncompromised in any circumstance. However, various implementation practices, such as turning over suspected employees to the local police, may be altered or dropped when it appears that the essence of a Key Belief or principle in the Code of Conduct would otherwise be distorted.

The point is simple but vital. Cultural differences **do** make a difference. Any manager who thinks that being ethically straight means doing the **same** thing in Egregia that is done in Detroit is transculturally incompetent. This case, then, is one that underscores a key fact of cultural wisdom: Even though a corporation must not compromise its core ethical values, this does not always entail "photocopy" behavior in the implementation of those values in a given host culture.

Approaches Primarily Used: Justice and Fairness, Consequences.

[RCS] This case illustrates a number of concerns about the nature of a transcultural approach to ethics. There are certain moral precepts that apply more or less universally, although perhaps with very different local emphases from one host culture to the next. The interplay between the universal and the local can often be confusing, complicated and even, as in this case, tragic. In both Egregia and the United States, theft is clearly both illegal and unethical. But attitudes toward theft in the two countries vary considerably. For example, in Egregia, theft might be taken to be an instance of a more serious offense, disloyalty, which may explain the harsh punishment meted out.

By contrast, in the United States, many companies now admit to as much as a 10 percent inventory loss through employee theft. Most of this pilfering goes unpunished. Many managers and employees strongly object to the security measures (video monitors, metal detectors, body searches, lie detector tests) that might significantly cut down on insider theft. Indeed, in many United States industries, employees caught stealing from the company are quietly permitted to resign. Reports are rarely made to the police, and even when reported, rarely prosecuted. Perhaps most shocking of all, the growing number of "wrongful termination" and "defamation" suits forces most companies to keep silent about such behavior, even in their letters of recommendation to other companies considering hiring the same dishonest employee. Given the rampant existence and lenient treatment of insider theft in the United States, it is no wonder that the death penalty for the same offense in Egregia is shocking to Americans.

The larger issue is a basic question of what is called "retributive justice," namely, when does the punishment "fit" the crime? In the eighteenth and nineteenth centuries in England, a man could still be hanged for stealing a loaf of bread for his starving children. Philosophers and social writers such as Jeremy Bentham and Charles Dickens (and Victor Hugo and Emile Zola in France) wrote passionately about such injustices. If Euro-American societies have now left those brutal punishments behind, one should remind oneself that it is only by a hundred or so years.

Is death a "fair" punishment for theft? Most readers would immediately agree that it is not. (Nor would one approve of that form of justice that recommends the somewhat milder punishment of the loss of a hand or two.) But the harshness of Egregian punishment and the lack of what Americans consider "due process" in Egregian justice should be no surprise to anyone who keeps up with the press. In this sense, Cosmotronics' transpatriate manager was at fault for his naivete or ignorance if nothing else. If the offense had been murder, his action would have been justified. But in a case of theft of company property, it probably would have been handled much better as an internal matter by firing the employee and demanding restitution if that were reasonable.

This case also raises questions about the meaning of "integrity." Imagine that the corporation in this case actually were Motorola. If Motorola were to define Uncompromising Integrity as meaning that the corporation must follow certain policies and procedures — developed in the United States and routinely implemented without qualification everywhere else — then "integrity" smacks of ignorant ethnocentrism and personal insensitivity, and can readily lead to tragedies such as this one. Integrity is not "compromised" when local conditions and customs are knowledgeably taken into account.

Moreover, the case invites a review of security procedures in this corporation's Egregian operations, particularly in its hiring practices and its own sense of what can be expected of its Egregian employees. Is this an isolated incident? Are there special features of the case that would point to other concerns to be addressed by the corporation (for example, some cultural expectation that has not been satisfied, some sense of injustice that has been provoked unwittingly)?

There is another lesson here. Business doesn't always take place in violence-free surroundings. Any global business might well find itself in situations where it is forced to take sides in delicate but violent situations. There are civil wars, insurrections, separatist movements, and the usual on-going and sometimes centuries-old ethnic conflicts. Companies can try to remain above the fray but, almost inevitably, they will find themselves involved to some degree with one side or another. A mere decade ago, many global companies had to make decisions regarding their policies concerning South Africa and apartheid: whether or not to invest in that country or deal with South African businesses. The arguments were complex — did divestment help or hurt South African blacks, for example — but every company had to reach its own decision. Today, there are similar dilemmas, such as with Shell Oil in Nigeria, and with Freeport-McMoran in Indonesia. Both companies, in order to operate in those countries at all, are compelled into complicity with unjust, dictatorial, violence-prone governments.

Motorola would do well to avoid such situations wherever it can. But countries like Egregaria are potentially enormous markets for Motorola products, making involvement unavoidable. From this will follow a long series of ethical decisions, ranging from "customs clearing" fees to more objectionable demands in the future concerning the political use of Motorola technology. All of this requires continued vigilance, cultural awareness, up-to-date political knowledge, and sensitivity to circumstances. Motorola's insistence on Uncompromising Integrity and Constant Respect for People remains unchallenged, of course, but the meaning of these values, and how these standards should be implemented in the different locations, are matters requiring concern, care and competence.

***Approaches Primarily Used:
Rights, Justice and Fairness, Virtue.***

Case 2
The Phantom Air Ticket

Karl Kelly is an American transpatriate assigned to Motorola's facility in a former USSR satellite nation in Eastern Europe, called *Ruritania*. Karl has found the Ruritanian culture strange and experienced a bit of culture shock, which explains why he arranged to have his wife *Kathleen* join him as soon as possible. Kathleen arrived in Ruritania ten months ago, eagerly looking forward to spending more time with Karl than was possible back in Florida. She was rudely surprised. In those ten months she was able to spend "quality" time with him on exactly seven weekends!

Then came some good news. Last month Karl was told that for the next four weeks he would be assigned to Surabaya, Indonesia. Kathleen, who had a long-standing interest in Javanese arts, wanted to go along. That way, on weekdays she could enjoy local music, dance, drama, painting and sculpture, and on week-ends she and Karl could finally snatch some quality time together in nearby Bali.

But there was a problem. All three of the Kelly children were in college, and their combined tuition payments were a huge financial burden, making it difficult to afford Kathleen's airfare to Indonesia.

Yaroslav, a Ruritanian colleague of Karl's, offered to help them out. Yaroslav got in touch with *Easy Virtue Travel*, a most obliging local company. That evening Easy Virtue delivered two round-trip coach tickets to Surabaya for Karl and Kathleen, along with a bill for just one round-trip "business class" passage for Karl. This way, Karl would bill Motorola for business-class reimbursement, while he and Kathleen would fly coach. Karl would be personally out of pocket only an extra $27.94 for Kathleen's seat. "Not bad," exclaimed Karl. "That will make up for all those lonely weekends," added an eager Kathleen.

That night, though, Karl had trouble sleeping. "Deserve it or not, this is probably against some corporate regulation. I'd better check with Sam."

Sam Smoothover was Motorola's HR manager for Ruritania. Sam had had long experience in the former satellite countries and suspected that local Ruritanian travel agencies often did things that were technically frowned upon by foreigners, yet actually humane in their consequences. Sam also enjoyed an enviable reputation for putting the well-being of Motorolans high on his list of value priorities — certainly higher than formal compliance with the details of regulations set by headquarters 4,000 miles away.

Sam's reaction was, "OK, Karl, you and Kathleen make the trip this time. But just don't go around talking to people about it."

However, a few days later Sam had his own second thoughts and decided to check with corporate officials in Schaumburg, just to make sure it really **was** OK.

Discussion Questions...

1. What should Karl have done? Since he accepted the two tickets (instead of one business-class ticket), should he follow Sam's advice not to "go around talking to people about it"?

2. What do you think the corporate officials decided as to the propriety of Karl's deal?

3. Would you agree with that decision? Why or why not?

4. Could this whole issue be resolved by a general policy — for example, one that would permit an employee's spouse to go along on business trips longer than a given number of days — with Motorola paying for two coach-class tickets instead of one business-class ticket? Why or why not?

Commentaries on Case 2

[RCS] This familiar case is deceptively innocent, and belongs to a class of cases that involves more than just airline tickets. The reason these questions most often come up regarding air tickets may be that international business-class travel costs almost exactly double international coach fares, inviting the "two-for-one" dilemma. But the real issue comes down to misuse of company funds — not dishonestly, perhaps, but nevertheless affecting a company's sense of its own integrity. (Case 9, "Personal Luxury or Family Loyalty?", involves some of the same considerations and effects.)

In approaching this case, one should note that different organizations have varying policies about air travel. For instance, some allow the spouse to accompany the employee, with both traveling "coach," if the trip is for three weeks or longer. The rationale is that the extra wear and tear of coach travel is compensated by the comfort of marital companionship.

If Motorola's policy were simply that the traveling employee is entitled to spend the amount of money equal to a business-class fare, to be used as desired so long as he reaches the destination in question, then this case would present no issue. Of course, few companies have such free-wheeling policies. The purpose of travel money is to get the employee from point A to point B and back. In this case, it is to get Karl Kelly from Ruritania to Surabaya and back again, as efficiently and as inexpensively as possible.

The extra expense for business class on international trips is justified for the sake of efficiency. Any traveler who has flown coach class internationally can testify to the difficulty of getting straight to work upon arrival. Even if the cost is the same, the purpose and intent of the added company expense has been violated.

Of course, matters might not be so simple. If Karl is one of those happily married managers who would and could, in fact, fly several thousand miles just as restfully with his wife sitting next to him in coach as he would alone in business class, it is not so obvious that the purpose of the policy is thwarted. With this in mind, manager Sam (the corporation's HR man for Ruritania), who puts the well-being of Motorolans "high on his list of value priorities," might well want to endorse the arrangement. But this brings the analysis back to the question of integrity with regard to corporation policy. Sam's judgment might be fair and sensible, but making exceptions such as this is always a dangerous precedent. His warning not to "go around talking to people about it" indicates that he is clearly aware of this. There is nothing about the Kelly trip that would warrant its treatment as a "special" case. (Moreover, it is unlikely that Kathleen's trip to Indonesia will remain a secret.)

A corporation's policy must be made **very** clear, regarding the types of exceptions that will be **explicitly** allowed. Which policy is mandated depends on many factors (expense, employee morale, general policy toward the family) but, whatever it is, it must be understood and followed.

Two added notes here:

- The suggestion of "fairness" from Kathy indicates a troublesome attitude toward the corporation, namely, "they've put such a burden on me that they owe me something in return." In a truly cooperative enterprise, such "keeping score" and "getting something in return" should not be so obviously evident. But the existence of such feelings on the part of a spouse also suggests that there is some reason for Motorola to consider more flexible travel arrangements so that families will not be separated so often or so long.

- A company is known by the company it keeps. For that reason, Motorola should NEVER do business with an outfit called "Easy Virtue Travel," or one that pursues an easy virtue approach.

Finally, suppose Karl, a "frequent flier" from his many travels, buys Kathy's ticket at his own expense, using his accumulated miles or "companion award" coupons that airlines occasionally send to their best customers. In such an instance, all of the above questions concerning the use of Motorola funds do not apply.

Approach Primarily Used: Virtue.

[RTD] Sam may be a humane person, and Karl Kelly and his wife might truly need quality time together. But the point here is that the travel agent is falsifying an invoice and that both Karl and Sam are knowingly in complicity. That is the unethical action in the case.

Since neither Karl nor Sam wants Motorola to pay more than the amount of Karl's business class airfare, they rationalize that they are not stealing from the corporation. Motorola pays out the same amount of money in either event. No harm is done the corporation, and both Karl and his wife — and perhaps his work also — will be better off. Nonetheless, the sticking point remains the falsification of the invoice and of the official record.

Motorola will pay the same amount whether it pays for Karl's business-class airfare, or whether it pays for his coach-class ticket and almost all of his wife's ticket, so why should Motorola care? Look at the situation a little more closely. Conceivably Motorola might have a policy that requires employees to travel only coach class, and that they must purchase the least expensive ticket available. This restrictive policy would often be counterproductive. Although it would cut travel expenses, traveling coach rather than business class on long trips probably means that the employee:

- gets less work done en route;
- gets less rest;
- will be less efficient upon arrival; and
- will be less inclined to travel in the future.

Motorola permits business-class travel on long trips because of these negative effects. The policy is reasonable, and it is ethically permissible although not ethically required.

It would not cost Motorola any more if it adopted a policy that allows employees on long business trips to travel either business or coach class, and receive the difference between the two fares in cash or as a contribution to a companion's ticket. But it is difficult to imagine why any company would make such a rule. If business class is justified because it promotes efficiency, that end is not achieved by the employee traveling coach and pocketing the difference. Nor is it achieved by the employee traveling coach and being accompanied by a companion or spouse. Surely the U.S. Internal Revenue Service would consider both the business-class or the coach-class ticket a legitimate business expense. But it would consider the difference between the two tickets, whether given in cash or used toward a companion ticket, as income, for that is exactly what it is.

It is unlikely that any company would allow an employee to choose whether to travel business class or coach and get the difference, so if Sam checks with corporate officials in Schaumburg, it is doubtful that his request would be approved.

This does not mean that Motorola would refuse a policy that allowed trips for spouses under certain conditions. Such a policy might even be a good one to adopt. But that is not what Karl and Sam were requesting. Because of Karl's situation and the unusual amount of traveling that he must do, Motorola might consider his position to be one of special hardship and decide to pay for his wife's airfare so she can accompany him. But that is different from agreeing to the falsification of records or to the payment of false invoices.

Sam's comment that Karl should not talk about this matter is fairly clear evidence that he believes what Karl is about to do is not quite right.

The basic issue is not really Motorola's policy but the fact that falsifying documents or paying invoices that are known to be false is unethical.

Approaches Primarily Used: Duties, Consequences.

Case 3
"Nurturing" a Deal

Motorola has sent *G.I. Quick* from the United States to an economically developing nation called *Developia*, to develop the market for a promising Motorola product, the new *X-4 Chip*. There are two other multi-national companies in direct competition with Motorola for the Developian domestic chip market, namely *Red Hot* and *Blue Lightning*.

Quick is not only a fine manager but also a brilliant technologist. He has spent the better part of a year in the new host country and has made considerable progress. He knows that Motorola has a much better product to offer, and has made this persuasively clear to prospective local buyers. He is working especially hard to ensure that the top officials of a large Developian company, namely *Supremo, Inc.*, will give a large order for X-4s to Motorola, rather than buy from Red Hot or Blue Lightning.

The fact is, though, that at present Supremo buys some products of this type from Motorola, some from Red Hot and some from Blue Lightning. The ostensible reason for this is that Supremo wants to spread its business among three suppliers as a hedge against possible failure of supply — even though, according to rumor, it regards the X-4 as superior on all major counts. Still, G.I. persists in his dogged efforts to make Motorola Supremo's sole supplier.

One day G.I. is called in by *Mal Diidh*, Supremo's vice president of purchasing. Mal tells G.I. that he is willing to cancel business with Red Hot and Blue Lightning, as he clearly sees that Motorola offers a better product. Then he adds a vague statement that G.I. has trouble interpreting, but which seems to mean that discreet, covert "friendship gifts" are a rather common business practice in Developia. Quick begins to suspect that Mal might have accepted under-the-table gifts from the two other companies. Slowly, subtly, Mal seems to indicate that if G.I. will provide a gift of about 8 percent of the sale price, Motorola will become his exclusive supplier. If Motorola refuses, however, he will keep the present Motorola contract at its existing level, but expand his business with Red Hot and Blue Lightning, who seem to "understand our Developian culture quite well."

Discussion Questions...

1. Should Quick refuse the apparent request for an under-the-table gift? How should he do so? Or should he continue to pursue the order from Supremo? If so, what should he report to his superiors?

2. Should Quick (and Motorola) go public with news of Diidh's request? Do you think that making such information public would force Red Hot and Blue Lightning to lose their contracts? Would this be ethical, if the purpose of reporting the request were to secure an advantage for Motorola?

3. Regardless of your answer to Question 2, does Motorola have an ethical **obligation** to make public the presumed bribing activity of Red Hot and Blue Lightning?

4. How much loyalty and responsibility for mutual integrity and fairness does Motorola owe to its fellow multinational companies in Developia's business community?

5. Does Motorola, which already has a strong reputation as a leader in business ethics, have a right to serve as a conscience for other companies?

6. Does it have a duty to do so?

Commentaries on Case 3

[RTD] Motorola's policy in this case is clear: It does not make under-the-table payments in order to get business. Such payments are not only against Motorola's stated policy, they are also unethical. Hence G.I. Quick should have no difficulty in knowing that he cannot give Mal Diidh any such payments. If he does think so, he is working for the wrong corporation.

But once that is agreed to, G.I. still must decide what to do. The case raises a number of questions. First, one assumes that G.I. has not made any under-the-table payments to Mal Diidh in the past, so Motorola has been receiving orders from Supremo because of the quality of its products. This shows that Supremo wants those products and up until now has been willing to buy them without any kickbacks or unethical payments. Mal Diidh seems to claim that Red Hot and Blue Lightning have been making payments to him. G.I. does not know whether this is true. Suppose it is. Then perhaps Mal has been buying chips from them because of their payments, not because of the stated reason of wanting a hedge against possible failure of supply. Or perhaps he has been buying from them as a hedge, but found that he could also get pay-

ments from them. The other possibility is that Red Hot and Blue Lightning have not been making payments, and Mal just says this in order to persuade G.I. to make such payments.

The next question is why does Mal now propose to cancel business with Red Hot and Blue Lightning? If it is because Motorola has a better product, then this is true whether or not Mal receives under-the-table payments. So G.I. is not in as bad a spot as it might at first seem. Mal might, after all, already have been told by his superiors to switch the whole account to Motorola, and might simply be seeing if he can make some personal income in the process. What G.I. has to determine is whether Mal is telling the truth or whether he is bluffing. The best way to find out is to refuse unconditionally to make the requested payments, explain the reason why, point out the advantages of using Motorola's products, and see Mal's response. If Mal is bluffing, he will increase his order with Motorola. If he is telling the truth, or if he is simply trying to get G.I. to make him payments — whether or not what he says about Red Hot and Blue Lightning is true — then G.I. knows the kind of person he is dealing with. Knowing that, what should he do next?

G.I. does not know whether Mal is acting on his own or as a representative of Supremo. He knows that in the past Motorola has not had to make under-the-table payments. So there is no Supremo policy saying that the company only does business with those who make such payments. One option, therefore, whether or not Mal gives G.I. the increased order, is to go over Mal's head to the president of Supremo. This is not ethically required. Motorola employees have no obligation to report requests for such payments to the superiors of those making the request. G.I. must consider the possible results of such a move, and he would do well to inform his own superiors about the situation before proceeding. If he does make the approach, he might find that the president is neither shocked nor bothered by Mal's request. It would then be clear that the company tolerates such practices.

At this point, whether Motorola wishes to do any business at all with such a company is up to Motorola. In some instances it has refused to do business with such companies, although not ethically required to do this. What **is** ethically required is to refrain from making such payments. Motorola has, in the past, dissociated itself from companies that ask for kickbacks in order to preserve its reputation for integrity, since companies that act unethically in one area cannot be trusted to act ethically in other areas. Working with such companies is not good business in the long run.

If G.I. does approach the president of Supremo, Mal might deny that he made any such offer. Before going to the top, therefore, and after conferring with his superiors, G.I. might well inform Mal that since the Motorola product is superior to the others, if Motorola's share of the Supremo market is reduced, he will be forced to report this to his Motorola superiors, who might in turn take the matter up with Supremo's president.

G.I. might, of course, also try to determine if representatives of the other companies are in fact making such payments. If they are, there is little point in G.I.'s trying to influence them. He has no leverage. If they are, it might or might not be the policy of their companies to make such payments. But that issue is between them and their companies. G.I. has no ethical obligation to make their actions known, even if he has some hard evidence that they are making such payments. From an ethical point of view, to require him to do so would be to require everyone to police the affairs of everyone else, and each company to police the affairs of

every other company. Such a requirement cannot be ethically demanded because it would be impossible to fulfill. If G.I. does have evidence that Red Hot and Blue Lightning are making under-the-table payments, he might use it to back up his claims with the Supremo president.

Finally, should G.I. go public with this information? He should not do so unless he has evidence beyond Mal's claim. To do so without hard evidence is to harm the reputations of Supremo, Red Hot and Blue Lightning without justifying cause. If he does have evidence, he has no obligation to make this public. Provided no serious harm is threatened to anyone, people have no general obligation to make public the known wrong-doings of companies. If he still decides to go public, G.I. should first check with his superiors. The implications of going public are serious for all parties, including Motorola. Also, if in Developia under-the-table payments are widespread and broadly tolerated, then going public will not be news, and so will produce little interest and probably bring about no change.

Although it is clear that G.I. should not make the requested payments, there are a number of options open to him concerning what to do next. Ethical considerations alone will not

tell him what to do, since no particular action — going to the president of Supremo, reporting Mal's request, reporting the payments by Red Hot and Blue Lightning, canceling all further business with Supremo, going public with information about under-the-table payments — is ethically required. All are ethically permitted. Which of those ethically permitted options are best must be decided on the basis of business considerations.

Approach Primarily Used: Duties.

[TD] It would be wonderful if bribes were rare, but they are not. In many parts of international business, bribery is a cold, ubiquitous reality. In some countries, bribery emerged from earlier practices of gift-giving. In others, it was encouraged by colonial powers. Whatever its source, bribery constitutes a formidable managerial challenge, for with it, a new, erratic factor enters the business game. No longer can the best product, backed by the best marketing and the best service, be predicted to win. Bribery changes the game itself.

Even more common than bribery are laws against it. John Noonan, author of the most comprehensive book ever written on the subject, notes that every single country has laws against bribery — even countries in which the practice flourishes.

Bribes have two principal drawbacks, and each harms both society and the company. First there is a problem of **duty** (page 30). Bribery constitutes a violation of the duties that employees have to their organizations. This is especially true of the person who accepts the bribe, since the money being paid for the goods or service in the transaction belongs to the organization, and eventually to the owners of the organization, rather than to the employees. This can be seen by considering the fact that if a

business were a sole proprietorship, and there were no tax problems with accepting a payment made to the employee, a separate payment would not be a **bribe.** What makes it a bribe is the violation of a special duty (called a fiduciary duty) owed by the employee to the organization. If owner and organization are one and the same, bribery becomes difficult to define.

The second drawback is related to the first, but is a problem not of duty but of **consequences** (page 29). When bribery becomes a practice, it has negative consequences for societies and for companies. Even the most elementary course in economics teaches that markets might not be capable of doing **everything** (such as ensuring that the poor are fed), but that they do **one** thing extremely well, namely, allocate resources efficiently. A great strength of capitalism as a system is that these capital allocation decisions are made without central direction. Efficient companies get more money to expand their efficient technology for the benefit of society. Inefficient companies get less money and are forced to become more efficient in order to survive. And it all happens through the impersonal magic of the market.

But — and this is a large **but** — capitalism's remarkably efficient mechanism of allocation only works when customers and other

market participants buy on the basis of price and quality. When people and companies begin to purchase services and goods on the basis of how much money they can pocket in a clandestine transaction, watch out! The market is no longer running rationally. The most inefficient companies might be rewarded and, in turn, encouraged for the future since they are receiving revenues based on their willingness to accept bribes. In fact, it is almost necessary that the activity be **less** efficient, since the bribe payer must shoulder a cost (the bribe) that is not part of production and which, were it used to improve production, would result in a better product.

In the Lockheed bribery scandal of the mid-70s, Lockheed, Boeing, and other companies were all competing to sell airplanes to the Japanese government. In the end, the Japanese government opted to buy the planes from Lockheed, but only because Lockheed was willing to pay millions of dollars in bribes to Japanese government officials. The point is straightforward: While there is no reason whatsoever to think that the Lockheed planes were superior to Boeing's planes, the Japanese public might well have purchased overpriced, less safe airplanes — all because of bribery. When such actions are multiplied thousands of times over, day in and day out, the result can be widespread economic corruption that prevents even large economies from attaining a decent standard of living.

These considerations are an important part of why Motorola takes a visible and strong stand against bribery. Its stand is reflected in its Code of Conduct, Key Beliefs and long history. In the present instance, Motorola's philosophy and history show why G.I. Quick should under no circumstances make the gifts requested by Mal Diidh. Its Code of Conduct (Appendix One) states under section A.1 that "the funds and assets of Motorola shall not be used, directly or indirectly, for illegal payments of any kind." At a deeper level, a bribe to Diidh would represent a violation of Motorola's Key Belief in Uncompromising Integrity.

Approaches Primarily Used: Consequences, Duties.

Case 4
Profits and People

This case occurs in the United States. It involves *Ephraim "Speedy" Fast*, an American Motorolan with expertise in cycle-time reduction. Over the past several years, Speedy's skills have paid off handsomely for Motorola. He has led task forces that have addressed efficiency and productivity issues for his sector, resulting in considerable cost savings. As the head of these task forces, Speedy has involved all his team members in the pursuit of these goals. He has encouraged challenge and criticism, and empowered team members to set and achieve new goals.

Recently, top management has assigned Speedy to head a special task force to assess a wide range of issues on which he is an acknowledged expert. Some of his long-time associates and subordinates serve as members of this task force and all of them, out of loyalty to Motorola and respect for Speedy, have participated enthusiastically and unselfishly.

As the work of the task force has proceeded, it has become clear to Speedy that productivity and cost-effectiveness will best be served, at least in the short run, by abolishing two key managerial positions and several in middle management, which due to technological progress are no longer needed. To make matters especially delicate, it turns out that three of these redundant positions are held by members of Speedy's own task force.

Of even greater consequence, the evidence gathered by Speedy and his group suggests that a Motorola facility in the United States should be totally closed down, and moved overseas to *Latafrasia*, a developing nation where labor availability and market access factors are especially favorable.

Speedy is deeply troubled. He is keenly aware that many of the employees who would be affected by these changes originally joined the corporation because of a strong sense of family, which they perceived to be a basic part of the Motorola Culture. What should he do?

Discussion Questions...

1. What is the relevance of the fact that through the years, many members of Speedy's task forces have, in good faith and with good will, brought about numerous job changes and reductions, to the benefit of the corporation but not necessarily themselves?

2. How should Speedy's task force present their recommendation so that both the good of Motorola and the well-being of the redundant members are optimized?

3. To what extent should Motorola employees view themselves as a family that must look after its members through good and bad times?

4. As a U.S.-based corporation, does Motorola have a special obligation to hire Americans, or to retain its U.S. locations, despite lower costs elsewhere?

5. How does Motorola reconcile the need to make a profit with observing Constant Respect for People and maintaining its employees' loyalty? How does one weigh the interests of the stockholders against the interests of employees and managers when the two collide? What sorts of considerations should be given priority?

Commentaries on Case 4

[RTD] "Speedy" Fast is paid to do his best for Motorola. He has done a good job, and is recognized for it. His obligation is to continue to do so. The answer to the question of what he should do, then, is basically an easy one. He should submit the most objective report he can. He may, of course, express his concerns about the people who will be affected by the abolition of positions and the closing of the U.S. facility. But to report any other result from his study would be to falsify the results and, as a violation of his duty, it would be ethically wrong.

Consider first the elimination of the managerial positions, and then the closing of the U.S. facility.

Motorola, like any other company, has no ethical obligation to retain unnecessary positions, to keep open inefficient plants, or to guarantee lifetime employment unless it has contractually agreed to do so. How it treats its employees, however, is an ethical issue. Motorola is committed to Constant Respect for People. Therefore it cannot treat people as expendable parts of a machine.

Of the positions recommended for elimination, three are held by members of Speedy's own task force. It is to the credit of all the members of the task force that the eliminations did not hinder their judgment. Eliminating positions, however, does not automatically mean firing the people who hold them. Motorola must ask itself whether the people in question are valuable enough to transfer elsewhere. The task force is not recommending a reduction in force, only the elimination of a number of unneeded positions. If Motorola wished to reduce its managerial force by the number of jobs eliminated, it might do so by attrition, by encouraging voluntary retirement, or by other means. If cutting the positions automatically means the elimination of the people from Motorola, it is unlikely that many future task forces will advise downsizing their own jobs.

If some Motorolans are let go as a result of the recommendation, and if there is no way to meet these numbers by attrition and voluntary retirement (which seems unlikely here because the numbers are small) then Motorola must treat those who leave with respect. This means providing them with appropriate separation packages — severance pay, continued health insurance for a specified period, out-placement help and so on.

Plant closings are not unethical in themselves, and so the recommendation that a U.S. Motorola plant be closed and moved to Latafrasia is not necessarily unethical. There are two separate issues to consider. The first is the closing of a facility by a corporation that is not in financial difficulty. The second is the moving of a facility to a location outside the United States. Both have been challenged as ethically suspect by some critics.

Assume that the reason for closing the U.S. plant is that it is no longer cost-effective. Is this ethically justifiable? If one argues in the negative, then that would require any profitable company to continue operating unprofitable segments until the company as a whole faces financial difficulty. When considering the consequences, we see that any such requirement is unreasonable and promotes inefficiency. Companies are allowed to close down inefficient operations if they wish. In the United States, the 1988 federal plant closing law mandates that any business with more than 100 employees must give at least 60 days' notice. Some states have more stringent laws requiring retraining, continuation of health insurance for three months, and other benefits. These are legal attempts to ensure that companies treat their employees with basic respect in plant closings.

Motorola is committed to treating its employees with respect and has the duty to do what it can to ease the blow of a plant closing on those who will be terminated, on the community in which the plant is located, and on others adversely affected. What it does might vary from employee to employee. The central points are that plant closings are allowed and that in a plant closing, adequate care must be taken to implement Motorola's commitment to Constant Respect for People.

The other issue is whether it is unethical to move U.S. facilities abroad. As already indicated, it is not unethical to close a facility. By similar reasoning, it is not unethical to close a facility in one location and open one in another location if doing so promotes efficiency and profitability. Unless companies did so, they could not remain competitive. This would undermine the system of competition and free enterprise, and would in the long run produce more harm than good for most Americans.

Closings, however, must be done in such a way as not to violate anyone's rights. If a plant were moved from the Northeastern part of the United States, where wages tend to be higher, to the South where wages tend to be lower, there would be some complaint. But generally the argument can be made that what one portion of the country loses the other portion gains, thus offsetting overall harm to U.S. workers and to the economic well-being of the country. However, this argument is challenged when a U.S. plant is closed

and replaced by another in countries such as Latafrasia. Nonetheless, that challenge is doubtful. Business has become international, whether some people like it or not. From an ethical point of view, if all persons deserve respect, then jobs for people in Latafrasia are as important to them as they are for Americans. Just as people in the Northeastern part of the United States might lose while those in the South gain, so some Americans might lose while some Latafrasians gain. Additional gains are made by the increased efficiency of the corporation and by the controlled or reduced costs as a result of the move, for customers, shareholders and other stakeholders.

To claim that companies should not be allowed to move production abroad is much too stringent. Although an American company has more obligations to the United States than to other countries, the proposed protection of U.S. jobs would do more harm than good. Other negative effects:

- it would impede efficiency;

- it would increase the cost of products to consumers;

- it would make U.S. companies less competitive; and

- it would slow the development of less developed countries and of markets within them.

Having provided justification for plant closings and for the elimination of unnecessary positions, one might ask whether jobs should be cut in order to raise profits, or whether Respect for People requires that positions not be sacrificed to profit enhancement. May a company ethically cut 100 or more positions to reduce costs and at the same time award its top managers with pay raises for having increased profits and shareholder wealth? The details of the answer are complicated. But a short version is that downsizing can be done in such a way as to respect those being laid off, and that the elimination of positions to increase profits might be ethically justifiable. Raising profits might be necessary to keep a company competitive or to keep it from being taken over, with possibly less desirable effects for more employees. The issue of pay increases for top managers is a separate issue. It might be justifiable, but it certainly does not help the morale of the remaining workforce.

Having said all of this, the end result is that Speedy should produce the best, most honest and most objective report he can, and that in implementing that report, Motorola must remember its commitment to respect its employees.

***Approaches Primarily Used:
Duties, Consequences, Rights.***

[RCS] In recent years, major companies have made headlines because of deep cuts in human resources that are intended to make the business more efficient. The headlines on the financial pages were often positive (and the value of the stock followed accordingly), but the editorials and the news reports painted a much bleaker picture. Concern for profits and concern for the people of the company sometimes come into conflict.

On one hand, there is the argument for efficiency and the bottom line. A company exists, in legal terms, in order to make as large a profit as is fair and reasonable. On the other hand, there is the concern for the people — many thousands of them — who found themselves out of a job. Many of them had been loyal employees for 10, 15, even 20-plus years. They had done a good job, and they assumed — wrongly — that their positions with the company were safe and secure. In many instances (according to recent statistics), these people did not find work for another year or more. Many found themselves working for significantly lower wages. Much of modern life is defined and supported by work. Consequently, lives were disrupted and sometimes shattered. Couples got divorced. Families broke up. People genuinely

suffered, and many of the quick profits celebrated by executives and stockholders disappeared. What looked like efficiency turned out to be a disastrous demoralizing of the workforce. Instead of loyalty, prudent employees and managers kept their ears alert and their resumes polished. "Profit Improvement" in the short run often meant a weaker organization in the long run.

The case involving "Speedy" Fast is far less dramatic than the radical downsizings that have been carried out by several of Motorola's peers in the telecommunications industry and elsewhere, but the principle is still the same. Efficiency and profitability are being given priority over people's jobs. Thus the question: Should a company sacrifice its employees and/or managers for the sake of cost-effectiveness? Even if one assumes such cuts are indeed cost-effective, does a company have an obligation to retain personnel who have become "redundant" (as one recent euphemism would have it)?

The question of "obligation" is extremely tricky. If what is meant is a legal obligation, then the answer is certainly no. Employment carries with it no legal guarantees except those explicitly specified by contract or imposed by law. If an ethical obligation is implied, however, then the answer is more com-

plex. Much of it has to do with the concept of loyalty and the rightful expectations of the company.

If the company has made very clear in the past that good employees can expect job security (except, of course, in the direst economic emergencies), then that creates, over time, something of an ethical obligation. If an employee must be terminated, one might expect financial support, retirement programs, "out-placement" services and continued respect for the individual. But, more to the point, one might also expect the company to retain jobs whenever possible, rather than treating managers and employees as dispensable parts in a money-making machine. That, more than anything else, is what is meant by Constant Respect for People.

In the current case, the problem is localized. One small group of managers is affected, and one particular plant is inefficient and not cost-effective. The corporation as a whole is doing quite well, and, in fact, is adding employees and expanding. This provides an easy answer to one aspect of the case. Closing a plant and eliminating a few positions do not require anyone to lose their job. Constant Respect for People means, among other things, giving every individual their due, including an opportunity to stay with the corporation in precisely such cases as this one. Very likely, the managers in question can be placed in other positions, since it is far more cost-effective to retrain an already loyal manager who knows the corporation than to hire someone new from the outside. Treating people with respect means honoring their ability to learn and adapt themselves, both in their own interest and that of the corporation.

A second aspect of the case involves even larger policy questions. Should a facility be moved outside of the United States for the sake of cheaper wages and costs? Again, studies show that the savings are not always as high as expected, given the complications of relocation and the common problems associated with a less experienced, sometimes untrained and culturally different labor force. But, again, let us assume that the savings are sufficient to justify such a move by even a very successful company.

The ethical questions here are well-known and profound. On the one hand, business at the end of the 20th century is essentially international. Markets are increasingly free, and every U.S. company has the right to set up business where it wishes. On the other hand, there is a "proximity" qualification in terms of relationships.

It is the nature of everyday social life that one feels closer to some people than others, and consequently feels a greater sense of responsibility toward them, as in the issue of "jobs for Americans." One might argue that Motorola is doing the Latafrasians more of a favor than it is doing U.S. employees. The standard of living is much poorer in Latafrasia, and the chances of finding a job slimmer, so that modernization of that country would be a considerable boon. But one cannot dismiss an American's obligations to other Americans as mere prejudice or chauvinism. There is a sense in which Motorola, as a U.S.-based corporation, has an obligation to provide employment first of all to the people who made its initial success possible. At the same time, Motorola is operating as a citizen of the world. Thus, such decisions become increasingly problematic.

None of this, however, directly addresses the personal dilemma that Speedy faces in his assignment. The above considerations are intended to outline the implications of the alternatives he and his group are considering. His personal concern, no doubt, is with the Motorolans of his own task force who stand to lose their jobs because of his (and their) recommendations.

It goes without saying that the assessment and report should be honest and straightforward. The report should clearly express both this personal concern and the larger ethical issues. Optimally, the report would also contain positive recommendations for alternative actions.

This is an exemplary case for what some business ethicists have called "moral imagination" — going beyond the limited options that first appear as alternatives and looking for others that serve both profits and people.

Approaches Primarily Used: Virtue, Duties, Ideals.

Case 5
Friendship or
Mutual Bribery?

When Motorola assigned *S.T. Kiosh*, an American, to the European nation of *Abendland* on his first overseas assignment, S.T. and his family soon became good friends with *Bartholomew*, a tried-and-true senior employee in the same department, and a native Abendlander. Their families, too, became good friends who genuinely enjoyed spending leisure time together. They would entertain each other on birthdays, holidays and other occasions. At first this entertainment was modest, but gradually it has become more and more lavish, with Bartholomew escalating the lavishness. However, some would say this is unexceptional, since Abendlanders have traditionally placed great emphasis on making foreign colleagues feel welcome and comfortable.

Over a period of months it gradually becomes clear to S.T. that Bartholomew would dearly love to get his oldest son, *Florian*, into a good university in the United States. Bartholomew could afford the tuition, but there is a problem: Florian is only an average student.

It so happens that S.T. is a graduate of, and contributor to, the famous business school at *Ivytwine University*. Although the standards of this old, established American university are not of the very highest, they are still quite respectable. And Ivytwine's business school is renowned as an excellent place for students

from all over the world to form friendships and alliances that will help them throughout their careers. For that reason, Abendlanders vie to get their children admitted there.

The Ivytwine admissions office has considerable integrity, but is not averse to giving a measure of special consideration to the applications of children, relatives or friends of generous alumni. It occurs to S.T. that with a strong recommendation from a generous alumnus like himself, Florian could probably get into Ivytwine.

As time goes on, the situation within the local Motorola facility evolves in such a way that S.T. sees that he has a splendid opportunity for a major promotion, right there in Abendland. However, there are also several other strong candidates for this position, and whether S.T. succeeds will depend in part on the support he receives from Abendlander Motorolans — such as Bartholomew.

Meanwhile, S.T. has contacted the admissions office at Ivytwine, and, by persistence and the hint that in due course he might have a sizeable gift to bestow upon his *alma mater*, he has managed to get Florian admitted. Since Florian could not have gotten into Ivytwine on his own merit, S.T. has in effect given Bartholomew something of substantial value. All of this has been handled quietly. Other employees are not aware of it.

Discussion Questions...

1. Since Bartholomew has escalated the mutual entertainment, can S.T.'s help getting Florian into Ivytwine be regarded as simple reciprocity between friends?

2. Does Bartholomew's lavish entertainment of S.T. constitute a possible violation of the corporation's "no gifts" policy?

3. Is it reasonable to suspect that S.T. is in effect bribing Bartholomew into supporting his own candidacy for promotion?

4. Should there be a clear articulation of policies in matters where Motorolans help each other in areas outside of their Motorola duties?

Commentaries on Case 5

[RCS] What makes this case particularly intriguing is the fact that it involves not so much financial exchanges, but "favors" of a less tangible but in some ways far more substantial nature. It is fairly easy to put limits on gifts and forbid financial exchanges that can be construed as bribes, but much more difficult to regulate or even detect the sort of favors that are at issue here.

It is clear, insofar as S.T.'s behavior can be considered a bribe — and not a bribe to give a competitive advantage to Motorola but for sheer personal advancement — that his behavior is unethical. (Depending on his abilities relative to the other candidates, his behavior could also be said to be detrimental to Motorola.) If he deserves the promotion, then he should get it without the "favor." If he does not deserve the promotion, then he should not get it.

What is not entirely clear (but of considerable importance) is the extent to which Bartholomew may have solicited S.T.'s help. If he had suggested that S.T. might be able to help his son enter a good business school, and in return he would influence S.T.'s promotion, then his behavior would have been clearly unethical.

Yet the nuances and implications of seemingly innocent social conversations create considerable subtlety regarding Bartholomew. If S.T., Bartholomew and their families have become good friends, then Bartholomew's expressions of concern about his son's future might well be a natural topic of conversation between the two of them, particularly if S.T. is known to be involved with a respectable business school of just the sort that Bartholomew would like to see Florian attend. A simple query like "Do you think that you could do anything?" might push this natural conversation into the realm of the ethically dubious, however, due to their relative positions. If Bartholomew had little or no say in S.T.'s promotion, such a query would remain innocent enough, a requested favor of one friend to another. On the other hand, if Bartholomew were S.T.'s superior, who would himself determine the promotion, then such a query would be clearly improper and coercive (somewhat comparable to sexual harassment situations).

But assume now that the ethical burden in this case lies entirely on S.T.'s shoulders, and that Bartholomew has made no such queries, nor has he anticipated his potential role in S.T.'s promotion. It is not improper to do favors for friends, and although one might well be skeptical about doing favors for friends in order to obtain a favor in return (even if no such tit-for-tat arrangement has been mentioned), such behavior is not in itself unethical. Of course, S.T. might fail in his effort — Florian might be unacceptable to Ivytwine even in the light of the promise of a future gift from S.T. Or Florian might get into Ivytwine, but Bartholomew, being a scrupulous manager, might not intervene as S.T. had hoped.

The main questions, however, concern S.T.'s own sense of integrity.

- Does he see doing favors for friends in order to advance himself at Motorola as a breach of friendship ("using" his friend)?

- Does he see himself as compromising Bartholomew's own integrity by putting him in a position where he owes S.T. a considerable favor?

- Does he see himself as compromising the policies of Motorola, which attempt to foster promotion by merit and not by connections?

- Does he see himself as willfully lying (or "padding the truth") in his recommendation of Florian to Ivytwine?

- Does he see himself as in effect offering a bribe to Ivytwine (or hinting that he will provide one in the future) in order to secure Florian's admission?

Finally, there is another realm of integrity that is at stake in this case, and that is at Ivytwine. There are many schools that have or once had an explicit policy of giving some preference to the children of alumni, assuming that they also fulfill all of the qualifications for admission. Florian, however, is not the child of an alumnus, and insisting on his status as the child of a friend of an alumnus is stretching the concept pretty thin. It is clearly the promise of the financial boon, not the ties of *alma mater*, that are the incentive in this case.

If S.T. is really the good friend he proclaims himself to be, he might offer to help Florian with his homework and help him get admitted on his own merits.

Approach Primarily Used: Virtue.

[WJE] S.T. Kiosh finds himself in a culture different from his own. For personal as well as business reasons he needs to feel as comfortable as possible in his new situation. What a delight then to meet Bartholomew and his family, who seem to blend in quite well in both the Abendlandian and American cultures.

But there are several murky areas in this scenario. Bartholomew's relation to S.T. is unclear. Do Bartholomew and his family truly share an interest in U.S. culture as such, and is this why he is so keen to get Florian into an American university? Or does he see the entire matter primarily in terms of helping Florian secure a good economic future? Or is Bartholomew's interest in S.T. simply a function of dynamics within the Motorola organization and culture? His relationship with S.T. will be quite different in each context.

If the context is that Bartholomew and his family have a genuine interest in U.S. culture that is reciprocated by S.T. and his family in Abendlandian culture, then Bartholomew's request to get Florian into Ivytwine might be viewed as a way of cementing a warm friendship.

But both Bartholomew and S.T. are employees of Motorola. While the Motorola Culture is concerned primarily with the workings of the corporation, it does deal with certain aspects of family and friendship relations, such as the exchange of gifts and favors. S.T.'s use of his influence and money in order to help get Florian into Ivytwine thus raises ethical questions. Although the many family gatherings could possibly have made S.T.'s action one of simple mutual familial support, the fact that Bartholomew and S.T. are colleagues at Motorola melds the dynamics of family into the dynamics of business. One cannot ignore the fact that S.T. might improve his chances for advancement at Motorola by getting Florian into Ivytwine. S.T. could possibly change the situation by informing Bartholomew that he neither intends nor expects that his work on Florian's behalf will have any benefit to him other than in the context of personal and familial friendship. But considering their working relationship, it is doubtful that such a statement could keep Bartholomew from feeling a debt of gratitude. At any rate, the absence of such a statement leads to the strong suspicion of an inappropriate *quid pro quo*.

Approach Primarily Used: Traditions and Stories.

Case 6
Constant Respect for —
Human Rights?

Dr. Tess Techster, 40, is a corporate officer responsible for research and development of Motorola's new *"Telekom SuperPackage"* of wireless telecommunications products. In recognition of her achievements as a technologist and business innovator, she has been chosen by the prestigious *Yarvard University Business School* to give its Annual Outstanding Young Technologist's Business Vision Lecture. The auditorium is packed.

The Speech

In her lecture Tess described the Telekom SuperPackage as an unprecedented achievement, combining features of user-friendliness, portability, durability, versatility, flexibility and affordability. Then she summed up:

> My vision is that Motorola's Telekom SuperPackage will revolutionize economic development in the Third World by allowing millions of isolated entre-preneurs, for the first time in history, to get timely and accurate market information and make business arrangements — all at a distance.

Then came question time. Tess was jolted when one student or professor after another rose to ask her about the ethics of Motorola's selling SuperPackages in

Amrubia. The climax came when *Holbridge Vanderbilt*, President of the Yarvard Chapter of the *World Student Confederation*, delivered a passionate threat:

> With due respect, Dr. Techster, I must disagree. You say Motorola is helping entrepreneurs, but in Amrubia you are primarily helping a bunch of corrupt *GRUNJ* generals to snoop on their own people. Motorola looks the other way and cannot see brutal despotism under its very nose! If Motorola continues to do this, do not be surprised if our Confederation launches a worldwide boycott of all your products, which will not do your global brand image any good.

Tess kept her composure: "I sincerely thank all of you for your input. Motorola prides itself on being a good corporate citizen. I will look into what you have told me."

The Amrubia Situation

Back at her office, Tess met with *Gordon Reeve* of Government Relations for a briefing. Here is what she learned.

The Republic of Amrubia, a British colony until 1955, is a poor nation of 45 million, ripe for develop-ment with its rich natural resources and adult literacy of 70 percent.

During their first 20 years of independence Amrubians enjoyed considerable personal freedom under a moderate government. Then in 1975 a military coup occurred, and a clique of generals called GRUNJ (Government Reconstruction and Unification Junta) took power. To promote "national reconstruction and unification," GRUNJ suspended elections, assigned military counterintelligence officers throughout the country down to the district level, and created informer networks in every village. Beginning last year, village informers have been issued Telekom SuperPackage equipment, often secretly. These informers are charged with reporting to the government all of their fellow villagers who express "subversive" opinions. Many Amrubians so identified have been imprisoned without proper trial, and some are known to have been tortured.

GRUNJ has also instituted rigid economic controls and stifled private initiative. Amrubia's gross domestic product has actually **fallen,** and is now one of the lowest in the world — $330 per capita. However, GRUNJ has permitted limited private enterprise, which explains Motorola's establishment of a sales office in Amrubia in 1985.

Amnesty International has strongly condemned the GRUNJ regime, as has the U.S. State Department in its latest annual report on nations violating human rights. However, the U.S. government has not prohibited U.S.-registered companies from doing business in Amrubia — yet, at least.

The Meeting

The next day Tess called a meeting of key personnel in her business. The agenda: What should be Motorola's policy in Amrubia and other host nations alleged to be violating basic human rights?

"Remain there!" says *Engelbert "Spike" Speer,* of Sales:

> We've had a sales office there for 12 years, but only last year did we start making real money. That's when the SuperPackage program got started. I've worked in the developing areas for nine years, and in my opinion this is a really unusual opportunity. The Amrubian government has indicated that it finds our new SuperPackages highly helpful to them in promoting order and development. We have sold about $11 million worth this year alone, and I think we can get about $19 million next year. But if we disengage, we will earn the lasting enmity of the Amrubian government, will lose our market share to non-American competitors who don't share our ethical standards, and will later find it very hard to re-enter that market.

"I'm not so sure," says *Sarah Sterling* of Law:

> Of course Motorola does not take sides in host country political issues, but the fact is that already the state of *Calichusetts* plus several European governments and American local governments have passed legislation boycotting **all** products of **any**

corporation that does business in Amrubia. And the World Student Confederation, with its intensive use of the Internet, has gained **global** political clout far beyond its numbers. Keep in mind that many very ethical companies like *Breineken's Beer* and *Pewlett Hackard* have already disengaged. The very least we should do, right now, is hire a good nongovernmental organization to do a prompt human rights audit for us in Amrubia.

"Get out of there!" says *Walt Welliver* of HR:

We would never do business with a **company** that treated its employees the way GRUNJ treats its citizens. The fact is that most of the SuperPackages would be used by GRUNJ, primarily to suppress their own people. GRUNJ wants SuperPackages because local village informers can **conceal** the equipment easily, so that other villagers won't know that they are informers. True, some businesspeople have been and will be issued licenses for SuperPackages, but they would almost all be people working closely with GRUNJ. GRUNJ will not allow any so-called "rising middle class" of business and professional people to have free use of SuperPackages. So far, only 20 percent of the SuperPackages in Amrubia are in private hands, and you should also know that almost none of these are owned by nongovernmental organizations. Even the *International Mercy Volunteers* cannot use a SuperPackage there except in case of an actual emergency.

Toward Decision

Tess summed up the meeting: "What I hear is that Amrubia is a country that **could** develop beautifully, but is being held back by a government with ethical standards very different from Motorola's. I hear you saying that our SuperPackages might help develop a democratically inclined middle class, but not much; and that it will help GRUNJ quite a bit more.

"Let's meet again next Tuesday to formulate a clear recommendation to senior management: to remain, to remain with qualifications, or to disengage. Please come prepared for a frank and open discussion."

Discussion Questions...

1. Should Motorola be concerned because Amnesty International and the U.S. State Department have documented that Amrubians opposed to GRUNJ have often been imprisoned without proper trial, and sometimes tortured?

2. Is the use to which a host government puts a Motorola product a proper ethical concern of Motorola's? Or does ethical responsibility stop the moment the ownership of a product is transferred?

3. Should Tess recommend total disengagement from Amrubia because similar violations of human rights and dignity by a private company would warrant Motorola's disengagement from doing business with that company?

4. In making its ethical decision, should Motorola take into account the likelihood that the World Student Confederation and other nongovernmental organizations could mount a boycott of Motorola products worldwide?

5. Would it make sense for Motorola to band together with other large multinationals operating in Amrubia in an effort to form a solid front against GRUNJ's use of wireless equipment to snoop indiscriminately on Amrubian citizens? Would such a front be likely to achieve solid results?

6. If Tess invited you to attend the next meeting, what policy would you suggest that she recommend to senior management?

Commentaries on Case 6

[RCS] Although this case raises deep and troublesome issues, the actual decision that Tess Techster must make — to recommend remaining in or disengaging from Amrubia (or taking some other course of action) — is straightforward. This is as it should be, for human rights are one of the most profound areas of international concern, and therefore unavoidably a central concern for a global and ethical corporation such as Motorola.

Yet there are many questions about whether this complex concept — often defined as a distinctively individualistic Western concept most famously formulated by such thinkers as John Locke — applies without modification (or at all) to **non-Western** cultures. For example, the argument is often distorted by such simple-minded accusations as "Culture X has no concept of rights," ignoring the fact that other traditions might have quite sufficient ethical standards, even though these might differ from the Western notion of **"individual** rights." In this connection, note that the case makes clear that prior to 1975 "Amrubians enjoyed considerable personal freedom under a moderate government." In other words, the GRUNJ group that took power that year by military coup obviously violated **Amrubian** cultural standards of human rights by imposing a corrupt and cruel regime on an unwilling people. The GRUNJ

regime is the very nightmare of unethical behavior. So, although the question of cultural and ethical differences is profound and difficult, it is not ultimately at stake in this case.

The key question is whether Motorola is willing to contribute to the efforts of the GRUNJ regime by making Telekom Superpackages available directly to it. The case would be substantially different if, for example, GRUNJ obtained the packages elsewhere through unspecified agents. An issue would still exist: Should Motorola hold itself responsible for the use of its products by people who are not its customers and in a country where it does not do business? But this is not Tess' issue. Her issue is simply whether to recommend remaining in or disengaging from Motorola's present involvement in Amrubia, or taking some third course of action.

The issue of standards, and of "who says so," is certainly a central concern. If it were only Amnesty International that had urged disengagement from Amrubia, that advice would be worth taking very seriously but would not, by itself, be definitive. (Indeed, the Amnesty International list would eliminate quite a number of the world's markets.) But when its list is coupled with those of the U.S. State Department, plus several foreign and local American governments, that gives the charges not only irrefutable legitimacy but the weight of patriotic obligation as well.

That the U.S. government has not yet prohibited American companies from doing business in Amrubia offers little consolation. Motorola prides itself on not only complying with the law but on cooperating with the spirit of international moral opinion — the difference between mere prudential legal obedience and true ethical behavior.

The question of market stakes is not, as such, an ethical question but a straightforward business matter. Nevertheless, business decisions concerning ethical matters are often influenced by considerations of market stakes. If Amrubia were not a country of 45 million but of 450 million, or perhaps even a billion, there is little doubt that the U.S. State Department would be heavily lobbied to issue "stern warnings" and other symbolic sanctions instead of closing off markets worth billions or trillions of dollars to U.S.-based businesses. Such questions are issues of continuing controversy, of course, but the question cannot be avoided here: What if Amrubia were a huge potential market, and, perhaps, a potent global market force? Would that make Motorola's position and Tess's decision more difficult? The honest answer has to be "yes." But the small scale of business in Amrubia, even given its upward potential, renders the weight of market stakes considerations negligible in the face of the ethical charges that Motorola is, whether wittingly or not, directly aiding an oppressive and brutal regime despised by its own people.

Spike Speer's argument that Motorola "will later find it very hard to re-enter the market" appears specious. If Motorola stays, and the GRUNJ regime is overthrown or replaced by a popular uprising and/or outside pressures, Motorola's name in the country will be hateful and its future business potential minimal. On the other hand, if Motorola were to leave, making known its reasons for doing so, it might find a welcome and grateful market when it returns, in part because of its proven reputation for ethical behavior and concern for human rights.

Likewise specious is Spike's facile warning that "we. . .will lose our market to non-American competitors who don't share our ethical standards." Yes, Motorola might well lose business temporarily to companies without ethical principles, who will then share the odium of the hated government and lose out when it falls. And history makes it clear enough: Oppressive, hated governments eventually fall. Why then take the chance of falling with them, when the probable benefits of doing the right thing so heavily outweigh the costs of stubbornly (but no longer blindly) holding one's ground?

Sarah Sterling's suggestion that Motorola should "at least" hire a good NGO to do a human rights audit, while no doubt desirable on its own merits and for the information it would provide (and not just

for Motorola), would by itself be of little significance. It would delay what should probably be a timely decision, given the pressures that are already mounting. And it would lend itself to the usual cynicism: "Sure, they are 'studying' the issue while they continue to make a profit from that obviously evil regime." The Lord Buddha said: "When a house is burning down, one does not stop to contemplate the meaning of 'house' or 'burning.' One puts out the fire."

Sarah also claims that "Motorola does not take sides in host country political issues." In an important sense, this is true. But some political issues are not merely differences of opinion, or power struggles between opposing parties. They are deep ethical and human rights issues, concerning which Motorola, like all of us, cannot help but take sides. To do or say nothing, to continue to carry on "business as usual," is in fact to take a side — the wrong one.

Some might contend that Motorola is not responsible for the use to which people put its products. Motorola pagers, for example, are used in various countries not only by doctors and businesspeople but also by drug dealers. And yet it would surely be false to say that Motorola is not concerned with the latter. The fact is that Motorola **does** take responsibility for the use of its products. For example, it has recently declared that it will do all in its power to ensure that its chips are not used in the manufacture

of anti-personnel land mines, which kill or injure thousands of people (mainly children) every year. Insofar as it is true, as Tess concludes, that the SuperPackages might help middle-class Amrubian entrepreneurs, but not much, and that they will help the hated GRUNJ much more, the argument that the packages are intended to help Third World entrepreneurs is eclipsed by the facts of the matter.

Tess should recommend total disengagement. The views of the World Student Confederation, combined with those of Amnesty International, the U.S. State Department and foreign and local American governments should be definitive, not only because of the threat of a worldwide boycott (although that is not an irrelevant consideration) but more importantly because such broad consensus points inescapably to the conclusion that disengagement is the morally obligatory thing to do. Moreover, Motorola should participate in larger attempts to prevent all such equipment, including its own equipment purchased elsewhere and smuggled into Amrubia, from being used for such nefarious purposes in Amrubia. In other troubled spots on the globe, the decision might be more difficult. But in Amrubia, the optimal business decision and the best ethical decision exactly coincide.

Approaches Primarily Used: Rights, Consequences, Virtue.

[RTD] Motorola's commitment to "Constant Respect for People" entails respect for the human rights of all with whom it deals. There is little controversy about this commitment on two levels: First, it entails respect for the human rights of all individuals — employees, customers and others — with whom Motorola deals directly everywhere in the world where it operates. Motorola should not and does not directly violate the human rights of anyone. Second, the commitment entails not indirectly violating anyone's human rights, for instance, by using suppliers who do not respect the human rights of their employees. Just as no company may ethically violate anyone's human rights directly, so it may not use as a supplier or agent any party or person who violates the human rights of others. For a company knowingly to work with such parties is to endorse, condone and be guilty of such violations.

Is the same thing true of a company operating in a country whose government is not only repressive, but which blatantly violates the human rights of its own citizens? Does a company indirectly violate human rights simply by carrying on business there? Since it is the government that is violating human rights, it might seem that unless a company worked with the government as a supplier, the company would be free to carry on its own affairs independently. Yet, although it might seem that simply operating in such a country does not automatically involve one in human rights violations, the situation becomes more complicated once we consider that a company may support a government indirectly by paying taxes, by adding respectability to the government by the company's presence, and, perhaps paradoxically, even by making life more tolerable for the people and so decreasing popular unrest. Hence we should look for principles that might be used in deciding whether or not to operate in such countries.

In searching for principles, we can consider the experience of companies that operated in South Africa during the period of apartheid. There those companies that directly supported the South African government, for instance through bank loans, were appropriately deemed as aiding and abetting apartheid. On the other hand, those companies that followed what were known as the Sullivan Code were able, at least for a number of years, to offer a plausible defense for staying in South Africa. Following the Sullivan Code involved refusing to follow the apartheid laws, and so refusing to violate the human rights of employees or others, and doing what the company could to break down apartheid from within by putting pressure on the government to rescind the laws. Moreover, the companies that signed on to following the Sullivan Code acted in unison, forming a group of important companies whose stance could not be ignored; and they acted openly, stating their policy to the government, to the people of South Africa, and to their shareholders and customers in the United States and elsewhere.

In the present case the government of Amrubia clearly violates the human rights of its citizens by imprisoning them without proper trial and in some cases torturing them. Amnesty International has condemned the GRUNJ regime for violating human rights, and so has the U.S. State Department. So the case is fairly clear for leaving Amrubia, unless one can develop something like the argument used by companies that stayed in South Africa during apartheid.

Engelbert Speer presents some of the reasons for staying. The government has used the new Motorola Telekom SuperPackages to promote order and development; if Motorola disengages, non-American competitors who don't share Motorola's ethical values will take over Motorola's market; and it will be difficult to return if human rights conditions change for the better. Speer, however, ignores the fact that the government has used the SuperPackages to promote order at the expense of human rights; he ignores the fact that since Amrubia's GDP has fallen, it is dubious that the government has promoted development and helped the people of the country; and he ignores the implications for Motorola worldwide if it continues doing business in Amrubia. He may be correct that some non-U.S. companies will gain market share. But he cannot complain about those companies not sharing Motorola's ethical standards because he is in fact arguing for a policy that ignores ethical commitments and responsibilities and takes into account only financial and market considerations. A company that acts in this way does not have any commitment to ethics. Such is not the company that Motorola has been and should desire to continue to be.

Sarah Sterling's position correctly states that Motorola should not take sides in host country political issues. But she notes that the State of Calichusetts, some local communities and some other governments have boycotted products of companies that do business in Amrubia; that some companies have already left; and that the World Student Confederation might take some action — mobilize a general boycott or the like. Although she gives these strong prudential reasons to consider leaving, she does not raise the ethical issues, except to suggest a human rights audit. Why she thinks another audit is necessary is not clear, since Amnesty International and a number of local governments have already obtained sufficient information for them to take action, and that information is widely known.

Walt Welliver makes some of the correct ethical points. But he does not state the general principles of which they are an application.

Two extreme positions concerning country engagement are: 1) to do business in any country in which a company is not legally prohibited from doing so; and 2) at the other extreme, to refuse to do business in any country that has been charged with any human rights violations. Both should be avoided. The first is in effect an abdication of moral

responsibility. It leaves all decisions about whether to operate in a country up to the U.S. Government and market forces. The second is unrealistic, since many nations, even the United States, have been charged with human rights violations.

Motorola in this and similar cases should take a position consistent with its Key Beliefs of Constant Respect for People and Uncompromising Integrity. Three principles can be applied:

• Never violate the human rights of anyone, either directly or indirectly. Just as Motorola does not aid and abet suppliers in violating the human rights of others, so it should not aid or abet any county in violating the human rights of its citizens. This means that Motorola should not sell its products to governments that it knows or has good reason to believe will use the products in suppressing or violating human rights.

• Do business in a country that is guilty of serious human rights abuses only if one can make a convincing case that by staying in or entering the country the company can significantly help the country's people; indirectly, at least, promote democracy; and help lessen human rights violations there. The test to pass is that of helping the people significantly more than helping the government, where "people" means the general population and not just some group of local elites. The case, when made, should be made publicly. The Sullivan Code in South Africa implemented this and the previous principle.

- If a company satisfies the two previous principles and remains in a country that violates human rights, the company should cooperate with U.S. and other companies in protesting the human rights violations and use its influence to the extent possible to change the conditions and the government's policies.

Although the principles are reasonably clear, each country to which they are applied must be assessed individually to make an appropriate decision. It will not always be clear whether a country's human rights abuses are serious and whether more harm than good is done to the people by continuing to do business in a certain country. However, in the present instance it is clear that doing business in Amrubia violates both of the first two principles. Hence the recommendation that Dr. Tess Techster should make to senior management is that Motorola should disengage from Amrubia.

Another lesson companies can learn from the South African experience is that there are better and worse ways to disengage. Because GRUNJ controls who has and who uses the SuperPackages, Motorola should not leave in name only and continue to market the SuperPackages through some third party. Tess should recommend complete disengagement.

Finally, since the conditions in Amrubia or conditions similar to them are likely to occur in other countries in which Motorola considers doing or is doing business, it would be well for Motorola to adopt a principled policy that it follows throughout the world. Otherwise, the company will be attempting to deal with each country in an ad hoc and possibly inconsistent and unprincipled way, and leaving decisions about whether or not to withdraw in the hands of the local managers without giving them adequate guidance.

Although the recommendation is basically an ethical one, it also makes good business sense and can be presented by Tess as such. Motorola will at least temporarily lose the Amrubian market. It may or may not be able to make a strong re-entry if conditions change. Nonetheless, Motorola will avoid a possible boycott of its products; it will improve its public relations and brand image with its stakeholders and its customers worldwide; and most importantly, it will preserve its integrity and its dedication to Constant Respect for People and Uncompromising Integrity.

Approaches Primarily Used: Rights, Consequences.

Case 7
When Is Information "Proprietary"?

This case occurs in *Industria,* one of the more technologically advanced nations of the Western world. The case involves Motorola engineer *Rex Bayard,* 37. Years ago, while still an undergraduate at *Industria National University (INU),* his country's premier institution of higher learning, Rex became friends with three of his professors. All of them — but especially his favorite, the brilliant technologist *Professor Kron* — urged him to go on for a doctorate in engineering. He did so.

One of the reasons Rex went to all the effort of earning his doctorate was to have the option of choosing a career in **either** academia or private industry — or perhaps both. The idea of **both** attracted him, and this is one reason why he sought and obtained a job at Motorola. He believed that by joining a leading technology corporation he could sooner or later have the best of both worlds.

During the next several years, Dr. Bayard performed excellently as a design engineer and achieved several patents. His future with Motorola looked bright. Through publications he also became well known in academic circles. Over the years, two or three good universities offered him full-time professorial appointments, but he turned them all down to remain at Motorola.

Three years ago Dr. Bayard did, however, become an **adjunct** professor at his old university, where his duties are to teach one practicum a year in his specialty, Computer-Aided Design (CAD), and to do a certain amount of student counseling. He genuinely enjoys this arrangement, because it provides an opportunity for continuing relationships with his old professors, as well as new relationships with some of their junior colleagues and graduate students.

Rex's old professors serve from time to time as consultants to various companies, including several that compete with Motorola. Often these consulting arrangements call for the professor to do a certain amount of proprietary research, usually assisted by one or more of their graduate students. Some of these students have enrolled in Rex's practicum, and he has generally found them to be bright and interesting.

Both in class and in informal contacts at INU, Rex has occasionally learned about work being done at these competing companies that was more advanced than the current work at Motorola. However, he has never shared any cutting-edge material about **Motorola's** technological development work with faculty or students at INU. He is, after all, an employee of Motorola, and only marginally a member of academe.

Rex understands that all this is in line with corporate policy, which basically provides that:

- Motorola will not allow others to steal its proprietary secrets.

- Motorola will not steal another company's proprietary secrets.

Last Thursday evening an unusual event occurred. Rex was developing instructional materials at INU's Computer-Aided Design Laboratory. He was tired and about to quit work when he inadvertently touched the wrong key sequence on his computer keyboard, and pulled up a CAD Lab file in which he recognized a design document by one of Professor Kron's graduate assistants, *Marianne McAlister*. Rex couldn't help noticing that Marianne had prepared this document for one of the companies with which Professor Kron consulted, namely *Mercury Electronics*. He also couldn't help noticing that the Kron-McAlister document was for the design of a product that would be competitive with a current Motorola product, and that was apparently **superior** to Motorola's in its functionality and user-friendliness. The document also included information relevant to pricing.

Rex printed out the Mercury document and put the printout into his briefcase. Then he promptly logged off. He did this more or less out of habit — yet with a strange dark feeling that he had crossed an ethical line.

Rex then left the CAD Lab and drove home, where he took an hour to study the printout. Yes, the Kron-McAlister design for Mercury indeed **was** superior, **but** in a way he could incorporate into a design he was developing for Motorola.

The following afternoon Rex showed the design printout to some of the members of his work group, including his supervisor, *Johan Streicher*. All of them found the document interesting and relevant to Motorola's own product development plans. Neither Johan nor any other member of the work group indicated or hinted that Rex had done anything wrong.

Nonetheless, all last weekend Rex felt troubled. Early Monday morning he went to see the director of R&D for Motorola/Industria (Johan's supervisor), *Antonio Romulo*. "Antonio," he said, "I think I might have crossed a line, and I need your advice and instructions. . . ."

Discussion Questions...

1. What should Antonio Romulo advise or require Rex Bayard to do?

2. What should be Rex's next step with Professor Kron?

3. What is the significance of the fact that Johan Streicher and other members of the work group did not indicate or hint that Rex had done anything wrong?

4. Speaking broadly, what is the proper relationship between academic research, and proprietary research carried out at universities for business clients?

Commentaries on Case 7

[WJE] Dr. Rex Bayard has been highly successful as a Motorola engineer. He clearly feels Motorola to be his primary loyalty, and Motorola/Industria to be his true professional home. At the same time, he feels a personal and professional need for continued contact with his former professors, and with their ideas, some of which are at the cutting edge of his field of Computer-Aided Design. Rex's adjunct professorship at Industria National University conveniently makes this possible.

The crux of this case concerns the relationship between the academic culture, and the business culture, found in Industria. One can conceive of an overall academic culture in Industria, but also a special variant thereof for INU. Similarly, one can conceive of an overall business culture in that country, but also a special Motorola Culture for Motorola/Industria.

The overall academic culture and the overall business culture of any modern industrial nation have many overlaps, but many differences as well. Primary among the differences is that in any major university in such a nation there will always be a strong emphasis on open procedures and the more or less prompt publication of research results. By contrast, in the business culture of such a nation

there will be considerable emphasis on generating **proprietary** information — and keeping it private at least until its commercial potential has been realized. Academe's more open approach is consistent with the fundamental mission of the university to discover and disseminate truth to **all** members of society (including of course its business members). Academicians such as Professor Kron who successfully contribute to this mission are rewarded by promotions, salary increases and other means. A business' more closed approach is likewise consistent with **its** fundamental mission — to its shareholders, employees and others — to remain profitable. Employees such as Dr. Bayard, who successfully contribute to this mission, such as by gaining and managing useful proprietary information, are likewise rewarded in career terms.

These matters vary from one national culture to another, and from one university to another, but the general fact remains that scholars such as Professor Kron are expected to do much of their research in areas where prompt and general publication will result. If Professor Kron had wanted to spend 90 percent of his time doing proprietary research or consulting, it is unlikely that he could ever have become a professor at a major university in the first place. By the same token, if Dr. Bayard had wanted to spend 90 percent of **his** time doing research for

dissemination to the general public (and of course to Motorola's competitors), it is unlikely that he could have remained very long at Motorola.

However, the separation between academic and business cultures is less than total. For example, it is well understood in most university cultures that once a professor has earned a permanent position, he or she may engage in a certain amount of proprietary research or consulting, subject to that university's general guidelines. Professor Kron is such a professor. Though he is willing to do consulting and research for such companies as Mercury, his primary loyalty remains with Industria National University, which requires that his work for Mercury be **subordinate** to his duties at INU. Nothing that he does for Mercury can violate his basic obligations to INU. At the same time, he must observe the terms of his agreement with Mercury, which will typically require him **not** to publish proprietary information, at least until Mercury authorizes him to do so.

Such consulting agreements can result in a certain constraining of a university's overall atmosphere of total intellectual freedom, and for this reason are properly subject to regulation by the university. Major universities in the industrial world are thus likely to have formal or informal codes governing such matters as the percentage of a professor's time he or she may devote to private consulting, or even the types of consulting he may do.

All this said, it must be stressed that many major universities **do** welcome a certain amount of the "right" kind of consulting, for the value that it can add. Thus, INU's connection with Mercury might well enrich the research atmosphere of some of its departments by providing fresh intellectual challenges from the "real world," and will often provide needed funding for useful research, and sometimes stipends for graduate students such as Marianne McAlister.

While some companies in Industria might regard the Kron-McAlister document as "fair game" to steal as long as they know they won't get caught, there is no doubt that the Motorola Culture defines such behavior as unethical and unallow-able. Motorola is intensely competi-tive, yes, but it places its **own** ethical limits on **how** it may com-pete. Rex clearly violated those limits by printing out Marianne's document and taking it home. It is not surprising that he had a "strange dark feeling" when he did so. After all, he didn't **have** to do this. Instead, he could have quietly discarded the printout and gone about his normal routine.

There can be little doubt but that the Kron-McAlister document is the private property of Mercury Electronics, the circulation of which Mercury has the right to restrict. One wonders why Mercury did not insist on one obviously needed restriction, namely the use of lim-ited-access provisions in the CAD Lab, such as security codes, passwords and the like. Perhaps Mercury assumed that Professor Kron would make the necessary security arrangements, and the busy professor simply forgot to do so.

Compounding Rex's ethical viola-tion is that if and when Mercury were to learn that one of its key proprietary documents had been shared with a competitor, Professor Kron might be subject to a lawsuit, or might lose his consultantship with Mercury, and perhaps suffer loss of much of his reputation as well.

Imagine a reverse situation, in which Dr. Bayard had arranged for Professor Kron and Marianne McAlister to do proprietary work for **Motorola,** only one day to learn that the resulting design document had somehow fallen into the hands of Mercury. Rex's career would be put at risk, and he would be justifiably furious.

When Rex showed the Kron-McAlister document to his work group, they must have quickly recognized that it was **not** a Motorola document. After all, Motorola documents have a

certain format and refer to Motorola matters, and here was a document probably in a different format, and certainly referring to **Mercury** matters, right down to pricing infor-mation. It is thus doubly surprising that "neither Johan nor any other member of the work group indicated or hinted that Rex had done anything wrong."

We are not told exactly what tran-spired at the work group's meeting, but it is conceivable that Rex did not volunteer to his colleagues any information about the source of the document, **and** that no one asked him. If someone did ask him and he lied about the source, his ethical infraction would be all the greater.

Professor Kron would certainly not knowingly pass along Mercury's current cutting-edge development secrets to Rex. The most that he, or Mercury, would be comfortable sharing with Motorola, or the public, would be information of a more general and abstract nature, rather than information in a form available for practical commercial use. Such a mutual sharing of information at a general level is a frequent practice, not only in academe but among corporations themselves.

What should R&D director Antonio Romulo do? He should advise and require Dr. Bayard to:

• Immediately withdraw the document from all use by Motorola.

- Inform all the members of his work team of the source of the document.

- Return the document to Professor Kron, together with a written statement that no copies have been made, and that Motorola will make no use of the information in it.

- Inform INU of what happened, and request a tightening of the computer-access security procedures in the CAD Lab, so that this type of incident will not recur.

- Ask Professor Kron what else he can do to cooperate.

Looking ahead broadly, it is clear that in tomorrow's global marketplace with its rapidly changing technology and intense competition for high stakes, ethical issues of this general sort are bound to arise frequently. It is important that major universities and research institutes around the world, and major multinational corporations such as Motorola, seek honestly and persistently to work out acceptable ethical standards for handling such issues, on a global basis if possible, or otherwise on a national or regional basis. This should be part of a deliberate ongoing ethical renewal process. One hopes that Motorola, as an ethical leader among the world's major corporations, will not shrink from the task.

Approach Primarily Used:
Traditions and Stories.

[TD] Intellectual property is one of the toughest ethical issues confronting domestic and multinational managers alike. Motorola has a strict policy for a good reason, namely that no other issue of competitive advantage is more crucial for Motorola's future success. Without intellectual property, Motorola is just another commodity producer. With it, Motorola can triumph over competition.

The debate on intellectual property pits two fundamental values against each other: the right to property on one hand, and freedom on the other. The clash between these two values has been played out in the courtroom as well as the board room. It has been arbitrated in international trade agreements and in private conversations between employers and employees who are signing "non-compete" agreements.

The obvious value of property, often created through great effort, is essential to any meaningful commerce. Intellectual property might not resemble property in the form of land or moveable possessions, but it has essential similarities. Without the rights that property conveys, there would be no incentive to develop a better mousetrap — or cellular phone. Without these rights, people would simply copy the hard-earned design of a brilliant inventor the moment it appeared on the market. Edwin Land, inventor or the Polaroid camera, once remarked that without protection of intellectual property, a "cesspool of secrecy" would exist. Sisela Bok, a well-known writer on property, describes how the porcelain factories of Germany in the 19th century had to maintain a near-police state at work, forcing employees to live within the walls of the factory, in order to ensure that their secrets of porcelain manufacture not leak out to German competitors.

This example gives rise to the other value at stake in intellectual property, namely freedom. Indeed, in **defending** the rights of property, invasions of liberty are all too common. Laws that assign copyrights and patents are not always enough to secure these rights in a world in which workers are increasingly mobile and able to carry a bundle of minor company secrets to competing workplaces. The development of legal instruments such as non-compete agreements is evidence of the need to protect intellectual property with explicit restrictions. And yet, freedom might be the loser in such arrangements. Suppose that a bright young engineer is required to sign a five-year non-compete agreement in order to get her first job. But suppose that within a few months the worker finds that she is totally incompatible with the company's management style. She has no intention of spreading trade secrets to another company — she just wants out of this one. Is she to be barred from **all** competitors in the same industry for the next five years? And if so, isn't this a violation of a value just as fundamental as property, that is, freedom?

In an attempt to strike the proper balance between the rights of property and freedom, prudent nations and companies employ a mix of law and ethics. Patent law, copyright law, trade secrets law, post-employment restraint agreements, and international trade agreements are all legal efforts to preserve intellectual property within the bounds of substantial individual freedom. But the law is powerless to reach into some of the most important corners of intellectual property protection. For this reason, it is important to create the right **ethical** climate to foster protection. International statistics on intellectual property show how important the moral "backdrop" is for the protection of intellectual property. Among European countries with similar intellectual property laws, the discrepancy between, for example, software piracy rates is dramatic; in Italy the rate is ten times that of Great Britain. What makes

the difference must, in part, be the differing cultural and moral attitudes that would-be pirates take toward software appropriation. The example shows that the surrounding ethical attitudes, whether in a particular company or a nation, have a great deal to do with maintaining intellectual property and the incentives it fuels.

In a similar way, an ethic of strict protection of Motorola's intellectual property, which, as noted above, is its chief competitive advantage, is best achieved not only through laws, internal rules, and non-compete agreements, but also through constant attention to avoiding leaks. Other companies have the same duties to protect their intellectual property. When their vigilance is lax and someone else learns of their success, there are rare instances in which it might even be permissible to use their information. The other companies might have inadvertently, as it were, put the information into the public domain. One can have little sympathy, for example, for a design engineer who talks openly with strangers at a bar about his new design — especially when he knows that the bar is frequented by competitors. The engineer must simply be more careful than that. It is noteworthy that even U.S. law dealing with trade secrets recognizes that people

who fail to protect their secrets have less of a right to complain when those secrets are stolen.

But passive reception of information in an instance where one's competitor has utterly failed to protect it should be sharply distinguished from the **active** pursuit of such information. And even the passive gathering of such intelligence is ethically acceptable only where deceit is absent, and where the only sources of information utilized are public sources.

But as soon as a competitor begins overflying another company's plants, or attempting to pry information from unsuspecting third parties, the lines of acceptable sleuthing have been crossed.

In the present instance, there is plenty of blame — and carelessness — to pass around. Even the relatively open atmosphere of the university doesn't justify Professor Kron or his assistant in placing proprietary information in a computer file that is accessible to others — at least unless a password is established to protect it. Professor Kron and his assistant might also be violating university policy that restricts faculty members from using university resources to aid in consulting projects. Many universities have such policies.

Yet whatever the ethical lapses on the part of Kron and his assistant, they pale by comparison with what Rex Bayard has done. Dr. Bayard seems intent on piling one bad decision on top of another:

- After inadvertently accessing the material on the computer, he examines it long enough to ascertain that it is a proprietary design for a Mercury Electronics product in some ways superior to a Motorola product.

- He then prints out a copy.

- He immediately leaves the CAD Lab and goes home, where he can study the printout without the danger that anyone from the university would see him doing so.

- He shares the printout with his Motorola colleagues.

By the time his conscience — or his fear of being caught — finally catches up to him, it is too late for anything but apologies and remedial action. Most of the damage has been done. Since much of the ethical issue turns on the level of harm (i.e., consequential impact), and since at any step in the process Rex Bayard could have limited that harm by refusing to progress to the next step, he has engaged in not only an instance but a **pattern** of unethical behavior.

It must be noted here that intellectual property is different from other kinds of property. If a person steals a refrigerator, he can at least make partial amends by returning it to its proper owner. But when Bayard steals intellectual property and shares it with others, the genie has escaped the bottle, and can never be cajoled into returning.

Bayard is right to report the incident. But at this late stage in the process, the only action that his supervisor, Mr. Romulo, can take is to push for a complete apology and an internal investigation. Motorola's law department should be contacted immediately, since critical legal issues are active in the incident. Moreover, from an ethical if not also a legal perspective, Kron/McAlister should be notified as quickly as possible, and any remaining copies of the material returned. Those Motorolans who inadvertently learned of the proprietary information must be counseled, and safeguards must be taken, to ensure that no Motorola work ever benefits by virtue of the theft.

Despite his final awakening, one can predict that Rex Bayard will be lucky to keep his job. Beyond question, he has engaged in behavior that provides grounds for dismissal.

Approaches Primarily Used: Rights, Consequences.

Case 8
"Hardship" and the Eye of the Beholder

M.B. Difchik was born and brought up in *Latafrasia*, an economically developing nation with a culture very different from that of the United States. Until two years ago, M.B. had spent his entire Motorola career in his native country. He had received steady promotions to the upper end of the middle management range, and had been identified as a "high-potential" manager.

A year ago Motorola asked him to move from Latafrasia on promotion to a higher position in Austin, Texas. M.B. was truly thrilled. He looked forward eagerly to this new challenge, and to advancing the good of the corporation in his new assignment. Although there had been some resistance to his appointment on the part of two or three other Motorolans who wanted the Austin position for themselves, a careful study of the matter had convinced top management that M.B. was indeed the most qualified person for the new opening.

M.B. had a wife, *Ada,* and two young children, a boy and a girl. Ada was happy about her husband's success and eager to be supportive in every way. However, she was full of foreboding about the move to the States, feeling that it would involve considerable culture shock and family stress.

She was right. And the culture shock and family stress that the Difchiks experienced in Austin were not just the kind that soon fades. No, the difficulties have persisted, and life has proven extremely difficult for the Difchik family, even though M.B. has done everything he could to make them feel at home in their new surroundings.

The key reason for the Difchiks' persistent malaise is that in Latafrasia, M.B. and his wife lived at a high social level, and his Motorola salary allowed the family to keep two live-in servants to do the household and child care chores. Indeed, even as children, both M.B. and Ada had grown up in families sufficiently affluent so that there were always servants around to attend to their needs. (Servants are quite affordable to middle-class citizens in low-wage Latafrasia.) It is thus understandable that M.B. and his family now feel a deep need for similar services in their new host country.

For such reasons, M.B., who ordinarily does not like to upset people, now submits a written memo requesting that Motorola provide him with an extra allowance for the hiring of two Latafrasian servants, explaining that this is "only fair." He is willing to pay their airfare from Latafrasia to Austin, but would like them to receive U.S.-level wages once they go to work for him in the United States "It will make every difference in the world," he explains in his request.

Discussion Questions...

1. If you were M.B.'s manager, how would you respond to his request?

2. Does Constant Respect for People mean that Motorola should allow M.B. and his family to continue living in the style to which they have been accustomed since childhood?

3. If M.B. and an American Motorolan of equal grade and position were today being transferred to, say, China, both would receive hardship allowance packages, but the American's would be more generous. Should it be?

4. How should Motorola respond to such cases in the future? Are there ways of avoiding the difficulties M.B. encountered? Should adjustments be made in Motorola's overall policies concerning standard-of-living differences?

Commentaries on Case 8

[RCS] This case could be viewed as an inversion of the "When in Rome. . ." sort of case, namely, whether one is **entitled** to keep up his/her personal (as opposed to moral) practices when in a different culture. The notion of "entitlement" is the key here, and in order to approach the case it is important to look at this much-abused concept. To be entitled is to "have a title," the right to make certain demands. But what demands, and **of whom,** might be delicate questions, and the origin of the entitlement is certainly relevant to the situation. Some entitlements — for example, the right to food and shelter, the right of children to be educated and brought up decently — are shared by all people by virtue of the fact that they are human. These entitlements are human rights, codified, for example, in the United Nations Declaration of 1948 (and in many national constitutions as well). Other entitlements are entirely specific, for example, the promises made by virtue of an employment contract. Thus an employee of Motorola is "entitled" to a certain specified salary and certain "perks" by virtue of his/her employment agreement, but there is also a presumption that all Motorolans at the same level of responsibility should be treated the same, no matter what their ethnic origins or cultural background. Some entitlements apply to every employee of Motorola, just by virtue of corporation history, policy and shared understanding. Everyone is entitled to a basic form of respect, namely to be treated fairly and equally (given their level of responsibility). Although this is now an explicit "Key Belief" on the TCS Card, it doubtless was in effect even long before it was explicitly formulated and written down.

Everyone is also entitled to a decent standard of living. This is not just an entitlement that applies to employees of Motorola, of course, nor is it stated as such in the rules and policies of the corporation. Rather, one might say, it is, for the most part, taken for granted. Motorola salaries are sufficient to provide more than a decent standard of living, and adjustments are routinely made where cost of living and personal circumstances require them. But there are a number of questions that enter here.

First, of course, there is the question of what constitutes a "decent" or an "adequate" standard of living. That question is, in part, subjective — dependent on the needs and experience of the person or people in question. But it is not — and this is the critical point — wholly subjective. It is in part a cultural question, in part a question of ethics. To take one terrible but uncontroversial example, if a manager at Motorola/Austin came from a country in which slavery was still an acceptable institution and slaves were a convenience in many households, he would certainly have no entitlement whatever to slaves as part of a "decent" standard of living in the United States. (Of course, he would not be entitled to slaves at home either, since the very institution of slavery is unethical.) Or, if a manager at Motorola/Austin came from a country in which racial segregation was practiced, he would have no claim whatever to be entitled to live and work in a work situation in which there would be no members of a certain race or color. Thus, while one might allow that what counts as a "decent" standard of living might vary considerably from person to person, family to family, culture to culture, personal expectations alone do not determine what is decent and what is not.

Second, there is the question of choice. Some people have extremely high expectations for material goods and comforts, but whether or not they are entitled to them surely depends on what they are willing to do for them, how hard they are willing to work, what skills they have to offer, what sacrifices they are willing to make. They can choose to work sufficiently hard and make sacrifices, but they can also choose to lower their expectations. One is entitled within a meritocratic context only to what one deserves.

Where there is less choice, the nature of entitlement might change. For example, a manager who is transferred to another culture not by choice but by necessity, who accepts the transfer out of loyalty to Motorola but clearly at great personal discomfort and sacrifice, might be entitled to "compensations" that another manager, who actively solicited the transfer, would not be. This is particularly true if the manager who solicited the job understood (or **should** have understood) that the transfer would carry with it certain burdens and sacrifices, such as a change in "lifestyle" and expectations concerning domestic chores and arrangements.

Now, to the Difchik family and their relocation in Austin. It is not entirely clear to what extent Difchik had a choice in accepting the transfer, although his enthusiasm suggests that he did not in any way resist the assignment. Insofar as he

had a choice, observers' estimates of the compensation he deserves for moving his family might vary, but nonetheless the observer would assume that a skilled Motorola manager (especially one with the responsibilities of a husband and father) would make himself aware, to as great an extent as possible, of the domestic living conditions of his proposed new home. But, of course, even if he did so educate himself, people often find something different from what they expected, and family culture shock is one of the most common problems in corporate transfers. Accordingly, it is essential that M.B. should be treated on a par with any other Motorolan at the same level of responsibility. But none of this is to say that the Difchiks are **entitled** to reproducing their Latafrasian living conditions in Texas (as M.B.'s phrase "only fair" makes quite explicit), and the question that permeates the description of the case is to what extent Motorola **requires** Difchik to be in Texas and to what extent it is his option to return to Latafrasia and his servants, and leave the Austin job to one of the Motorolans who craved it originally.

But, now, what about the domestic circumstances themselves? On the one hand, the Difchiks have a set of cultural and domestic expectations that are clearly out of the ordinary. True, many Austinites

have hired help in doing their domestic chores, particularly when both parents hold full-time jobs. But it is understood, as part of the general culture, that such help is not in any sense an entitlement. It is to be arranged and paid for by the family, and whatever sacrifices this might involve (not buying a new car, fewer dinners at restaurants), are a matter of choice and not to be compensated by either their employers or the government. Thus the Difchiks are certainly free to hire help around the house, but, within U.S. culture, it is understood that this is a personal choice, not an entitlement from the corporation. It is also true that many Austinites hire foreign help to do their domestic chores, and certainly there is no objection to Difchik's flying two servants from Latafrasia to Austin (at his expense), securing their proper immigration papers and paying them appropriate U.S.-level wages (along with payments for their social security, etc.). But is this an entitlement from Motorola, or is this a choice the Difchiks face like every other employee and manager of Motorola in Austin? Clearly, it is the latter. Of course, if Difchik's value to the corporation in Austin is such that he can demand and deserves a raise, that is a perfectly appropriate subject for negotiation. But an "extra allowance" for the express purpose of hiring servants would not seem to be an entitlement or a legitimate demand at all. Nor is it convincing to contend that the servant problem is indeed "the key reason for the Difchiks' persistent malaise." It might be that, despite Difchik's skills and proven performance with Motorola, the transfer to Austin was a mistake. One transfers not only a manager but an entire family, an established form of life. The Difchik's family "hardships" reminds one that the dimensions of one's position at Motorola are far broader than the narrow questions of job skills and performance alone.

Approaches Primarily Used: Rights, Virtue.

[WJE] The plight of M.B. Difchik is culturally complex. The ethical validity of the outcome can be determined only by considering his and his family's social and economic situation before and after the Austin move. In one sense M.B. is now financially better off, but in another sense not. He and his family now have more actual money yet are living at a comparatively lower social level. A raise in pay should bring a comparable increase in overall well-being, but in this case it does not.

Also of considerable importance here is M.B.'s clear dedication to Motorola. Some might say that it would be a form of Constant Respect for People to grant his request. In this way Motorola would help him maintain his social and cultural tradition.

But this is only part of the story. There is also the question of equity. Though granting M.B.'s request would help him preserve within his home a microcosm of his native culture, he would be out of step with the Austin culture where Motorolans of comparable rank do not have full-time live-in servants. This is made even more evident in his request that the extra allowance be sufficient to ensure that his servants receive at least the Texas minimum wage. Granting this request would tip the balance financially toward M.B. Not only would he make a salary comparable to his Motorola peers, but also an add-on sufficient to maintain a style of living to which his family has grown accustomed. But this would of course mean that he would be receiving perquisites not available to his peers. This must be justified.

Which is more important, that M.B. get the raise and promotion, or that he maintain his standard of living? He should have considered this question before his move. Should he and his family accommodate to the Austin standard? This is his decision to make.

M.B. might raise the matter of American Motorolans in China, who currently receive a substantial hardship allowance, and thus receive more money than some other transpatriate Motorolans serving there. Isn't the basic standard of fairness being applied in China that one should live at a level comparable to one's own home social and economic situation? In reply, however, one might contend that the very notion of a hardship allowance presupposes that the Motorolan has relocated to a country with a lower standard of living. That is not true of the Difchiks. Hence the analog with China does not hold.

What should Motorola's policy be? Perhaps little or no account should be taken of past and future social arrangements. Perhaps the standard ought to be strictly economic, and all Motorolans at a given grade level be given the same relocation allowance. It would then be up to each employee to decide how to use these funds in establishing personal and familial lifestyles. This would preclude any arrangements which in any given host country would allow Motorolans operating at the same grade level to obtain further funding to move themselves to a higher standard of living than that enjoyed by comparable transpatriate Motorolans.

It is conceivable that Motorola might have policies to encourage, and even financially support, transpatriate employees' initiatives to understand, and accommodate to, the host culture. Such a policy would encourage the opposite of what M.B. seeks, which is to some extent to encapsulate himself **from** the local Austin culture.

Whether or not Motorola were to adopt such a policy, in the present instance it has no ethical obligation to grant M.B.'s request.

Approach Primarily Used: Traditions and Stories.

Case 9
Personal Luxury or Family Loyalty?

Joe was a native of *Ganzpoor*, a megacity in the developing nation of *Chompu*. Joe entered this life as the first of five children of an impoverished cloth peddler. Against all odds, by means of sheer guts, hard work and ability, Joe had brought himself to the United States and managed to earn a prestigious degree in engineering from *Cornford University*. Motorola snapped him up a week after graduation, and during the next five years gave him challenging assignments in Florida, Phoenix, Scotland and Mexico. Joe had thoroughly "bought into" the Motorola Culture. Or so it seemed.

Meanwhile, Motorola's business in Chompu began taking off. The Chompu Group was eager for more engineers. But the Human Resources Office was having great difficulty finding candidates willing to accept assignment to Ganzpoor. The news of all this reached Joe, who soon began a vigorous campaign for a transfer. "Look," he argued, "I speak native Ganzpoori and near-native Chompunese, and can hit the ground running." HR saw him as a guy too good to be true: qualified both professionally and culturally. Joe got his transfer.

Upon his assignment to Ganzpoor, Joe was informed in writing that he was expected to reside in a safe and seemly residence of his choice, and would be reimbursed for the actual cost of his rent and servants, up to a maximum of $2,000 per month. "Joe, just give us your landlord's and servants' receipts, and we'll get you promptly reimbursed," explained *Pierre Picard*, a French Motorolan assigned as financial controller for Motorola/Chompu.

Joe found a place to live, but even months later, other Motorolans were not sure exactly where it was because he never seemed to entertain at home. Some of his colleagues thought this was a bit strange, but then realized that Joe hardly had time for entertaining, given his executive responsibility for sourcing contracts for the construction of a new office and factory complex.

Each month Joe would send Pierre a bill for $2,000, accompanied by a rental and service receipt for exactly that amount, duly signed by his landlord. Each month Pierre would reimburse Joe accordingly. This went on for several months, until one day, a traditionally dressed Chompunese man came to see Pierre. He complained bitterly that Joe was his Master, and that Master had cheated him of his servant's wages for the past three months. At this point Pierre, despite his personal regard for Joe, had no alternative but to check into the facts of Joe's living arrangements.

Pierre and the local HR manager, *Harry Hanks,* had trouble getting the facts of the case, so finally they got a car and driver and went looking for Joe's address. It took almost two hours. The address turned out to be on the edge of a slum area of Ganzpoor, where houses were poorly marked. When they finally got there, they were shocked. Joe was living in what was, by Western standards, not much more than a shack.

Their first concern was for Joe's safety. In this part of the world, there were good reasons why transpatriates chose not to live in slums. Also, they felt, Joe's unseemly residence was hardly good for Motorola's image. Aside from these considerations, though, was the fundamental matter of simple integrity.

Harry felt he had no choice but to report the case to the regional HR director, who had no choice but to order a full-scale investigation.

When Joe learned that he was under investigation, he exploded in fury. He complained to HR that his right to personal privacy was being invaded. Further, he argued that his receipts were legitimate, despite the fact that the investigation revealed that rent plus service in so humble a dwelling could not possibly have cost Joe more than $400 a month, and probably cost much less.

Joe finally explained: Yes, it was true that he actually paid "less than" $2,000 a month (though he refused to say how much less). But, he argued, just because he was willing to "make sacrifices" should not mean that he should receive less than the full $2,000, which "all of my fellow Motorolans receive." To clinch his defense, Joe argued, "Look, I'm a Chompunese as well as a Motorolan, and here in Chompu this kind of thing happens all the time."

The hearings officer pressed further. Finally Joe, near tears, explained that all four of his younger siblings were now of college or high school age, and that he was putting all four of them through school with the reimbursements he received from Motorola, plus a size-able chunk of his salary. "Look," said Joe, "My family is **poor** — so poor in fact that most Westerners wouldn't believe our poverty even if they saw it. This money can mean the difference between hope and despair for all of us. For me to do anything less for my family would be to defile the honor of my late father.

"Can't you understand?"

A week later Joe was asked to step into the director's office to learn his fate. . . .

Discussion Questions...

1. Did Joe act unethically? If so, what did he do that was unethical?

2. Joe defends his actions in terms of financial need. Could he have given a better defense?

3. Could Joe have achieved his end in an ethically acceptable way? If so, how?

4. Is Motorola's policy on housing, servants, and reimbursement in Chompu a reasonable and defensible one?

5. Is there a better policy that Motorola might adopt? If yes, what would it be? If no, should Motorola take measures to prevent other cases like Joe's from arising?

Commentaries on Case 9

[RTD] This case states Motorola's policy: Reside in a safe and seemly residence, and be reimbursed up to $2,000 upon presentation of receipts. Joe violated at least the second part of that policy. He presented false receipts for reimbursement and did not use the money he received as was intended. He clearly violated Motorola's policy of Uncompromising Integrity, leaving him appropriately open to discipline.

Joe's excuse, although not sufficient to justify his action, is that all his fellow Motorolans receive $2,000 for their living accommodations and that he should receive no less. He might also argue that although his neighborhood might not be safe for a Westerner, it is safe for a native of Ganzpoor, such as he. He might further argue that whether his residence is "seemly" or not is a matter of taste, and is something that Motorola has no right to determine for its employees. However, even if one grants all of this, Joe cannot explain away the fact that he submitted for reimbursement a bill he knew to be falsified. That is the crux of the matter, and Joe's explanation for doing so is no excuse.

The question naturally arises as to whether Motorola's policy is fair and wise. The policy offers each Motorolan up to $2,000 for housing and servants. Since there is no incentive to keep costs down, one can assume that each Motorolan tends to spend at least $2,000 each month. Joe was the exception. Joe operated as if Motorola's policy stated that each Motorolan would be given this amount as a cost-of-living allowance. If that were Motorola's policy, it would be a fair one. Some companies have such a policy. But it is not, with good reason. As the case states, Ganzpoor can be a dangerous place. Parts of it are slums. If Motorola's policy were simply to give each Motorolan a $2,000 cost-of-living allowance, some might skimp on their housing in order to pocket the difference. It might appear paternalistic for Motorola to wish its higher level people to live in safe housing. But given the situation in Ganzpoor, it is not unreasonable. By adopting the policy of reimbursement rather than a cash supplement, Motorola ensures that housing money is not used for other purposes. Motorola's intent is not to increase the salary of its employees but to make their stays in Ganzpoor reasonably comfortable and safe.

The expectation that each Motorolan choose a "seemly" residence is not unreasonable, given the amount of money that is made available for housing. If Joe had preferred to live in his shack and asked to be reimbursed for the $400 a month that he presumably actually spent, it is not clear that he would have violated Motorola's policy. If he was expected to entertain as part of his job, then that should have been made clear to him, and he might have been counseled for that reason to seek better quarters.

Motorola's policy thus is equitable and fair, and although somewhat paternalistic, it is reasonable. Joe cannot convincingly claim that the policy is unfair and that it should have been as he wished, namely, that of providing a $2,000 supplementary allowance.

Joe misappropriated Motorola funds. The fact that he was putting his four younger siblings through school is beside the point. If he still worked in the United States and did not get a housing allowance, the fact that he was putting his siblings through school would not justify his submitting false vouchers to get additional money from Motorola. Nor is it a valid excuse that he is Chompunese and that in Chompu "this kind of thing happens all the time." Chompunese or not, he is also a Motorolan, and he knows that falsifying records does not "happen all the time" at Motorola — and that it is never supposed to happen.

Joe could be reprimanded instead of fired. He could be made to return the difference between his actual expenses and the $2,000 a month he received. In addition, he could be placed on probation. Ethical considerations do not demand that he be terminated, but his falsification of receipts was a serious enough offense to warrant that. Termination would be ethically justified but not ethically required.

Approaches Primarily Used: Duties, Justice and Fairness.

[WJE] To his fellow Motorolans, Joe seemed to be very much part of the Motorola Culture. It is now clear, however, that this assessment was based more on his performance in the Motorola Culture's Key Goals and Key Initiatives areas, than on its more ethical Key Beliefs. Even in this latter area, however, there was no reason to question his commitment until he was assigned to Ganzpoor. One could argue that in Ganzpoor, Joe was adhering to his own version of Constant Respect for People, but there is no doubt that he was violating Uncompromising Integrity. Joe's actions manifest a deep cultural clash. It seemed that Joe was an excellent Motorolan with a high regard for the Motorola Culture. But his present actions suggest that he considers that culture as something to be exploited rather than respected. Joe has superficially complied with the standards of the Motorola Culture, while in fact keeping his own personal agenda foremost.

Joe's termination would be ethically justified. Whatever action is taken, however, it would be good ethical business practice to explore with him the social and cultural clashes operative in this situation in order to know how to identify and counsel future Joes.

Approach Primarily Used: Traditions and Stories.

Case 10
Performance Bonuses:
How to Allocate?

Suzanne Cure is an American who has been a well-regarded Motorolan for many years. She worked in a division of Motorola that was highly profitable. One of the reasons for her satisfaction with the corporation was that she had been involved in a fine performance bonus plan. The benefits she and her family enjoyed were more generous than those available to employees in a number of other divisions. She had often wondered about those discrepancies, but since her own situation was so good, she never took the time to look into the matter in any great depth.

Three years ago, however, things took a turn which made her look into it deeply indeed. Suzanne was given a promotion and assigned to manage an operation in *Pacifica*, a rapidly developing Pacific Rim nation. Her assignment was to build up the operation significantly, and she succeeded beyond most people's expectations. In the process, she got to know many Pacifican Motorolans quite well, and was struck by their strong commitment and loyalty to the corporation and to their work units.

In Pacifica, it was not the tradition for companies, local or multinational, to award performance bonuses, and Motorola conformed to this pattern. Suzanne noted that most local employees were quite happy to work for Motorola because they felt that they earned competitive wages and enjoyed good job security. Local Motorolans knew little about performance bonuses, nor were they aware that such rewards varied among different divisions and geographies within the corporation.

Suzanne decided to pursue an innovative pilot project, and, on the basis of her excellent track record, managed to convince her Motorola superiors to allow her to try it for a period of three years. The project was to introduce rewards for good performance, in the form of a quarterly bonus. What made the project truly audacious, though, was that each employee would receive the **same** monetary amount, regardless of salary level. (New employees with less than one year's service were handled differently, and the bonus was handled separately from merit raises, promotions in grade, etc.)

At the end of the first year, the total bonus turned out to be $456 for each employee, regardless of rank or salary. This amount was seen as trivial by the higher-paid employees but, in this low-wage country with considerable annual inflation, was eagerly welcomed by the lesser-paid ones. Suzanne had learned, from extensive dialogues with local employees, that they preferred to be rewarded as members of a unit. They would have regarded individual bonuses as unfair and divisive.

The program is now in the early stages of its second year. Already, the results have been encouraging. Productivity has generally risen. Employees, especially those at lower pay levels, seem enthusiastic. None of those at higher levels appear quite satisfied with the new arrangement, but few have complained formally. Various surveys conducted at this facility confirm that morale is generally higher, as measured by a number of quantitative indicators.

Discussion Questions...

1. If you were Suzanne, would you seek to continue the bonus program for the full three years? Would you recommend that other Motorola units adopt a similar program?

2. Should Motorola encourage performance bonuses around the world?

3. Fairness often implies uniform standards. Do issues of fairness arise when Motorola uses different standards around the world for bonus programs? Should Motorola adopt different standards in different parts of the world for other issues?

4. If Motorola allows different styles of bonus plans in order to accommodate particular cultural standards, how should it handle bonuses for transpatriates assigned to work in those particular cultures? Should these nonlocal Motorolans be bound by local rules?

Commentaries on Case 10

[TD] The key to solving "Performance Bonuses: How to Allocate?" is recognizing the importance of cultural differences in interpretations of fairness, and, in turn, in correct business decision making. Cultural notions of fairness can affect the way incentives are perceived, and, in turn, the best manner of structuring incentive programs.

Cultural standards of fairness vary around the world. Research in Hong Kong showed recently that while Hong Kong business people are somewhat more accepting of bribery than their Western counterparts, they are much less accepting of a superior taking disproportionate credit for a project heavily contributed to by subordinates. While such credit-stealing is frowned upon in the West, it can constitute a truly serious offense for some Hong Kong Chinese.

In many instances, of course, it simply makes no difference that cultural notions of fairness differ. Even if a culture perceives bribery as fair (which virtually none does, by the way), Motorola will not, and should not, allow this to affect its actions. But in some instances, cultural notions make an important ethical difference. For example, when what is at stake is a person's sense of reward, then it makes sense to tailor the reward to hit the mark. If a person feels no sense of reward from an encouraging remark, then a manager is well advised to choose another form of reward.

In the case at hand, employees at Motorola/Pacifica appear to have a different sense of fairness that impacts upon their sense of reward. The case states that the employees would have "regarded individual bonuses as unfair and divisive." The case also states that the new bonus plan seems to have raised morale as measured by a number of quantitative indicators.

On what ethical grounds, then, could one criticize the incentive plan?

• Does it conflict with American notions of individual merit? But even U.S. management programs are stressing the need to use team-related measurements.

• Is it that if Pacifica adopts a performance bonus plan, or any bonus plan with an egalitarian distribution mechanism, then **all** other Motorolan structures will need to follow suit? But, then, it has already been noted that what justified this plan was the particular **perception** of fairness and that perception's consequence on creating incentives in Pacifica. Surely not all host countries will share Pacifica's cultural standards.

Therefore, the performance bonus plan should be encouraged, so long as it does not create a negative incentive for other, better-paid employees.

Approach Primarily Used: Justice and Fairness.

[RTD] The analysis can start from two fairly uncontroversial principles. The first is that no company is ethically required to pay performance bonuses. It is ethically required to pay at least a living wage, and it is competitively required to pay as much beyond that as is necessary to get the people it wishes for its various positions. The second principle is that although companies should follow the rule of equal pay for equal work, this does not mean that a company must pay all those doing similar work the same amount, regardless of where they live. Pay is appropriately related to both the local standard of living and the local cost of living. If it were not ethical for a company to pay people according to the local standard and cost of living, it would make no sense for companies to operate in one place rather than another, where labor costs are less. For an American company to pay its employees in India the same amount as it pays its employees in Chicago for comparable work would make little sense, given the great difference in cost of living. To do so would make the Indian employees relatively rich, would undermine the local pay structure, and would open American companies up to legitimate charges of stealing the best workers and of driving the local competition out of business by raising wages beyond what they could pay.

These principles allow differences in pay by Motorola in different locations for the same kind of work. They also allow differences in whether performance bonuses are adopted and how they are adopted. But whenever they are adopted, due care must be taken that all those in comparable categories are treated similarly. Justice requires that comparable cases be treated comparably. It would be unfair in the same plant to have some people in a unit eligible, if others with similar positions and qualifications were deemed ineligible by the whim of their supervisor.

Motorola appears to have two principal concerns:

• The fact that different divisions of Motorola get different benefits, depending on productivity and profitability.

• The question of whether and how to implement performance bonuses worldwide.

With respect to whether performance bonuses may ethically vary according to productivity and profitability, the basis for answering yes has already been given — provided that all parties have been informed of the plan and have agreed to it as part of their compensation packages. Motorola has the obligation to pay all its employees a living wage, and is prevented from exploiting its employees. Performance bonuses are compen-

sation in addition to basic wages. They are not something that employees have a right to, unless agreed to in their stated conditions of employment. Performance bonuses are an incentive to employees, a reward for achievement, and sometimes a retention strategy.

Since performance bonuses are not ethically required, they may be structured in many different ways. What is not ethically permitted is any scheme that is arbitrary or that discriminates, or in other ways makes unjustified distinctions between people in similar situations. Two employees in the same grade doing comparable work rightly expect that they will share in performance bonuses in the same way and to the same extent. This does not necessarily mean the same monetary amount, although it does mean that the same criteria are used to determine that amount. The procedure used must not be biased by factors such as friendship, age, nationality, ethnicity or the like.

Suzanne introduces performance bonuses as a pilot project in Pacifica, and she ties them to productivity and morale. Since productivity has increased and morale, at least of those at lower pay levels, has improved, there is reason to believe that the performance bonus plan has produced the desired effects and is successful. Given these results, it would be counter-productive to terminate the plan after the three-year project. Yet if Motorola did terminate the plan, no injustice would be done to the employees, provided that they were informed from the start that the program was for three years, that it might be discontinued, and that the performance bonuses were in addition to their basic compensation and independent of it. After three years the Motorolans in Pacifica might have become used to the extra compensation and they might react adversely if the plan is not continued. That is part of the down-side risk in conducting the pilot project. But such expectations are not the same as contractual com-mitments and do not in themselves make performance bonuses ethically mandatory once started.

Suzanne is conscious of the local culture of Pacifica. It was employee preference that led her to reward all employees as members of the unit. Similar considerations led her to the decision that each employee would receive the same amount, rather than allocating the bonuses proportionally, based on salary differences. Is it fairer to give every-one the same amount, or to give everyone the same percent of their salary? Or is it fairer yet to give those who worked harder or

received better evaluations propor-tionately more? There are many ways of considering the criterion to be used in allocating bonuses, and each has something to be said for it. The scheme Suzanne adopted is fair, it is the one that seems to have satisfied most employees, it results from respecting their desires about criteria, and it has produced the desired effect. The scheme might not be the preferred one in a division located elsewhere, per-haps in the United States. There the employees might prefer individual rather than unit awards, with amounts set according to their salary levels, or the level of their positions within the company. From an ethical point of view, both schemes, as well as many others, are acceptable.

What is important is that if a performance bonus scheme is introduced, it should consider the wishes of those who will take part in it, it should be administered fairly, and its rules should be clear to all concerned before the plan is implemented.

The only apparent problem with the scheme Suzanne has adopted is that it does not seem to have energized the higher-level employ-ees, some of whom have com-plained quietly. It is not clear from the case whether these employees were included in the dialogues Suzanne had earlier, which indi-cated employees wished to be

rewarded as a unit. Nor is it clear why these higher-level employees would complain if their culture views individual bonuses as unfair. Are these employees transpatriates rather than Pacificans? Two conclu-sions regarding them follow:

- Since they have no right to a bonus plan in the first place, they have no right to one that yields more for them than for lesser-paid employees.

- Since a bonus plan that treats like cases similarly is ethically allowable, then one that treats team members one way, and higher-level managers who are not team members another way, would be fair.

Whether Suzanne's scheme would affect morale positively or negatively, whether it would ener-gize the higher-paid employees, and whether that would increase productivity, are all key questions. Suzanne is carrying on a pilot project. After three years she might wish to initiate another project along these lines.

Wages and compensation vary widely across the globe. Equal pay for equal work applies to specific locations and does not imply that Motorolans everywhere must in justice receive the same wage for similar work. Nor does it imply that Motorolans everywhere must enjoy a comparable standard of living. That is more than any company can guarantee, and so it is more than can be required of any company. Justice, and ethics more broadly, require the payment of a just living wage; they prohibit exploitation; they require equal pay for equal work in the same job market; and they prohibit discrimination and other kinds of unjust treatment in compensation. They do not specify particular wages, nor do they demand performance bonuses or require that such bonuses as are adopted be the same in all Motorola facilities throughout the world.

Approaches Primarily Used: Duties, Consequences, Justice and Fairness, Rights.

Case 11
The Golf Clubs That
Would Not Disappear

Sylvester is a Northwestern European who has been with Motorola for 21 years and risen through the ranks to be No. 1 in his business unit in the Asian nation of *Tropica*. His career is in high gear, in part because local demand for Motorola's new *TX-7* hand-held personal digital assistant practically gives the corporation a seller's market in Tropica. However, sales in nearby Asian nations have been spotty. Sylvester believes that with the right marketing approach this can be remedied.

Choop, a citizen of Tropica, is a shrewd, decisive businessman who is making good profits as the principal distributor of TX-7s. He is eager to work with the corporation on a wider scale.

Sylvester is impressed by Choop's obvious business acumen, and by his extensive business and kinship connections throughout this part of Asia, which could make him a key player in helping the corporation capture nearby national markets. Choop enjoys social contact with Sylvester, and is anxious to forge the kind of relationship of implicit trust that Asian businessmen habitually seek. Given this convergence of friendship and economic interest, before long the two men begin to see more and more of each other socially.

Much of this social relationship takes place at the exclusive *Plushmore Golf and Country Club*. The two men have about the same handicap, and whenever they need a foursome, Choop brings along his relatives and business friends whom he wants Sylvester to meet — some from Tropica, some from nearby nations.

In the beginning, though, there had been a problem: Sylvester had left his golf clubs back home in the States, and the "rental" golf sets available at Plushmore were old and inadequate. But not to worry: The ever-resourceful Choop solved the problem by providing Sylvester with a beautiful set of handcrafted clubs — worth, as it turned out, some U.S. $3,000 to $5,000 (including Tropica's stiff luxury import duty).

Meanwhile, back at the TX-7 facility, a local Tropican employee named *Gurr* was given a series of substandard performance reviews, and finally terminated. Gurr was outraged, and complained all the way to the Ethics Committee in Schaumburg that Sylvester was unfair and untrustworthy, as shown by the fact that he had accepted an expensive set of golf clubs as a bribe from Choop.

The Ethics Committee investigated and determined the following:

- Gurr's performance had in fact been substandard, and he deserved to be terminated.

- Sylvester had in fact been frequently playing golf with Choop and friends, over a period of two years, using this expensive set of clubs.

- Sylvester kept the clubs at his home when not in use.

- Sylvester, when questioned, said that the clubs had been just a loan, to allow him to bond socially with Choop and friends. To have turned down such a loan, he explained, would have been insulting in terms of Tropican culture.

- Choop, when questioned, also said that the clubs had been just a loan.

The Ethics Committee considered the following options:

1. Believe Sylvester's and Choop's stories that the clubs were in reality a loan.

2. Avoid any formal decision on whether to believe these stories, and let the matter go at that.

3. Plunge vigorously into a deeper investigation in an effort to dispel any ambiguity. (For example, the Committee could probe as to why Sylvester had not returned the "loan" to Choop.)

If the Committee found Sylvester not culpable, they would, of course, take no further action. Otherwise, the Committee had the following main options.

1. Decide that Sylvester was lying, and terminate him. However, his previous record was completely clean, and to terminate him would mean losing a valuable employee in whom the corporation had made a substantial investment. Moreover, such an action might ruin Motorola's contact with Choop, and the prospect of securing greater market share for TX-7s in nearby countries.

2. Demote him.

3. Neither of the above, but transfer Sylvester to another country.

4. None of the above, but penalize him financially.

The Committee proceeded to make its decision....

Discussion Questions...

1. Is the Ethics Committee paying too much attention to Gurr, given that he was terminated because of a series of substandard performance reports?

2. Are Motorola officials paying more attention to this case than is really warranted?

3. Should Motorolans avoid all occasions in which even the possibility of the appearance of a bribe arises?

4. Should distributors who may be suspected of bribery, such as Choop, be retained and even advanced as Motorola's partners?

5. Based on the available information, what action, if any, should Motorola take concerning Sylvester?

Commentaries on Case 11

[TD] Gifts are bribes, even in business contexts. The golf club case displays how gradually and silently unethical behavior can slip into a person's actions. The golf course was clearly a conduit to more than pleasant afternoons, and Sylvester was correct to see his golf association as a potentially beneficial one for Motorola. Choop's habit of bringing his friends along only intensified the business importance of the golf outings.

Friends help friends, and being loaned a set of clubs by a friend is not an unusual occurrence among golf partners. Add to that the fact that it can seem ungracious if not rude to decline a gift or offer of help, especially in a country where gifts and favors are a way of life. So when Sylvester received a set of clubs from Choop on the Tropican golf course, one can empathize with Sylvester's situation. Why not at least **play** with the clubs?

The problem is that most serious ethical missteps begin in just this fashion. A series of small, almost unnoticeable steps are taken in a certain direction until finally one awakens to find clear unethical behavior. In this case, that appears to be what happened, for even if Sylvester means to draw a line between **using** the clubs and **owning** the clubs, that line is apparent to nobody except himself. This is especially true in light of the fact that Sylvester has used the clubs for two years, and has kept them at his home when not in use. Sylvester has gone beyond the point where he can justify his behavior.

The critical point is that Motorolans, especially managers, must avoid even the **appearance** of impropriety. As a representative of an ethical corporation, a Motorolan such as Sylvester must live many aspects of his business life quite transparently. The disgruntled Gurr might be a poor performer and wrong about Sylvester. But he sees what he sees. And what he reports leaves a murky picture of Sylvester's ethics. Having seen such an example, Gurr and others might take liberties on their own that would be damaging to Motorola. Sylvester must not accept the clubs. As a Motorolan, and especially as a leader at Motorola, Sylvester has no choice but to lead.

Should Sylvester be punished? Because the line between using and owning the clubs is apparent to nobody except Sylvester, I believe Motorola has no choice but to discipline him. If unacceptable behavior is allowed to slide by without sanction, the lines of conduct for all Motorolans become blurred. True, the matter of Sylvester's intent may lessen the punishment needed. Did he only mean to borrow the clubs? Did he, despite appearances, mean to return the clubs at a later time? If the Motorolans responsible for assigning penalties in this instance believe this is possible, and if Sylvester's history of conduct and management performance is otherwise exemplary, then the appropriate punishment may be something less than termination.

Approach Primarily Used: Duties.

[WJE] To begin with, it should be noted that Gurr is an outsider to the Sylvester and Choop relationship. There is no evidence presented at all that Sylvester has been in any way unfair to Gurr. Yet Gurr insults Sylvester's character in general — citing as evidence the matter of the expensive golf clubs. The fact that these clubs are expensive sets the tone for the whole case. Even the long-term use of a cheap set of clubs would alter the ethical complexion of the case. Hence the ethical issue is ambiguous. Borrowing clubs in itself is not unethical.

One should not ignore the fact that this case takes place in the context of golf, a sport often seen as not merely mirroring the competitiveness of the business and political worlds, but also in a strange way as being integral to them. One must be a good, or at least companionable, golfer because many deals are actually struck on the course. Would this case be perceived differently if Sylvester had accepted the loan of an equally expensive set of equipment for some other game?

Sylvester is in fact doing a lot of business with Choop and other Asians on the golf course. Is this the best available means to attain his and Motorola's ends?

Why is it that nothing happens to Choop, who continues to prosper? As lender of the clubs, he is the reputed corrupter of Sylvester. What is at issue here is not so much the case of Choop himself, but rather the ethical practices of Tropica, in which he might be either a willing or unwilling participant. True, he cannot be terminated or penalized by corporate policy because he is not a Motorolan. But the case raises the question of whether Motorola should drop him as a distributor on grounds that he is untrustworthy.

Since Sylvester used the clubs over a period of two years, this falls more into the category of being a gift than a loan, and so comes under the prohibition of accepting a gift. As a result, the reduction of Sylvester's annual bonus and the placing of a letter of reprimand in his confidential file would be appropriate disciplinary action on the part of Motorola.

Approach Primarily Used: Traditions and Stories.

Case 12
Are Training Budgets Geographically Equitable?

Lisalotte Sauer, a young German Motorolan, has been assigned as training manager in a Latin American country called *Serenia*. She arrives in her new host country full of enthusiasm, having just been briefed about the corporation's policy of providing at least 40 hours of training annually to every employee worldwide — from the highest manager to the newest line employee. At last, Lisalotte thinks, she will have a chance to use her three years of experience at Motorola/*Saarbruecken*, plus the training she earlier received in a Master's Program in Industrial Apprenticeship Education.

On arriving in Serenia, Lisalotte begins working with her new assistant, *Maria Olarte de la Lopez*. Maria has had little formal education, but during her 16 years with Motorola/Serenia, she has earned regular merit promotions. Lisalotte soon learns to appreciate what a gem of an assistant Maria is, with her encyclopedic knowledge of how things work in her facility, and her habit of speaking the facts, no matter how painful.

One of the most painful of these facts concerns *Rodrigo Oliveira*, a 27-year veteran of Motorola and chief of the Maintenance and Repair Team. Just three months ago,

Rodrigo lost a finger in an industrial accident. The local management staff were shocked and apologetic, and promptly arranged an appropriate financial restitution for Rodrigo.

Most Serenian Motorolans tried to put this disturbing incident out of their minds. But not Lisalotte. She persisted in trying to find out why it happened. Though the details were complex, it soon became clear that lack of training was one of the key causes. A new type of machine, with intricate maintenance and repair procedures, had just been purchased from Japan and installed. The Japanese-language instructions that came with the machine were quite detailed, while the English-language instructions were ambiguous and flawed. There were **no** Spanish-language instructions at all. Also, no systematic training had been given to the local employees in how to maintain or repair this machine. One day the machine broke down. Rodrigo, proud of his title of chief of Maintenance and Repair, decided to try to fix it. He moved fast, but with a tragic false confidence. He placed his left hand into the machine, and a heavy element slipped from its mooring, crushing his little finger.

Lisalotte was scandalized by the lack of printed Spanish-language instructions and safety precautions — not to mention the lack of preparatory training. She was further shocked to learn that the per-employee budget for the annual 40 hours of training for Motorolans at this facility was vastly less adequate than at her previous Motorola post in Germany. This was despite the fact that the Serenian facility was actually more profitable, and that the dollar cost of training in Serenia would be lower. Surely, she felt, there ought to be **some** parity between the training budget in Germany and that in Serenia.

Lisalotte soon found herself viewing this low budget in terms that went beyond basic safety, and dealt with the broader matter of professional **development.** To her, a great corporation such as Motorola ought to foster training for the ongoing professional development of **every** employee, high or low. This made sense to her not only in terms of dignity entitlement for the individual, but also in terms of competitiveness and profitability for the corporation. She had written her Master's thesis about on-the-job professional development programs for German blue collar workers. In the course of her study, she had encountered many exam-ples of technological progress achieved by ordinary workers with limited formal education. She wondered whether Motorola/Serenia could offer training for professional development in this same spirit — to encourage and capture this natural potential among their Serenian employees. Wouldn't this be a "win-win" arrangement for all concerned?

Discussion Questions...

1. Is Motorola/Serenia ethically required to devise new training programs in basic safety? In professional development? Equally so?

2. How do the vastly less adequate per-employee training budgets in Serenia square with Constant Respect for People?

3. Given that these budgetary differences do exist, is it realistic to expect that employees in Serenia will realize their full productive potential as members of the Motorola family?

4. In judging the value that an employee adds, is it fair to expect employees in Serenia to add as much as employees in Germany or other highly industrialized nations?

Commentaries on Case 12

[TD] Discrimination exists and all Motorolans must constantly be on their guard against it. The issue of discrimination reaches deep into Motorola's shared humanity as well as affecting the efficiency of its business. To lower a person's opportunities because of a racial, cultural or gender characteristic demeans that person's humanity — even as it harms opportunities for company success. Of course, Motorolans in the United States are painfully familiar with racial discrimination and the deep scar it has etched on their national history. But even they sometimes have trouble spotting discrimination in other contexts, especially transcultural contexts where issues other than hiring and promotion are at stake. This case is especially interesting, for it involves the subtle issue of varying levels of support for training.

Few people would contend that the health and safety of Motorolans working on the Maintenance and Repair Team at Motorola/Serenia are less important than the health and safety of Motorolans in Chicago. To make such a claim would fly in the face of the Motorola Key Belief in Constant Respect for People. This same notion of "constant respect" is reflected in countless moral theories and religious traditions: from the German philosopher Immanuel Kant's Categorical Imperative that calls for respecting the inner humanity of people, to the Christian, Judaic, Islamic and Confucian support of the Golden Rule. Most of us follow the business principle, "Hire, fire, promote and reward on the basis of qualifications rather than irrelevant criteria such as race or sex." We properly regard following such a principle as a **duty.** For this reason, unequal training budgets for health and safety, assuming relevantly similar work contexts, can violate a key human — and a key Motorolan — belief.

Discrimination that affects the safety and health of particular Motorolans is also bad business. Injured, unhealthy employees cannot work, and a dangerous working environment lowers morale and productivity. These considerations exist independently from those of skin color, gender, nationality or culture.

However, it is important to understand that while it would be discrimination to have varying safety standards for similar work contexts, it is not necessarily wrong to provide different resources to different groups of people.

Companies would be imprudent, and eventually unethical, to pay precisely the same rates for similar work around the world. Not only do living standards differ, but the opportunity to pay lower wages is the fuel that drives the expansion of companies abroad, and with it the technological and monetary capital for poorer countries to advance. Different pay rates also help create incentives. Successful salespeople are usually paid more than unsuccessful ones in order to encourage more effective selling. Furthermore, relative need is sometimes a compelling reason for differing allocations of resources. If one has two children, one of whom is much sicker than the other, it is not unfair to give the sicker child a larger share of the medicine. If Motorola needs more skills at a given time in finance than in marketing, it is not unfair to give more training to Motorola's financial people than to the marketing people.

For all these reasons, it is important in this case to separate the issue of unequal safety and health training budgets from that of unequal professional development training budgets. It is discriminatory and wrong, as earlier indicated, to treat the health and safety of one employee as less important than another. But it is not necessarily wrong to provide different levels of professional development training to one group of people over another. With regard to this latter issue, only one thing is certain in the context of this case: The **reason** for having less professional development training in a Serenian employee group than in another Motorola group must not be that one group is Serenian and the other is not. To do this **would** definitely constitute discrimination, and a violation of Motorola's Constant Respect for People.

Approaches Primarily Used:
Duties, Consequences.

[WJE] Lisalotte comes on the scene very much as the outsider. Not only is she from another culture, but she is also a college-educated intellectual now at work in a world where many of her colleagues have little formal education. Lisalotte is highly appreciative of the quality of work being done by Maria and wants to help improve the situation for other Serenian workers. She maintains that there should be more training for Motorolans in the Serenia setting and that the budget for the annual five days of training should be genuinely adequate. Rodrigo and Maria would welcome such a development. Lisalotte's position is justified.

A critical issue surfaces here, and Lisalotte sees it clearly: If Motorola is truly going to prosper in its worldwide operations, it must ensure opportunities for continued training, learning and growth. If the budget for the annual 40 hours of training in Serenia is inadequate, not only will the employees suffer but so will Motorola as a whole. This is because, as Motorola has long realized, the key to its continued success and growth has more to do with intellectual capital than with technology itself. The corporation has always encouraged new approaches and ideas, often from unlikely sources. It would limit continuous training opportunities at its own peril.

Motorola's dealing with the problem of adequate training, for both safety and professional development, is the appropriate policy. Not only would such a policy help remove any suspicion of insensitivity on the part of Motorola, but it would also provide the occasion for a move forward on the part of all.

Approach Primarily Used:
Traditions and Stories.

Case 13
Rupert's "Royal" Gift

Omnilink, Inc. is a global microelectronic corporation headquartered in *Cupertino, California. Rupert ("Rupe") Rifflinger,* 62, is an Omnilink officer with extensive overseas experience. *Clara Skelton* has been Rupe's secretary for 13 years and is due to retire next month.

Rupe himself had planned to retire two years ago, but senior management persuaded him to stay on awhile, to serve as special investigator for cases involving theft of Omnilink's intellectual property. The present case has taken Rupe to the Omnilink facility in *Quang Phu*, where there is suspicion that three or four Omnilinkers might be covertly collaborating with a local organization of intellectual property thieves that has recently been selling, in several parts of Asia, a communication linkage device very similar in design and function to the Omnilink *J-14*. These devices are even labeled and packaged with the Omnilink logo.

Our story finds Rupe in Quang Phu on a Sunday afternoon. His business office is closed, and Rupe decides to go shopping. He wants to find a really special gift for Clara to acknowledge her long years

of truly extraordinary service. Of course, he knows about Omnilink's policy on gift-giving within the corporation, but decides that it would be OK to give Clara a nice gift a few days **after** she retires, as a token of his genuine appreciation.

Where to go? Suddenly Rupe remembers a recent conversation with *Frank Fairweather* of Omnilink/ Quang Phu, who mentioned a local shop with great bargains in watches and jewelry, called the *Caveat Emptor Emporium*. Frank had casually added that there was a rumor that not all goods sold by Caveat Emptor were necessarily genuine — "but never mind, Rupe, even if what you buy there **is** an imitation, it'll be so good that not even an expert could tell the difference."

Rupe soon finds his way to Caveat Emptor. It is a place of beauty and sparkle, crowded with customers. There he is greeted by a dignified and immaculately dressed saleswoman who quickly ushers him into a small back room where she unveils a dazzling array of 50 or more luxury watches bearing the logo of the famous Swiss company, *"Royal."* Rupe is stunned by the beauty of one *"Lady Royal"* model, especially when he notes that it costs less than half of what would be its price in

Zurich. "Just the thing for Clara," Rupe says to himself. He ends up buying it plus two lesser models for other office assistants, plus one for an Omnilinker in another department. All four timepieces are emblazoned with the "Royal" logo.

Back in Cupertino, the three Omnilinkers who received the lesser models expressed delight over Rupert's thoughtful gift. And the following month Rupe officiated at Clara's retirement party. The next weekend he delivered the Lady Royal to the Skelton home, where Clara and her husband *Elmer,* also a retired Omnilinker, were stunned by its beauty. Rupe returned home from his errand glowing with satisfaction. "That imitation, if that's what it is, is so clever that it will probably last longer than a real Royal from Switzerland," he mused.

A few months later Rupe met Elmer for a game of golf. But things did not go well. Elmer seemed not quite himself. "What's the matter, Elmer?" asked Rupe later, over martinis at the clubhouse. The two men had been closely associated at several points during their Omnilink careers and had a good relationship that permitted frankness.

"Rupe, the crystal fell off Clara's Lady Royal so I took it to *Palo Alto Royal* for repairs, and the jeweler there told me it was not a genuine Royal. What's going on, my friend?"

"Relax, Elmer," replied Rupe. "I checked it out personally with the shopkeeper in Quang Phu. There's no doubt about it, it's the genuine article. Take it from me."

Elmer was disturbed, but in the interest of preserving his relationship with Rupert, he let the matter drop. However, when he got home, he vented his feelings to Clara. "Why does Omnilink allow its employees to do this sort of thing?" he asked, "especially employees like Rupe, who are supposed to be responsible for preventing **other** companies from stealing **our** intellectual property?"

Clara thought a moment, not wanting to upset her husband or to be unfair to Rupert. "Well, Elmer," she finally said, "I don't really think it's any of Omnilink's business what Rupert does off the job and on his own time. Do you?"

Discussion Questions...

1. If this case involved Motorola instead of Omnilink, would Motorola's policies cover Rupert's gift-giving behavior? If so, would Rupert's actions be in conformity with these policies?

2. If the company were Motorola, would there be any difference between Rupert's giving the watch to Clara and giving watches to his other corporation colleagues?

3. If the company were Motorola, would it matter whether the gifts that Rupert gave these people were imitations rather than genuine Royals?

4. What does it say about Rupert's credibility as an employee charged with preventing the counterfeiting of an Omnilink product, when he buys these watches without actively assuring himself that they are not counterfeits?

5. Suppose you and Rupert were fellow Omnilinkers and you learned about his behavior in this case. To what extent would that incline you to be concerned about the integrity of his **other** on-the-job behavior?

6. To what extent does a company such as Omnilink or Motorola have a legitimate interest in the ethics of an employee's **off**-the-job behavior?

Commentaries on Case 13

[RTD] This case raises four questions. The first question is whether Rupert Rifflinger paid for the watch and gave it to Clara as a personal present or whether he paid for it with Omnilink funds. If he paid for it with his own money and gave it to Clara after she retired, he broke no Omnilink rule. Giving personal gifts in this instance is ethically permissible and not prohibited by the policy of most companies. Since Rupert knows Omnilink's policy on gifts (he waited until after Clara retired before giving her the watch), it is fair to assume that he paid for her watch with his own money. He also bought watches for two other office assistants and an Omnilinker in another department. Did he buy those with his own money or with Omnilink's? Once again, let us assume he bought them with his own money. But in this case the three are still Omnilink employees. How and when did he give them the gifts, and under what conditions? Any Royal watch is expensive and worth more than the limits on gifts allowed by most company policies. More on this later.

The second question is whether Rupert lied or otherwise acted unethically either in presenting the watches or in replying to Elmer. If he did not "check it out personally with the shopkeeper," he lied in his response to Elmer. He is also foolish to insist that it is a genuine Royal if the Royal dealer claims otherwise. His insistence is not going to make the dealer return the watch to Royal or replace it with a new Royal. So his friend cannot simply "relax." Elmer will be forced to conclude that either Rupert is a liar or that he was duped in Quang Phu and doesn't seem to care.

Did Rupert act unethically in giving as a gift a watch marked "Royal" if he knew it was not a Royal? He had no obligation to give anything, so the giving is not at issue. He acted foolishly thinking a watch that cost less than half the Swiss price was either really a Royal or that it was "as good." "As good" as the original is not the same as being an original. Rupert wanted credit for giving Clara an expensive watch without having to pay the cost of the watch. If he had bought an original Royal on sale — say, from a Royal dealer who was going out of business — there would be nothing wrong with his giving Clara the watch, even though he paid less than the retail price for it. The deception does not consist in his paying less than retail. It consists in giving a watch that he suspects is an imitation as a gift, and in expecting to get credit for giving Clara an original. Rupert had no obligation to give Clara a gift, much less an expensive watch. Clara had no right to receive an expensive watch from Rupert. That's what makes this a gift. But Clara and Elmer might well feel that they have been deceived, as in fact they have.

Should this concern Omnilink? So far we have discussed the giving of a gift by an Omnilinker to a former Omnilinker. Since Clara no longer works for Omnilink, what gifts she does or does not receive or that Rupert does or does not give to her are of no concern to the company.

What of the watches Rupert bought for the other Omnilinkers? Assuming he bought them with his own money, and assuming he gives them as personal gifts, the matter of their being fake Royals is not a concern of Omnilink. He did not spend corporate funds or claim reimbursement for mismarked goods. If he expects that the recipients will think that the watches are genuine, then he intends to deceive them. They, in turn, will feel some obligation of gratitude commensurate with an expensive gift, causing a potential conflict of interest. Creating such conflicts of interest would be a violation of most company policies on gifts, and it would have exactly the effect that the company policies wish to preclude: namely, that employees will not make the best business decisions based on the facts, but will be influenced by a feeling of obligation.

On the other hand, suppose Rupert says to each of the Omnilinkers to whom he gives a watch: "Here is a phony Royal that cost less than $25.00, but you might get some good use out of it. It looks real, and if you want you can fool people into thinking you have the real thing." He and they might consider the gift a joke, not implying any obligation, and not violating Omnilink's policy on gifts.

It is unlikely, from the response Rupert gives to Elmer, that he gave the watches as jokes. If he did not, then he can be faulted for violating Omnilink's presumed policy on gifts. Moreover, his actions are doubly unethical in that he both deceives the recipients as to the real worth of the watches, and imposes on them a burden of gratitude which must somehow be repaid.

The third issue concerns the phony Royal itself. Whoever produced that watch violates the Royal Company's patents, and by producing an inferior product under the Royal name, harms its reputation for quality. Those who sell the watches further the unethical activity by providing a sales outlet. Is it also unethical

to buy the watches, knowing or believing they are fake? With no buyers, the manufacturer could not remain in business; so buying the watch helps promote the unethical activity.

Yet, Rupert might claim that buying the watch does not rob Royal of any profits because he would not purchase a genuine Royal. He bought fakes, and as long as he does not try to deceive anyone, he is not really causing anyone any harm. If all concerned know they are fakes, the poor quality of the watches does not harm Royal's reputation. This is, therefore, different from buying a product that is a duplicate of the original and that replaces the original. Finally, Rupert might add, buying fake watches is so minor a matter that it hardly deserves to be called unethical.

Nonetheless, by his purchases he is supporting the unethical activity of patent infringement. The irony of the case is that he is in Quang Phu to investigate pirates of Omnilink's J-14 and he does not see the similarity between that and the phony Royals.

The fourth issue is what this incident says about Rupert and his relation to Omnilink. Although Clara is correct that it is not any of Omnilink's business what Rupert does off the job and on his own time, his actions reflect traits of

character and judgment that, should they become known at Omnilink, might appropriately influence the way others in the company think of him. Someone who is known to lie in some circumstances cannot be trusted to tell the truth in any circumstances. Someone who is willing to bend the rules in one instance might well bend them in another. Rupert has worked for Omnilink for a long time and has proven himself so valuable that he has been persuaded to stay on to serve as a special investigator. Presumably his past record has been very good. Nonetheless, if his present actions were known, they might well lead some in the company to look at his work for the company more closely, to trust his word less, and to be more cautious in relying on his judgment.

Overall, Rupert Rifflinger should have known better. He should have been aware of the ethical quality of his actions and conscious of the fact that his actions might be taken as a model for others to follow.

Approach Primarily Used: Duties.

[RCS] Ethics and etiquette often become issues together. Sometimes lying is not so much immoral as it is discourteous, and sometimes deception is not so much unethical as it is a matter of bad taste. The present case involves **both** unethical behavior and bad taste. It also spills over into the more serious area of patent infringement and, therefore, theft. But while patent infringement is clearly wrong, the dubious nature of the person who supports such crimes presents some challenging subtleties.

As a gift to his much valued secretary of 13 years, Rupert has the gall to give her a phony watch. What does it say about their relationship all of these years that, at the very end, he lies to her? His "token of genuine appreciation" is not genuine at all. Not only is the watch a phony; Rupert is a phony, too.

What should Clara and her husband think of her former boss now that they have discovered the fraud, and what suspicions should they rightfully harbor concerning his integrity and fair-dealing with them over the past decade or so? Did Rupert think this was merely a joke? If so, why didn't he share the joke with them? (If he had, they might still have apprehensions, but at least there would be no reason for suspicion that the deception was aimed at them.) But Rupert did not deceive only Clara. Three other Omnilinkers also received phony Royals. And to top it all off, instead of confessing or finessing his poor judgment and bad taste, Rupert unabashedly lied to Elmer.

It is a bit of a surprise that Rupert did not buy himself at least one phony watch. Did he understand the demeaning significance of the phony watches and so avoid wearing one himself? One thinks the worse of him for palming them off on others. He appreciates the clever imitations, but would he similarly appreciate the skill of the Asians who copied Omnilink products?

The question of whether or not Rupert paid for the watches with his own or with Omnilink funds is a secondary matter. If he declared a false amount of expense, the case would, of course, become one of straightforward fraud. If company policy forbids the giving of substantial gifts to fellow employees, then his act is a violation of company policy. (Though Clara is no longer an employee, the other three recipients are.) But Rupert would have acted unethically even if his clumsy deception did not violate any Omnilink policies. (Although it would be surprising if there were not some sort of unwritten policy concerning the avoidance of illegally manufactured goods.) Given his duties within the corporation, he is supposed to be particularly alert and conscientious about counterfeit goods. If he is not so in his off-the-job behavior, one should be doubtful about his conscientiousness on the job as well.

One might insist that Rupert's off-the-job behavior is "none of the company's business," and in other instances it would not be. Rupert's religious practices, for example, are none of the company's business. But his behavior in this case is not exactly "off-the-job." His purpose in buying the watches was to express his appreciation for a fellow Omnilinker who has just retired, plus three others on active duty. Even more to the point, the parallel between his duties on the job and his behavior in gift-giving gives the company a perfectly legitimate interest in the case. The fact that he saw nothing wrong with supporting thieves is the very opposite of integrity, since the costs of trafficking in fake goods should be especially appreciated by someone whose job it is to protect the intellectual property of the company.

Approaches Primarily Used: Virtue, Rights.

Case 14
Facing Face

This case takes place in the recent past in *Chikorpan*, an East Asian nation with a culture deeply influenced by the Confucian tradition. Motorola's business has been booming in Chikorpan, outpacing the corporation's ability to find and train qualified Chikorpanese Motorolans to handle the rapidly growing management workload. Consequently, it has been necessary to assign a large number of transpatriate Motorolans to Chikorpan. These transpatriates are enormously expensive, and partly for this reason corporate leadership is sponsoring numerous "localizing" initiatives to recruit, train, and upgrade high-potential Chikorpanese Motorolans, and to induct them as quickly as possible into the corporate culture.

Among these initiatives are several by Motorola University. For example, MU has sent *Frank Blunt* to Chikorpan to offer training to the Human Resources (HR) staff. Frank's assignment was to serve as moderator and primary resource person for a two-week seminar in Fusan.

Frank is from the American Midwest. In his 35 years with Motorola he has built an enviable reputation as an HR specialist, both in the United States and also, for briefer periods, in Europe.

A keystone of Frank's working philosophy of HR is honesty and openness in performance evaluation. For some years he has passionately advocated putting an end to the practice in which a supervisor gives a marginal employee a high performance evaluation in order to get rid of him/her by arranging his/her transfer to another, unsuspecting, department. "Such fraudulent evaluations betray trust and are a danger to Motorola and a favor to no one, including the employee," Frank has said.

Frank feels pretty much the same way about terminations. "If the employee isn't cutting it, he should be terminated, and told why," he told the Fusan Seminar participants. "Integrity necessitates nothing less."

Among the participants at the Fusan Seminar were *Siew Chee-Wah* and *Ingrid Marklund*. Chee-Wah, 43, known informally among his Westerner friends as *"Chuck,"* was former chief of HR at the corporation's *Mei An* Facility. His performance was good, and the need for qualified Chikorpanese HR specialists was urgent, so that after only two years at Mei An, Chuck was promoted and transferred to a top job in Fusan. There was at the time no Chikorpanese Motorolan available to replace him at Mei An, so his job went to a Swedish transpatriate, Ingrid Marklund, 29. Chuck thought highly of Ingrid, who, among all his foreign colleagues, seemed to be the one with the deepest understanding of "the Chikorpanese culture."

During the Fusan Seminar, Chuck politely and indirectly asked Frank whether it would be OK to terminate a substandard Chikorpanese employee by **both** gently pointing out the employee's shortcomings **and** making some vague reference to the possibility of re-employment at some future time — "if and when demand for the product requires upsizing the force."

Frank replied with apparent incredulity, "Well, Chuck, let's see, that would be lying to the employee, wouldn't it?" Chuck immediately sensed that he had gone too far, and made a vague reply of polite demurral.

At this point the normally cool Ingrid spoke up heatedly: "But if I send a man of 30 or 40 back to his family and village without giving him **some** means of saving face, he and his family will lose the respect of people who have been part of their lives for decades, even generations. Why can't I just give him some kind of a — what you Americans call — a 'fig leaf'? My study of Chikorpanese culture tells me that even if he himself doesn't really believe the fig leaf story, as long as it has a surface plausibility back in the village, he can use it and everybody will feel better that way."

Frank was obviously taken aback by Ingrid's apparent support of Chuck's apparent disagreement. But Frank held his ground: "What I say is, integrity is integrity. Here's the real test: If Chuck can look at himself in the mirror in the morning and feel good about lying to an employee he is about to terminate, maybe that is OK. But I could not. Could you, Ingrid?"

Ingrid paused. Was she about to commit an enormous political mistake? But she decided to be gutsy: "Well," she said, "I think termination must be handled sensitively, and if the culture requires certain cosmetics, I am prepared to use them, provided that there is no legal risk in doing so, and that in doing so I do not sacrifice the essence of my own true integrity."

Frank was getting excited: "But Ingrid, that is precisely the question: Just what is true integrity? If you did that, Ingrid, would you be showing true integrity to yourself? If not, then I would advise against it."

Discussion Questions...

1. Imagine yourself in a situation similar to the one described in this case. You believe that it is necessary to terminate a substandard Chikorpanese employee, in a situation where you believe he/she will encounter a serious loss of face in his/her home village. How would you handle the situation?

2. Is integrity measured by one's subjective sense of rightness, or is there a more objective measure?

3. In the broad scale of things, must Uncompromising Integrity sometimes be optimized with Constant Respect for People in the context of the host culture? Does one of these two values usually have priority over the other?

4. How can Motorola's policies best address the issues encountered in the "Facing Face" situation?

Commentaries on Case 14

[WJE] While the first of the two Key Beliefs listed on the TCS Card is Constant Respect for People, often the first one actually appealed to in a particular case, such as this one, is Uncompromising Integrity. Frank Blunt is regarded as the embodiment of this latter belief, a belief stemming ultimately from some deep ethical traditions of Western European culture. In Frank's mind, to be ethical is to operate in the context of quite rigid principles. While it is not stated in so many words on the TCS Card, it seems clear that for Frank, Uncompromising Integrity implies that one should always tell the truth, period — regardless of the cultural context. Therefore he is appalled at even the slightest suggestion that perhaps one should not be so rigid on this matter in the Chikorpanese context. If one invokes only this ethic of principle, the decision is clear: The Chikorpanese substandard employee should be dismissed summarily. This Frank thinks will also further the business interests of Motorola in Chikorpan.

Ingrid demurs. She too is deeply committed to Motorola's business interests but thinks that they can best be served by invoking in some sense the last of the Motorola Key Initiatives. Real "Empowerment for All in a Participative, Cooperative and Creative Workplace" will demand much more of an understanding of, and adaptation to, the standards of Chikorpanese culture. One of the most important of these is an almost desperate need to save face. So, she argues, Motorola should hold out some hint of further employment even though this is so unlikely as to be virtually impossible. What Ingrid is really doing in terms of ethics, is appealing to the undoubted richness of the centuries-old Chikorpanese culture. To be ethical in Chikorpan is to sense oneself as part of this tradition. In sharp contrast to the consequentialism approach central to Western ethics (page 29), which look always to the future, Chikorpanese ethics are more oriented to the past.

Culture often manifests itself not directly but obliquely. Not surprisingly Chuck makes his suggestion to Frank obliquely and tentatively. Principled Frank, however, wants to face the issue head on. But consider with Chuck a few possibilities. If the employee were allowed to save face, he would leave Motorola reasonably content, or at least be able to face his family and friends with honor. The reputation of Motorola in these and other Chikorpanese circles might well be enhanced, and a sense of community within Motorola also enhanced, making it a more truly Participative, Cooperative and Creative Workplace. The reverse would be true should the employee be terminated summarily.

Moreover, in this case it might be entirely possible that the friends and family of the terminated employee who hear that there is a very slight chance of re-employment will hear this as a gentle way of saying that in fact there is none. An understanding of Chikorpanese culture will make it clear to the outside observer that in this case Motorola would essentially be engaging not in a lie but rather in an understood politeness.

So while all cultures as well as all stories contain a certain amount of untruth, these factors should never be valued as ends in themselves but only as means to greater truth. One would personally hope that in Chikorpanese culture over a period of time this practice of gently understood deception will yield to a tendency toward more straightforward statement of the truth. In this case Frank Blunt and Motorola should for the time being go along with Chuck's suggestion, but also quietly make clear their conviction that certain of the values and standards of the Motorola Culture, such as Uncompromising Integrity, are of such universally recognized utility that they are worthy candidates for eventual incorporation into Chikorpanese culture, or at any rate into its business subculture.

Approach Primarily Used: Traditions and Stories.

[TD] At bottom, this is a case about truth-telling and integrity. It contains, of course, a dimension of cultural difference that might affect how truth is perceived, but then most difficult questions of truth contain dimensions of context that affect how truth is perceived. For example, when people make false statements in a game such as "Twenty Questions," the context excuses the false statements from being lies. Even social contexts can affect one's interpretation of what counts as a lie. When the father of a bride approaches one at a wedding with the bride on his arm and asks "Isn't she beautiful!", one would doubtless reply "yes" no matter what one's true impression. So too, the ethical issue of truth-telling arises when one asks whether an advertiser who "puffs" a product, is guilty of lying about it. Surely the context of advertising is one of puffery, but does that context make certain stretchings of the truth permissible?

In turn, the issue of "Facing Face" is simply that of whether the context, that is, Chikorpan, makes it something less than a lie, when terminating a substandard Chikorpanese employee, to **both** gently point out the employee's shortcomings **and** make vague reference to the possibility of re-employment — even though the employee himself will not believe

it. The point of the white lie, of course, is to help the employee "save face" in his home village — and saving face is more important socially in Chikorpan than in the United States or France.

This case is partly one of an issue of duty versus consequences (pages 29, 30). It is the **consequences,** that is, saving embarrassment and shunning in the village, that presumably justify evading the **duty,** that is, refraining from lying. One should next remember, as noted above, that not every false statement is a lie. Indeed one characteristic in the example of making false statements in the game of "Twenty Questions" that might be present in the act of telling the Chikorpanese employee he might be rehired, is that no one will believe the false statement. And yet the mere fact that no one will **believe** a statement cannot in itself be sufficient to justify making a false statement. For example, one might not believe the claims of a hardened criminal, but it does not follow that the criminal is justified in lying.

What is it, then, that makes a false statement a lie? The German philosopher, Immanuel Kant, was probably correct when he said that what makes a false statement a lie is (1) that the person making the false statement intends to deceive, and (2) that the person hearing the false statement had a **right** to the truth. A close look at the Chikorpan

case reveals that both these conditions are met with respect to the "white lie" in question. When a manager "makes vague reference to the possibility of re-employment" there must be some intent to deceive, otherwise there would be no point in making the claim. This is not to say that the intent is to persuade or to remove all doubt that re-employment will occur. It is only to say that "saving face" means creating at least mild uncertainty about whether the termination was permanent. Otherwise, no face would be saved.

So too, the second condition is met. Perhaps people in the village should not ask embarrassing questions of returning workers. Perhaps they have no right to receive an answer — or a direct answer — even if they ask such questions. But insofar as they ask questions and receive answers, they have a right not to be lied to. The only situations in which one's right not to be lied to could be eclipsed are those in which another, stronger right is at issue. For example, in Case 1, "'Uncompromising Integrity' and Egregian Justice," in which a company employee was summarily executed by local government officials for stealing from the company, if lying were the only way to save the life of the employee, then lying to the local officials might be justified. Hence it is clear that, as painful as it might sometimes be to implement Uncompromising Integrity at Motorola, this Key Belief means just what it says: not compromising on the integrity of what one says. Another way to see the same point is to use the age-old test for determining an ethical principle: "Ask what the world would look like if everyone followed the principle." Once one sees the pernicious, hypothetical consequences of Motorolans **always** helping people save face when being dismissed or evaluated, one's own obligations become clearer.

We should keep in mind, however, that it might be possible to arrive at an imaginative solution that manages to save the employee's face while it preserves Motorola's integrity. For example:

• A memo explaining the termination of the employee for incompetence could be entered into his confidential file, as a safeguard against the possibility that another HR manager, some months or years later, might receive an employment application from him.

• However, the corporation could still give the employee a nice note thanking him for his service and wishing him well in his future career. He would then be free, if he chose, to show this to his family and fellow villagers.

Approaches Primarily Used: Duties, Consequences, Rights, Justice and Fairness.

Case 15
Just When Is a "Tip" ONLY "To Insure Promptness"?

Legend has it that the British invented the word "tip" as an abbreviation for "to insure promptness." The key question of this case is: When is it simply that, and when is it something more than that — enough "more" so that it verges on violating the Motorola Key Belief in Uncompromising Integrity?

The setting is the city of *Palatinsk*, capital of *Slavinia*, one of the Slavic-speaking republics that became independent when the USSR broke up. Motorola has recently established an office in downtown Palatinsk, and is eager to get going. But the going is not easy. Motorola must face remnants of the partially defunct Soviet **culture,** in which bribery was expected and tolerated. As if this were not enough, the corporation must also face the current Slavinia **situation,** in which even those Slavinians who strongly hold to the value that bribery is wrong, often find that they must engage in it to some extent merely to feed themselves and their families in the disorganized, inflation-ridden, crime-plagued reality that is Slavinia today.

One of the new hires at Motorola/Palatinsk is *Natasha Sakharov*, age 24. Natasha speaks native Slavinian, excellent Russian and adequate English. She is proud of her qualifications as an industrial engineer, openly disdainful of the unproductive Soviet past, and eager

to make her contribution, through Motorola, to a "new Slavinia" where people will be rewarded on the basis of merit — NOT connections. True, the Slavinian job market is such that she would have taken a job even with a company not perceived as outstandingly ethical — but in her three months on the job she has obviously "bought into" the Motorola Culture, and proudly refers to herself as a Motorolan.

Enter *Bernard Yeats*, a senior Motorola manager out of Phoenix. Bernard arrives in Palatinsk on a Wednesday intending to stay six days and then leave for Germany — but on Thursday he suddenly receives a fax directing him to be in St. Petersburg, Russia, on Saturday to trouble-shoot a crisis.

Problem: Bernard must somehow get a Russian visa in time to leave on Friday. Most foreigners in Slavinia must wait two weeks to secure a Russian visa, during which they are forced to spend endless hours in the Outer Waiting Room of the Russian Embassy, located in downtown Palatinsk — ironically in the building that was once the headquarters of the Soviet Secret Police.

In an effort to assist Bernard, Motorola's Palatinsk office manager immediately tries to contact *Josef Fixzitup*. Fixzitup is a native Slavinian who speaks adequate Russian and broken English. He is a high school graduate and was recently superannuated out of the Soviet Army after 26 years, with the rank of senior sergeant of quartermaster. His pension is tiny, so he has become an independent "administrative broker" who specializes in getting governmental clearances for foreign companies.

Alas, at this moment Fixzitup is off on an errand for another of his foreign clients, *Burger Heaven*. Palatinsk does not yet have a paging system, so no one can find out exactly when Josef will be back.

Desperate, Bernard turns to Natasha. The latter, though knowing nothing about visas, is eager to establish herself as a "can-do" Motorolan. So, she jumps into a taxi with Bernard and off they careen for the Russian Embassy.

There, in the Outer Waiting Room, reality confronts them. Fifty-seven foreigners of all nationalities, ages and appearances are patiently waiting their turn to be admitted to the Inner Waiting Room, where they will have a good chance of receiving a visa within several days. Twenty make it, and then the door closes. The others are told brusquely: "Come back tomorrow."

Next problem: How to get Yeats into the Inner Waiting Room, even though the door has been closed? The key player is obviously the Russian guard, one *Igor Kipoutskii*, who speaks native Russian, minimal Slavinian, and virtually no English. Like most Russian government personnel, Kipoutskii's salary has been reduced by inflation to a mere pittance, and he could not possibly feed his family in high-cost Palatinsk unless he had additional sources of income.

Natasha quells her nerves and approaches Kipoutskii. She explains in Russian how important Motorola is to both Slavinia and Russia, and how important Yeats is to Motorola. Then she hands Bernard's visa application to Kipoutskii, along with an envelope from which a U.S. ten-dollar bill is slightly yet visibly protruding. Kipoutskii shakes his head vigorously to indicate that he is not interested in the envelope, but he immediately places Yeats' application in a special wire basket, and bids Yeats enter the Inner Waiting Room. There, after answering a few routine questions and paying the official $40 visa fee — no more — the dumbfounded Bernard receives his visa, all within 15 minutes!

As Bernard and Natasha are about to leave the embassy, in rushes Fixzitup. Eagerly, he learns from Natasha that Kipoutskii refused the ten-dollar bill. "Please give it to me," he barks, and immediately takes it to Kipoutskii who, after a sidelong glance or two, readily pockets it.

That evening, Yeats is having a vodka tonic with a group of Motorolans who have worked in various parts of the world. "Hey," he asks, "did Natasha and I violate Uncompromising Integrity?" The consensual answer was no. "Why?" "Because, Bernie" replies *Dieter Weltlich* of Motorola/Latinia, "all you were doing was asking for promptness — **not** for something that they wouldn't have done for you anyway, sooner or later. What you did was legal, according to the U.S. Foreign Corrupt Practices Act."

"Legal, of course," pressed Yeats, "but was it **ethical**? And, to hell with Fixzitup and Kipoutskii, what I want to know is: Did I corrupt **Natasha** in the process?"

"Maybe, a little," interjected the scholarly *Lim Key-Boon* of Motorola/Hong Kong, "but I think it was OK nonetheless, because Natasha seems like a real serious post-Communist 'New Slavinian,' and probably sees her behavior as merely coping with a temporary situational **norm,** without endorsing it as a cultural **value.** As soon as the situation improves, she will no doubt act with Uncompromising Integrity. And further-more, by helping Motorola in this way she is helping establish the corporation as a permanent player in Slavinia, and this in turn will help produce a future Slavinian culture in which people are rewarded for their merits and not their connections."

"Besides," added the demure *Kazuko Takeuchi* of Motorola/Sendai, "if you will excuse me for saying so, shouldn't we remember that 'Uncompromising Integrity' is not the only value on our TCS Card? Don't we also need to take seriously the Key Initiative of 'Total Cycle Time Reduction'?"

Discussion Questions...

1. How should Yeats have responded to the situation? Should he have attempted to stop Natasha from offering the money? Should he have attempted to stop the process later? What should he have said to Natasha?

2. Tipping is common in many countries. Was the payment to Fixzitup a tip or a bribe? Who, if anyone, is harmed by a bribe? Who, if anyone, was harmed in the situation described in this case?

3. Later, at the informal meeting with his fellow Motorolans over vodka tonics, Yeats seeks an understanding of what happened and why. He receives three explanations. Which of the three makes the most sense to you?

Commentaries on Case 15

[TD] Underpaid government employees are a fact of life in many countries. Their pay is sometimes so low that they cannot even feed themselves and their families on their salaries. Sometimes it even appears that governments deliberately set these salaries at a low level, assuming that the officials can always gain supplementary income through bribery. Often the bribes are assessed in accordance with a set of informal, but evenly applied, rules.

It should also be noted that the U.S. Foreign Corrupt Practices Act (FCPA), enacted in the 1970s and amended in the 1980s, prohibits U.S. companies and their agents from paying anything of value to a foreign official, political party or candidate for the purpose of influencing an act or decision in order to obtain or retain business. The Act **does** allow facilitating or expediting ("grease") payments to secure the performance of a **routine** or **ministerial** government action. Examples include granting permits or licenses to do business in a foreign country, processing visas and customs applications, providing phone service, etc. It is noteworthy the United States is the only country in the world that even **has** a foreign corrupt practices act.

Nonetheless, the practice of bribery does have pernicious consequences. Even when the amounts are small and the tip might be construed as a "tax" or informal salary supplement, the resulting economic uncertainty can have disastrous consequences for companies. In the present case, Bernard Yeats desperately needs to leave in order to reach St. Petersburg to trouble-shoot a crisis. The fact that he cannot count on the visa that is absolutely necessary for getting there creates dramatic inefficiencies.

Indeed, to digress momentarily, so serious are the uncertainties associated with bribery that one U.S. company took unusual steps to avoid it in Brazil. The company was having its crates regularly pilfered on the docks of Rio de Janeiro by handlers. The handlers took about 10 percent of the cargo, which was destined for customers in Brazil. Not only was the loss significant but, even worse, the U.S. company never knew **which** 10 percent the handlers would take. In a novel move, the company began sending two crates for every one they had sent in the past. The first crate contained approximately nine-tenths of what their earlier crates had contained; the second contained approximately one-tenth. The plan worked: The handlers began taking the small crates and leaving the larger ones untouched. The company still had its goods pilfered, but it now at least knew which 10 percent wouldn't make it to customers! (This solution is not recommended for Motorola.)

Yet another reason why bribery creates inefficiency is evidenced in this case. Note the extra **time** taken in arranging the bribe. This is time that could have been spent doing something useful!

Clearly there are ethical issues in the context described in this case. The prevalence of the practice means that, in general, those with the most money get the best access to government services, and the money goes to those who don't deserve it: an odd consequence for any government whose aim is supposedly to serve its citizens with justice. Clearly, any government that discriminates against those who follow the rules, and, moreover, allows its duly appointed agents to pocket money that — even if interpreted as a "fee for service" — belongs to the government (and indirectly to the citizens of the state) is not serving its citizens with justice. Note also that Kipoutskii is doubtless violating his duty, for almost certainly, the pocketing of bribes breaks Russian law as well as his explicit terms of employment.

Writers who have dealt with bribery note that a key issue separating a tip from a bribe is that of the so-called "prior condition." One's tip to a waiter is not a bribe in part because it was not a condition for one's receiving food, and the fact that the money is given after service rather than before is not important. When a bribe or a tip is made is not ethically significant. Hence even though the payment to the guard is made after the fact, it is still a bribe because it was a condition for getting the visa. Bernard never could have gained entrance through the outer waiting room without the selective cooperation of the guard.

It might be argued that the payment is made only for the sake of speeding up the process, not circumventing it, and that for this reason the actions do not violate the Foreign Corrupt Practices Act. The FCPA explicitly allows that payments made for services that should have been rendered by host country officials anyway (and that meet a few other conditions) may be legally acceptable. Such payments are commonly called "grease" payments.

But this line of argument cannot offer an ethical green light. Even if the payment were to escape the strictures of the FCPA, it still may be wrong on ethical grounds. In fact, three considerations show that the payment made in the case is wrong. First, the fiduciary **duty** of the Russian officials accepting the bribes, that is, their duty to serve their government faithfully, is violated in the process. The Motorolan

employees in the case are helping encourage a government agent to violate his official duty. Second, while some say that small payments made to officials who refuse to do their job **at all** can sometimes be ethical, the officials in the case are not making such a refusal. Here the payment is made to obtain **special treatment**. Bernard is able to obtain service that is dramatically faster than any ordinary Slavinian would receive — even if the officials were doing their utmost. Finally, as explained earlier, any pattern of bribery, including this one, has long-term **consequences** that create inefficiencies for an economy, and a lower level of welfare for the people in a country.

Hence, no matter how much of a mess the Russian system is in, and no matter how unfair it might be that Bernard is denied his visa, Bernard's allegiance to Motorola's Uncompromising Integrity means that he must neither participate in, nor tolerate, the bribe. In this instance Natasha's role is worse than Bernard's since she knew the entire picture. But even Bernard should have balked at two points: first when the money was offered as a bribe; and second, when it was demanded by Fixzitup.

For better or worse, Uncompromising Integrity means Uncompromising Integrity.

Approaches Primarily Used: Justice and Fairness, Duties, Consequences.

[WJE] Natasha wants to play a strong role in developing a new culture for her recently freed Slavinian society, and she sees Motorola playing a helpful role in this transformation. This new society, quite unlike its communist predecessor, is to be solidly business-based. However, Natasha is also still influenced by the practices of the past. So when Bernard Yeats suddenly and urgently needs a visa, she knows that the one effective tactic is to slip a little money to the gatekeeper.

The case is loaded with complexity and ambiguity. Here, though, are a few comments. Take Bernard first. He might be playing a number of roles only one of which is really clear to him. That one role is to further the interests of Motorola. Good ethics are not likely to result in situations of such great ambiguity. What is important ethically is knowing what one is doing and why.

And Natasha? She is certainly somewhat better informed, but is probably also rather confused by the initial refusal of the bribe. But she quite likely understands the dynamics of the situation once Fixzitup arrives on the scene. She also probably feels that his intervention does not contribute to the eventual healthy growth of business ethics in Slavinia. Should she take some action to curb Fixzitup and to stop Kipoutskii from taking the bribe? Or does she think that Kipoutskii will be helpful to Motorola in the future, so that she should go along with his unethical behavior? But if she does this she will herself be engaging in actions detrimental to her country's ethical growth, and to Motorola's values. The actions of Fixzitup and Kipoutskii have now probably made it clearer to her that her own initial offer of the $10 was ethically wrong.

The three final commentators each reveal weak ethical thinking:

- **Weltlich**, in appealing to the law, plays into a fundamental confusion between law and ethics. He takes the position that if something is not illegal then it must be ethical. He sees law as the only real constraint on human practice. This position neatly ignores the fact that law, even international law, is nation- and culture-specific, growing integrally out of these contexts, and is itself sometimes ethical, sometimes not. In the present case, probably not. Moreover, Kipoutskii's acceptance of a bribe probably violates some Russian law.

- **Lim** brings into play something of a consequentialist analysis. He notes that a little bad practice now and then can and probably should be indulged in, because it will eventually produce more good than bad for everyone involved. This clashes directly with a more principled ethical approach which cannot allow bad means to produce good ends.

- **Takeuchi** is the ultimate ethical opportunist. She seems to see the sets of Key Beliefs, Key Goals and Key Initiatives not as hierarchized but rather as all equal. They are game rules for business which can and should be played, one off the other, applying now one and now the other, as most helpful in winning. This comes dangerously close to being no ethic at all.

Approach Primarily Used: Traditions and Stories.

Case 16
Paying "Respect for People" in a Red Envelope

In 1988, *Godwin Pei*, a Motorolan from Bangkok, was assigned to be Human Resources director at the corporation's facility in the Asian nation of *Shimpo*. People assumed that Godwin's Asian origins would give him a head start in learning the Shimponese business culture.

And indeed it did. Take a simple example. Godwin knew that in the Shimponese tradition, the color red symbolizes good luck and long life, and that placing a gift in a red envelope thus takes on special symbolic meaning.

However, Godwin still had more to learn about just **how** much special meaning a red envelope could carry. He learned this lesson rudely one night when his bedside phone rang at 3:00 AM. An anonymous (but obviously Shimponese) voice urged him to come immediately to the facility. There had been a fire on Soldering Line Four, and the local fire brigade had been summoned.

"Is the fire out?" Godwin asked.

"Yes, the flames are out but there's still some smoke," replied the voice.

"Have any of our people been injured?"

"No, Mr. Pei," came the answer. "But I still urge you to come here right away. It is important."

"Well, if the fire is out, and all Motorolans are safe, why can't the night shift foreman just handle it, so I can come in at my usual time around eight o'clock?" queried an impatient Godwin. Godwin had worked late the previous evening, and needed his sleep.

"With respect, Mr. Pei, you should come here now. It really **is** an HR issue."

Reluctantly, Godwin dressed and got into his car.

Arriving at the facility, Godwin was careful not to let anyone know that the phone call he had received was anonymous. He made no effort to find out who the caller had been. Instead, he plunged into his investigation. He satisfied himself that no Motorolans had been injured; that the property damage was limited to the immediate area around Soldering Line Four; and that the rest of the facility was unharmed.

Godwin also noticed that the firemen of the local fire brigade, about 24 of them, were still on the scene. Curiously, they seemed to be just hanging around and not doing very much. They were apparently waiting for an order to return to their station.

Soon Godwin learned why all of this was a Human Resources issue. It turned out that *Da Shin*, the night shift foreman, had already solicited a collection among the shift employees, and was just about to place a substantial amount of money — equal to about U.S. $400 — in a red envelope, to give to the fire brigade captain. This would serve as a token of the employees' respect for the firemen who had "risked their lives to protect Motorola life and property."

As Godwin spoke to Da Shin, he struggled to control his feelings. "Look, Da Shin, Motorola pays taxes, plenty of taxes, and those taxes support the Fire Department. We have already paid for its service many times over!"

In return, Da Shin gave a smile of sheer embarrassment. He explained to Godwin that the money was **not** Motorola's money. It represented "voluntary contributions" from the employees of Soldering Line Four, out of their own pockets. "It's just our Shimponese tradition, sir. All the other big multinationals here in Shimpo observe that tradition, and the local people expect Motorola to observe it, too. After all, it's our way of showing sincerity, respect and appreciation. It doesn't hurt anybody. The firemen will just use it to have a nice catered banquet and celebrate a little bit."

"True, Da Shin, but it will still **look** like Motorola's money, and you know very well that would violate our Code of Conduct."

Godwin persisted in his questioning. Then he learned something that shocked him deeply: In essence, Da Shin was afraid that if the red envelope payment were **not** made, the fire captain might suddenly "discover" that Line Four needed more water, and order the hoses turned back on, with the result that there could be great water damage — maybe even greater than the fire damage.

To make matters worse, under Shimponese law, if the monetary value of the **total** fire damage plus water damage reached a certain level, the Shimponese government was empowered to declare the whole matter to be a threat to public safety — and shut down the entire Motorola facility until the High Court could get around to handling the matter. And that could take months.

"No wonder those employees want to show their so-called 'respect' to the Fire Brigade," Godwin mused to himself. "They are afraid of being laid off or having to work reduced hours." And of course all the other local Motorolans would also lose out if the government shut down the whole facility. That would make Da Shin lose a lot of face. And to make matters worse, the media would pick up the entire affair, and it could turn out to be a public relations disaster.

Godwin took Da Shin aside and asked him to keep the red envelope and the money in a safe place, and, to the extent possible, to make a record of who had contributed how much.

Then Godwin took a deep breath and summoned all his diplomatic skills. He approached the fire brigade captain respectfully. "Sir, I hope you'll appreciate that Motorola is from another culture, and that our corporation has certain strict rules. Please trust me. Motorola wants to work with you. I will do the right thing. Just allow us a few days."

At this point communication got a bit vague. Anyway, the firemen did soon leave the scene. And the captain also left, **without** a red envelope.

Godwin promptly conferred with General Manager *Fidel Vigil*, a Filipino transpatriate. Fidel and Godwin decided to phone the Ethics Committee in Schaumburg and ask for a quick decision on what to do.

Within 48 hours they had their answer. . . .

Discussion Questions...

1. What is the evidence (if any) that the threat against the facility was real? How would one find this out:

- at the moment of the apparent threat itself?

- in retrospect, after the incident is over?

2. Was Da Shin acting properly when he solicited money from the employees?

3. Should Godwin have returned the money to the employees immediately after the firemen had left, rather than "keeping the envelope in a safe place"?

4. Would the money given to the Shimponese firefighters have violated Motorola's Code of Conduct? Why or why not? What extenuating circumstances would make you change your answer?

5. If it were to become evident that the fire captain's intentions were to threaten the facility with further damage unless he received an adequate payoff, what should Godwin have done? What should Motorola have done?

6. If the fire captain also refused to leave — or to order his men to leave — until the payment was made, what should Godwin have done? (This obviously would be a much more dangerous situation.)

7. If practices that Motorolans recognize as extortion are widespread and generally accepted (even though not liked) in a particular host culture, to what extent (if any) should Motorola respect and honor those practices?

Commentaries on Case 16

[RTD] The case starts with a puzzle: Who called Godwin Pei and why? The answer to that puzzle leads us to the ethical issues in the case. The phone call was almost certainly not made by Da Shin, the night shift foreman, who gives every indication of feeling he was in charge of the situation. So the caller was probably one of the employees. The reason for the call was either that he or she felt the payment being made was contrary to Motorola's policy, or that the employees were being asked to make a contribution that the caller thought was inappropriate. The first possibility is unlikely, since there is no Motorola policy about employees giving gifts of their own money to firefighters or anyone else.

So the likely alternative is that the collection was not a spontaneous expression of gratitude, but the result of a less-than-free solicitation, which the caller felt was unfair. That feeling is justified, and any solicitation under the circumstances amounts to coercion. Forcing employees to make a contribution of this sort (and of most other sorts) is unfair to them. If the employees feared that unless they made a contribution, the firefighters might damage the plant so much that it would be closed down and they would be laid off, we have an explanation for their actions. But it is not the responsibility of the employees to donate money to make sure the plant stays open. The collection was not taken among all the facility's employees, but only among those unlucky enough to be working that night. That they should have to pay for the benefit the facility received from the firefighters, or for keeping the firefighters from doing harm, is unfair to them.

Godwin therefore acted correctly in telling Da Shin not to give the money he had collected to the fire brigade, and to make a record of who had contributed how much. Because the money should not have been solicited in the first place, it should be returned to the donors as quickly as possible. Returning the money immediately would have been better than holding it for even a day or two.

At some point Godwin should find out how the money was collected and seek to prevent a recurrence of the event. Since Da Shin listed the contributors, in most cultures it would be appropriate to write each of them a letter thanking them for their willingness to help Motorola, even though the money was returned. And since they were directly involved, it is fitting to keep them informed of Motorola's actions. Whether such a letter would be appropriate in Shimpo depends upon many factors within that culture, since Motorola would not want to add insult to injury.

If any money is to be given in gratitude to the members of the Fire Brigade, Motorola should make the contribution, since it is the Motorola facility in which the fire occurred and it is Motorola's property that was saved.

The further problem the case presents is that it is not clear exactly what is going on. Da Shin indicates that "It's just our Shimponese tradition. All other big multinationals here observe that tradition, and the local people expect Motorola to observe it, too."

At that point Godwin would have done well to pursue the details of that tradition, since Da Shin's statement is ambiguous. Is it the tradition that whenever firefighters put out a fire, the property owners give them a present for their efforts, like a tip for good service? Or is the tradition that only multinationals do that? Among multinationals, is the tradition that the employees working at the time of the fire express their appreciation through a voluntary contribution, or is it that the multinational gives the gift? Since a tradition is mentioned, knowing the details would be useful. But even with the limited information we have, it seems safe to say that any payment should involve Motorola and not the individual employees on a particular shift.

Is such a tradition one that Motorola can ethically follow? Giving gifts to civil servants — and the firefighters in this case are probably civil servants — is usually inappropriate. If given before the fact, it would appear to be a bribe to get them to perform their duty. But in this case, the firefighters had already put out the fire, so the payment was not a bribe. Yet it was not required, nor would there be a bill. Therefore, the payment will not be accounted for in the usual business manner, which makes paying it counter to Motorola's policy. Godwin acts appropriately in seeking an interpretation of corporate policy from the Ethics Committee. While giving a gift of gratitude is not unethical in itself, because this gift may violate Motorola's policy, its senior management should be consulted to see whether they wish to allow an exception in this case. No group — executive or otherwise — can make an unethical action ethical. But managers who make policies have the authority to allow exceptions, provided the exception is not in itself unethical.

The Ethics Committee should know that Da Shin was worried that unless a gift was given, the firefighters might in retaliation resume pouring water on the plant, causing possible damage. Such a threat amounts to extortion, and extortion should not be encouraged by giving in to the extortioners. Whether Da Shin is accurately reporting on the firefighters' intent is difficult to say, since they do withdraw without any payment. Though the firefighters were waiting for their expected reward, they were not like the typical extortionist who carries out the threatened damage when payment is not forthcoming. And they could hardly have come back to the facility three days later to drench it with water. So whether their delay in leaving was really an attempt at extortion, or merely a strong hint that they expected a monetary expression of gratitude, is not entirely clear.

Motorola must, of course, weigh the possibility that if there is another fire, and if the corporation has not followed the traditional practice of expressing gratitude, it might not get the best service. In the final analysis, it is not inappropriate to express gratitude to the firefighters. For instance, if the money is usually used for a banquet, Motorola might host a catered evening for them. It would also not be unethical to give them the money to arrange their own banquet, assuming that the money does go for that purpose and not into the pocket of the fire brigade captain. Such gifts are not unethical if they are done openly and are duly approved and noted. To prevent any possible uneasiness about giving in to possible extortion, the presentation of the gift should clearly indicate that it is purely an expression of gratitude to the firefighters. Although Motorola is not ethically required to make such a gift, it is not ethically prohibited from doing so. And, since it is ethically permitted, and it may also be insurance that the fire brigade will promptly answer any future calls, Motorola has a good business reason to follow the tradition.

Finally, if Motorola learns that there is no such tradition, that the practice is actually extortion, and that willful damage has been done to the facilities of other companies by the firefighters, then the corporation should do what it can to combat the practice. This might involve going to the fire chief, city officials or higher government officials, possibly together with representatives of other multinationals. Motorola should also adopt a clear policy so that Da Shin and all its other managers and employees know what to do and not do in case of future fires.

Approaches Primarily Used: Justice and Fairness, Duties, Consequences.

[RCS] At first glance this case appears to be another instance of a demand for illicit payments, which under Motorola guidelines are strictly prohibited. But on further reading, the situation is far less clear. Depending on certain background information (which might not be accessible), the case could be a matter of innocent misunderstanding, or it could be a matter of extortion. No doubt both the principals in the case, Godwin and Da Shin, were conscientious and thoughtful in their perception of the situation at the time. It seems clear that Godwin made the right decision, namely, to politely encourage the firemen to leave, thus ending the apparent threat, and then immediately appealing to the Ethics Committee in Schaumburg, Illinois, for an authoritative ruling. What remains unclear is the actual degree of danger from the firemen's unspoken threat. A background of criminal activity in Shimpo would make the fears of Da Shin and Godwin more believable. There are, at least, two ethical questions here:

- How does one handle the threat of criminal activity (about which Motorola's rules are quite clear)?

- How does one determine the truth in an ambiguous and culturally unfamiliar situation?

For the two major participants, Da Shin and Godwin, the case unfolds like one of those current "thrillers" that begins with an innocent, everyday sort of emergency but suddenly crosses the line into the horrible, with the threat of extortion and violence unless certain payments are made. What makes the matter worse is that the threat comes from a civic department upon whose services we depend. It is one thing if mobsters threaten to destroy businesses if they are not paid. We do not expect to depend on mobsters. They are an intrusion. But if we cannot trust the fire department to preserve and protect our businesses, then the very structure of society is undermined. The implied threat of future slow responses is a serious cause for worry. But with the immediate threat to cause damage by turning their hoses on Line Four, Da Shin and Godwin are dealing with extortion and corruption on a larger scale.

What is not clear, however, is the full extent of the threat. We are only told of Da Shin's fear, but not of the evidence for that fear, so it is hard to judge the accuracy of what he reported to Godwin. One would like to know exactly what the custom of red envelope "gratitude" payments involves, and what sort of social penalties typically result from a failure or refusal to

pay them. Many more questions arise: Was the suggestion that the fire captain might "discover" that Line Four needed more water a real threat? Had such things happened before? Why was Da Shin afraid? Was his fear based on knowledge of previous incidents? Was the "hanging around" of the firemen as ominous as he believed, or were the men who had just risked their lives resting briefly before departure, perhaps waiting for a possible tip? Was there any substance to Da Shin's and Godwin's fears of the entire facility being shut down as a threat to public safety?

It seems unlikely that the firemen, even in the worst-case scenario, would extend the damage more than enough to "send a message." They would have no reason to destroy the facility, and many good reasons not to. They might very likely be arrested or at least investigated for such irresponsible behavior. (There are, of course, witnesses to the fact that the fire had already been controlled.) The government of any country sophisticated enough to support high technology would not look kindly on the unnecessary destruction of one of their best companies, and the incompetence of the firemen would not go unnoticed. Nor would Motorola simply sit by and wait for High Court proceedings once the details of the incident became clear. We are told that Shimponese law regarding public safety is strict enough to shut down the plant as "unsafe." As long as this is not an intentionally discriminatory act against Motorola, one would surmise that the same law would be hard on those public servants who abuse their civic authority. So, with the luxury of hindsight, one wonders how much of an ethical emergency this case actually reflects, and instead, to what extent it reflects the difficulties of dealing with an agency, organization or government that is not itself trustworthy. If Da Shin's fears had any foundation, then this would reflect a serious and possibly enduring ethical problem in doing business in Shimpo. It is rare to find, in a given country, only one isolated civic agency that is corrupt. Corruption is a contagious disease, which unchecked, tends to become a pervasive part of the culture. Nothing in this case, however, suggests that this is so in Shimpo. Thus, one wonders about the validity of the threat and the possibly coercive nature of the demand for "gratitude."

But whatever the real nature of the threat, Godwin acted correctly by politely getting the firemen out

of the facility and stalling for time. His ability to do so with such grace shows the importance of firm corporate ethical standards and policies. All too often, managers in companies without such policies get swept away by events. Having a firmly set policy against making any such payments allows managers at every level to resist and refuse such demands, and, in this case, provided the excuse to prevent what could possibly have been a major catastrophe.

The difference between a bribe and a gratuity is itself a matter of some interest. The first precedes a favor (even if the favor is a perfectly legitimate action, approval or business endeavor). It is an illicit enticement, that undermines the institution that it subverts (be it a system of justice or a free market). A gratuity is more complicated. Coming **after** the favor (even though the favor was, as in this case, the duty of the firemen), it cannot be seen as an illicit enticement, nor does it obviously undermine institutions. The implication of any such payment might be either that:

• This is a "special" favor, therefore something out of the ordinary; or

• This is a bribe meaning, "if you want our help at the next fire, you'd better reward us now."

A gratuity is usually a matter of proper appearances. Tipping in restaurants is a familiar example. As a matter of custom it might be innocent enough. When one frequents a good restaurant, one might tip generously as an expression of satisfaction. However, when the tip is in response to an implied threat of poor service in the future, then the extortion element creeps in.

The problem in such cases is that the would-be receiver of the bribe or gratuity might not **say** anything explicit about a threat. A larger frame of reference is needed to evaluate the seriousness of implicit threats. This is where local custom comes in — and where Godwin might have pursued his inquiry. For example, in the small Texas city where this commentator lives, citizens receive yearly phone calls from the fire department — which is paid for by their property taxes — requesting an annual "donation." The amount is not unreasonable, but local residents deeply (though silently) resent the call. It is not the annoyance of the call (always at dinnertime) nor the amount (always quite reasonable) nor any lack of appreciation for the importance of the fire department. Rather, it is the implication that, if there were a fire and one had not responded to the appeal, the possible delay in answering the call might be devastating. Of course, the friendly voice on the other end of the line in no way suggests such an implication. Nevertheless, the threat is real enough, even if unstated and unintended.

In the Shimponese case, the implied threat that the fire brigade might not return in future emergencies, and of actually increasing the damage with more water, is a step into the realm of overtly criminal activity. That is why one must be wary of accepting Da Shin's and Godwin's fears, and a bit suspicious that their initial reactions were unwarranted.

This case has other considerations besides the threat of extortion:

- However the case was resolved at Motorola headquarters it would be intolerable for shift employees to bear the burden of payments to save their jobs. A policy against illicit payments means nothing if the burden is shifted from the corporation to its employees. So, one absolute ethical requirement is that the employees must not be left in this situation.

- Another consideration has to do with the gift in the red envelope that is part of Shimponese tradition. This seems perfectly legitimate, in the same way that other culturally appropriate gifts are legitimate under the Motorola Code of Conduct. There is nothing wrong with providing a "token of respect for the firemen who had risked their lives to protect life and property." Since the firemen did, in fact, leave the premises after putting the fire out, there is nothing wrong with following local custom and showing gratitude.

Approaches Primarily Used: Virtue, Duties.

Case 17
Is Motorola Its Agent's Ethical Keeper?

Shamus O'Shaunessy was an aggressive engineer of Irish nationality who had won steady promotions at Motorola/Dublin, and at age 42 was promoted to be director of the Motorola facility in a host nation with a culture very different from Ireland's, namely *Exotica*. The corporation trusted in his strong reputation as a no-nonsense guy who challenged conventional wisdom and got to the bottom of issues. Shamus had never before worked outside his native Ireland and relished the challenge of his new transpatriate assignment.

A week after arriving in Exotica, Shamus began taking a hard look at every major cost figure. One item that quickly caught his eye was "freight forwarding costs." Shamus understood how important it was for Motorola to get its materials, parts and products cleared through the Exotican Customs Service quickly, conveniently and predictably. But there was a problem. He noticed that the fees charged by Motorola's freight forwarders had been escalating steeply for the past seven years — for **no** apparent reason.

Shamus called in *Peter Plassitt*, the manager in charge of shipping and logistics. Peter was a native Exotican who had been with Motorola for 21 years. He had the reputation of being forever eager to keep everything smooth and harmonious. Peter told Shamus that when Motorola established its Exotica facility 22 years ago, it made use of three local freight forwarding companies, namely *Golden Wings Expediters, Quikshot Brothers,* and *Magic Touch, Ltd.* It became clear that the corporation got the best service from Magic Touch, and so that company grew to handle about 80 or 90 percent of Motorola's freight forwarding business in Exotica. The converse was also true: About 75 percent of Magic Touch's business was with Motorola. Peter explained: "Magic Touch understands the culture of the Exotican bureaucracy. They know how to handle all the messy details so we don't have to."

Later that day, Shamus felt troubled. Just what **were** those "messy details?" Why did it cost so much to handle them? And why did Peter seem so reluctant to talk about them?

Before Shamus could answer these questions to his own satisfaction, *Ray Brainright* answered them for him in a story in Shamus' favorite newspaper, the *International Gold Street Journal*. Ray was a character: a brash, ambitious 28-year-old reporter who served as the *Journal's* Exotica correspondent. In his analytical reports, he enjoyed shocking the international business community by making fun of what he called their "hypocrisy."

And in this case, Ray certainly succeeded in delivering a shock. When Shamus read Ray's story he exploded with frustration.

> (Exotic City, Exotica, March 15) The foreign business community in this Exotican capital is buzzing with stories about the escalating cost of so-called "freight forwarding" services. Most officials of the Exotican Customs Service are known to be willing to accept under-the-table payments. They are masters at the art of dragging their heels when a foreign company does not "understand Exotican culture" and resists making such payments under the table.
>
> More than a few Exotican freight forwarders have been feeding in this corrupt trough for years. They make their best money serving multinationals whose products require short deadlines. They often charge foreign companies two or three times the going rate for local Exotican firms.
>
> As an illustration, take the case of Magic Touch, Ltd. This company has only about a dozen employees and operates out of a headquarters that can only be described as modest, yet it earns a prodigious annual income by representing Motorola, as well as certain other multinationals. It is reported that

> Motorola personnel feel that they have no reason to suspect Magic Touch of any wrong-doing. Can such an excellent corporation really believe this? One wonders.

Shamus took several minutes to cool off. Then he called a senior staff meeting for 13:30 the following day, with a single agenda item: "How to Handle the Brainright Affair."

Shamus feverishly prepared himself for the meeting. He pulled together the following facts:

- When Motorola first entered Exotica 22 years ago, it received written assurance from the Exotican Ministry of Development that this sort of practice did not go on and would not be allowed. Other multinationals received similar assurances.

- The situation has changed. Inflation rates have been steep and the Exotican customs officials' raises have fallen short of the inflation rate. This has led to a loosening of discipline among the officials.

- The Exotican government seems to assume tacitly that it is unnecessary to raise customs officials' salaries to keep up with inflation, because they can find ways to collect part of their income from under-the-table payments.

- Within the past few years five senior and middle managers at Motorola/Exotica have quietly expressed the opinion that paying "forwarding fees" might be poor ethical practice and, therefore, poor business practice.

- Two of these managers have also contended that Motorola must take a "brother's keeper" position whether it wants to or not, because Magic Touch is identified with Motorola in the public perception.

- Finally, all five are concerned that **unless** Motorola takes some kind of action, it might lose its reputation for Uncompromising Integrity, and with it an important business advantage.

His research completed, Shamus typed the following agenda for the staff meeting.

1. Investigate facts. Is alleged corruption real?

2. If corruption is found to be real:
   a. How did we get into this? Whose responsibility?
   b. How has/will it affect Motorola reputation?
   c. How has/will it affect Motorolans' morale?

3. What should we do re Magic Touch?
   a. Ask them to change behavior?
   b. Fire them and get a different forwarder?
   c. Do our own forwarding?

4. What should we do re public relations?
   a. Ignore whole matter and hope it dies?
   b. Issue our own press release?

5. What should we do with or against other multinationals?
   a. Nothing?
   b. Assign partial blame to them?
   c. Cooperate with them to reform the customs service? If so, how?

6. What should we do re Exotican government?
   a. Nothing?
   b. Complain privately?
   c. Complain publicly?
   d. Take legal action?

Next day at 13:30 the meeting began. . . .

Discussion Questions...

1. Knowing that freight forwarding charges were escalating, what was the responsibility of Motorola's management in Exotica?

2. Assuming that Magic Touch was in fact making under-the-table payments, what should Motorola have done? Is there a linkage between Motorola's ethical position and that of Magic Touch? Is Motorola any more responsible for Magic Touch's ethics than Magic Touch is for Motorola's ethics?

3. Assuming that the reports of corrupt payments are true, should responsibility be placed primarily on Magic Touch, the customs officials or the Exotican government? Which group is most likely to effect change and how?

4. Who in Motorola should have asked more questions? When? What questions?

5. Assume that a Motorolan learns about such under-the-table payments and reports them to his immediate supervisor. If no remedial action results, should the Motorolan then report this information directly to higher corporate levels?

6. The Exotican Ministry of Development originally assured Motorola that such corrupt practices did not occur and would not be allowed. How then, might Motorola have gotten into this situation?

7. The local justification for such corrupt practices is that customs officials are so poorly paid that they are expected to supplement their salaries by their personal efforts. Is this justification similar to the justification for paying waiters very low wages because they are expected to supplement their salaries with tips? Why or why not?

8. Are there circumstances under which Motorola/Exotica should go public with its position on this issue?

9. Under the U.S. Foreign Corrupt Practices Act, it is not illegal for a U.S. company to make a "grease" payment to a local government official in order to receive promptly the **same** service that it would otherwise receive more slowly. Does this legal fact make under-the-table payments by Magic Touch ethically acceptable?

Commentaries on Case 17

[RTD] A common rule of thumb in testing the ethics of an action is to ask whether you would feel comfortable if the action were described in the local newspaper. Shamus O'Shaunessy explodes with frustration when he sees Motorola linked to Magic Touch's activities in the *International Gold Street Journal*.

In creating the agenda for the senior staff meeting Shamus called, he appropriately starts by investigating the facts. These are essential in any case study. Part of that investigation should include the circumstances of freight forwarding in Exotica and how and why they have changed. Shamus might assume that any actions taken by his predecessors and by Peter Plassitt were taken out of concern for Motorola's best interests, rather than for their personal gain but that does not mean they acted ethically or wisely, or that their actions benefited Motorola.

There are two issues in the case. One is clearly ethical, and that is the issue of whether Motorola is its agent's ethical keeper. The case, with Ray Brainright's article and Shamus' reaction, clearly implies that it is. We should see whether this is correct and why.

The second issue is how to use public relations to deal with the situation. Although this should be done ethically, ethical considerations will not yield a specific answer and will only rule out certain unethical alternatives.

Regarding the question of whether Motorola is its agent's ethical keeper, we can start with a clear statement. Motorola does not pay or condone paying bribes or any fees under the table. Such payments are prohibited by the Motorola Code of Conduct because they are unethical and because they are poor business practice. Paying bribes undermines the free market system by basing business decisions on payments to individuals rather than the quality and price of goods and services. Doing so misallocates goods and services. Bribery is inherently unfair, or unjust, to a variety of people: those who are discriminated against because they do not make such payments and those who do not receive the best products available for their money. In addition, bribery undermines the morality of those engaged in the practice and helps to corrupt them. Frequently it leads to the need to falsify records. Once a company starts making such payments, it gains a reputation for making them, and is expected to make more payments to people who expect similar treatment. Aware of these and other similar

consequences, Motorola wishes to preserve its integrity — one of its Key Beliefs — as well as its reputation.

The question Shamus correctly asks is: How did Motorola get itself into the situation described in this case? When it entered Exotica it was assured that this sort of practice did not go on and would not be allowed. So the initial question is: When did it become necessary to use a "freight forwarding agent"? If Motorola did so from the beginning, was it assured that the agent was not making under-the-table payments? If so, at what point did the forwarding fee rise to cover such payments, and why was nothing done at that point? One thing to be learned from this case, and something of which Shamus is aware, is that somewhere along the line one or more poor decisions were made, probably without thought of where the extra money was going or why fees were going up. The best time to handle unethical payments is before any are made. If Motorola was not assured by its agent that no unethical payments were being made when it first hired the agent, then such assurances should have been sought and obtained upon the first hint or suspicion of the possibility of such payments. A serious problem, or at least a failure to take

Motorola's values seriously, is indicated by the ethical concerns of five managers that were ignored. What was Peter Plassitt's part in this? That must be part of the investigation.

This analysis started by stating that it is Motorola's practice not to pay or accept bribes and that paying bribes is unethical. Since it is unethical to do so, is it also unethical to do so indirectly through one's agent? Some might argue that it is not Motorola that is paying the bribes. Motorola is simply hiring an agent and paying the agent a legitimate fee. What the agent does with the money he receives is his and not Motorola's business. As long as the fee is considered a reasonable business expense and the agent is effective in moving shipments, his dealings with local customs agents and with other local people are not Motorola's business. That is why the agent is hired. This seems to be Peter's view.

Although some might argue this way, the argument is unsound. Imagine that one's agent is completely ruthless, kills people who get in his way, and threatens others with death or serious harm in order to get them to expedite shipments. It is clear that Motorola could not condone such actions, and should not pay anyone to perform such

actions, even if the actions benefit Motorola. Agents act for the principal or the people who hire them. The principal cannot control and is not responsible for everything an agent does; but the principal is responsible for the actions taken by the agent on the principal's behalf. If paying bribes is unethical, then Motorola cannot escape responsibility for paying bribes if its agent pays the bribes to expedite shipment of Motorola's goods.

Yet, Motorola does not **know** that the agent is making such payments. Some Motorolans simply suspect that the agent does so. Some might argue that since Motorola does not know, it is not responsible for the payments made, if any are made at all. This defense is defective. If Motorola does not know, then once someone in the corporation suspects that the agent is acting unethically, Motorola has the responsibility and obligation to determine the facts. Motorolans in Exotica failed to determine these with respect to Magic Touch.

The claim that Magic Touch's payments were facilitating payments and allowable under the U.S. Foreign Corrupt Practices Act carries little weight. Motorola does not condone such payments and sought and received written assurances from the Exotican Ministry of Development that such practices would not be allowed. Hence it is on record as opposing them.

In its investigation, Motorola should determine whether all freight forwarding agents in Exotica make such payments. If only some of them do, are those who do not ineffective in handling shipments? If all of them make such payments, then are such agents necessary? If its agents are making unethical under-the-table payments, Motorola's policy is clear and the practice must stop.

What is less clear is what Motorola's options are once that decision is made. If Brainright's report is correct, Motorola must immediately distance itself from Magic Touch and look for another freight forwarding agent who can be effective while operating ethically. If no such agent is available, Motorola can raise the issue with the local authorities who guaranteed that such practices would not be allowed. Perhaps some accommodation can be made for Motorola. Motorola might contact other companies to see if jointly they can protest the practice and effect some change. In some instances, companies have agreed to pay higher government charges, if the money raised is used to increase local customs officials' pay. The company saves the money it pays in higher fees by not having to pay bribes. There are other possible avenues to pursue and the local Motorolans must use their imaginations and initiative.

In the end, if nothing is possible and Motorola cannot operate ethically in Exotica, then it cannot operate there at all.

The second issue is how to handle the situation from a public relations point of view. The article in the *International Gold Street Journal* has already threatened Motorola's reputation by attributing to it naiveté or a lack of integrity. Ethics require that Motorola act ethically in facing and responding to the charge. It should not cover up or deny wrongdoing if its agent acted as reported. If Motorola determines that its agent acted inappropriately, and if it separates itself from that agent and handles its subsequent transactions ethically, it is ethically permitted but not required to make this known publicly through news releases and by other standard public relations efforts. It may not ethically excuse its ethical lapse by shifting blame only to the agent, or to the government, or to other multinational or local companies, even though it **may** make whatever factual statements about these entities that it wishes. Ethical considerations alone will not show how to

best handle the public relations aspect of the case, and will only limit what Motorola may not do.

An important lesson to be learned from this case is that Motorolans should be careful not to get themselves into this kind of situation in the first place. Somewhere along the line someone did not ask questions that should have been asked, or chose to ignore signs that should not have been ignored, or refused to accept responsibility for the actions of Motorola's agent. That failure led to the issues the case presents.

Approach Primarily Used: Duties.

[RCS] Bribery, in all of its forms and under any number of euphemisms, such as "clearing customs" or "freight forwarding fees," is the continuing focus of many pronouncements and policy disputes. It is also the subject of many misunderstandings. As the focus of debate in transcultural ethics and global company policy, it has often become the unfortunate model of the saying, "When in Rome, do as the Romans do," the thesis sometimes known as ethical relativism. That is, it is right to act in accord with the customs and mores of the local culture.

Ethical relativism should be distinguished from cultural relativism, the thesis that different cultures have different social practices. Cultural relativism is no longer a matter of serious debate because cultural differences are a fact. Ethical relativism adds the stipulation that two or more opposed moral practices — that is, the most basic interpersonal and principled practices in the society — can be **correct,** each in its own culture. But whether it is possible for a practice to be morally permissible (or even obligatory) in one locale and not in another, is a far more complex philosophical question than the factual question of whether different societies have different practices.

One can take at face value the stated facts that it has become a custom in Exotica for agents to charge "freight forwarding fees" that are "unreasonably high," and that part of these payments is used to supplement the pay of Exotica's underpaid customs officials. The fact that the case involves a **change** in local cultural expectations, and that Motorola originally entered Exotica with the assurance that such practices were not allowed, ought to make us go beyond this assumption.

The two approaches to such cases — exemplified by the "When in Rome . . ." position on the one hand and Motorola's absolute policy against paying bribes on the other — provide a framework for an investigation, but only if one is clear what kind of ethical question one is asking and what kind of ethical approach one is considering. First, it is important to ask whether this is an **ethical** question at all. If there were a religious-cultural practice requiring that all men wear hats and all women cover their shoulders when traveling or doing business in Exotica, one could agree that this is not a moral question but rather one of courtesy, and courtesy would dictate that when one is in Exotica, one should do as the Exoticans do. But this is often taken to be the status of the bribery situation as well. There are companies and policy makers who think of bribes as "part of the cost

of doing business" in Exotica and not as an ethical issue. The question becomes whether the cost is worth the benefits of doing business in Exotica. The future of corporate policy and of the custom becomes nothing but a product of market forces — are companies willing to pay the increased fees or not? Such an approach is dangerously misleading and self-defeating. Bribery is not just bad for business. Bribery, under any name, is unethical. Bribery is **wrong.** But what makes bribery wrong and unethical and what constitutes bribery are by no means straightforward questions.

What is bribery? How is it to be distinguished from legitimate levies, fees and payments that might cost just as much? How does one distinguish "bribery" from other seemingly similar — but ethically different — practices such as "forwarding fees," local tariffs and taxes? The short answer is that bribery is **corruption.** It is a destructive social practice that eats away at and destroys the culture it is part of **from the inside.** The fact that it presents an **internal** danger to the host culture is what renders the "when in Rome. . . " argument irrelevant. The question of bribery is not just a matter of Motorola respecting the social practices of other host countries. It is a matter, in part, of not doing them harm. While it is true that some less industrial nations have developed

rapidly despite widespread corruption among their officials, the record makes it clear that corruption generally hinders true development and that nations with less corruption do better.

One can draw a parallel here with the courtesies and concerns between individuals. Acting in accordance with a friend's desire or respecting a friend's intense dislike of certain behaviors such as profanity or loud and boisterous laughter is perfectly proper and an essential part of friendship. But encouraging or contributing to a friend's self-destructive habit, such as buying a drink for a problem drinker, is very different in kind and not an act of friendship at all. So, respecting the customs and practices of another culture is essential to building a business relationship, but contributing to the destruction of that culture through bribery is not part of that business relationship but its very opposite.

The frame of the investigation must be enlarged to include individual acts of corruption and the entire system in which these acts take place. This is where so many discussions of the bribery question and intercultural differences go wrong by looking at only the particulars and their consequences rather than business as a whole. In a culture that had no commerce or where commerce played a minimal role, there could be no such practice as bribery. There might be gifts, and in turn, obligations of many kinds. There might be solicitations and payments of tribute to those in power in exchange for certain favors. But there would be no bribery. Bribery is a particular, clandestine payment within a society of the type that proscribes bribery.

That general environment, which is rightly, but sometimes misleadingly, called free enterprise, presumes a level playing field and competition on the basis of price and quality, among other things. It is essential to the idea of business that such openness and competition be unencumbered. This is not to say that there cannot be proprietary information, sealed bids, secret strategies or private arrangements, but all of these are defined and restricted by the practice of business. Intimidation, coercion and violence, for example, are clearly forbidden by the practice. Bribery is also forbidden because it endangers that openness and free competition by its nature.

One might use a utilitarian approach here to argue that the consequences of widespread bribery are bad for almost everyone, including the customs officials, who are locked into a system in which the government feels no obligation to pay them a living wage. This misses the main point, which is that the corruption of the practice itself — not just its consequences — is the ethical violation. There might be societies with no interest in business or free markets, but then there would be no dilemma, because Motorola would not want to do business there. Unfortunately, the world is much more complicated than this, and what is or is not a market society is now seriously contested. In many societies, especially those referred to as "the Third World," there is fierce internal conflict over this question, often confused by the misleading term "Westernization." But the question of whether a society wants to encourage free markets and the consumerism they produce is a major issue in much of the world. The prevalence of bribery and the attitudes toward it often indicate these basic conflicts. It is difficult to measure "utility" in such cases because it is the culture's values as such that are in dispute. This is one of several objections to a pure utilitarian treatment of the case. The primary objection is the fact that bribery is a knowing violation of the most basic principles of a free market, not just a practice with bad consequences.

One must be concerned about the wrongness of bribery both in terms of its effects on the host country and on the company asked to pay bribes. For a company with a stated principle not to pay bribes of any kind, making such payments is a violation of its own integrity, and is perhaps hypocrisy as well, particularly if the bribe is "rationalized" as "not being really a bribe at all." Acting consistently with one's principles is essential to any adequate sense of integrity. But it is more than this. When a company is concerned for the well-being of another culture, rather than cultural exploitation for gain — it is an essential sign of that company's character. Respect for one's practice is a sign not only of good sportsmanship but also of integrity.

This brings the analysis back to the "facts" of the case as stated. The case involves a **change** in the customs of Exotica and "a loosening of discipline." Therefore, by their **own** established standards, Exoticans believe bribery is improper and not permissible. Again, the "When in Rome. . ." argument breaks down, and one can argue that it is not in any way improper for Motorola to address the powers that be in Exotica and attempt to rectify the situation. Indeed, it is Motorola's responsibility, if it is to take a major role in the economy of Exotica, to make clear "in a quiet firm way" that it will not participate in such practices, and to engage in efforts to change them.

"Going public" is itself a transcultural issue of some delicacy. In a democracy, this might be the most effective way of bringing about change, but more often discreet, nonconfrontational negotiations that do not cause public officials to lose face are much more effective. The fact that Motorola originally entered Exotica with the "assurance" that such practices were not allowed brings this case into the realm of promises made but broken, inviting efforts at redress and rectification. One should not confuse this with blame. The effort it takes to pin the blame on one party or another usually distracts from, rather than contributes to, the solution of the problem.

The history of such cases is important. To understand Exotican culture is to understand its past and present, its development and current customs. One wants to know why and how local customs have changed and why discipline has loosened in the face of the promise of increased prosperity. More importantly, one's integrity as a Motorolan does not involve just compliance with one's policies and principles, but an understanding and appreciation of the corporate culture that has evolved around key values and insights contributing to the corporation's success. The case of bribery in Exotica is foremost a routine test of Motorola's character as a corporation. It involves Motorola's history and integrity, its recognition of its essential place in the world of business, its appreciation for the integrity of the free enterprise system and its concern for the ultimate well-being of the cultures in which it is doing business. The more common but mistaken treatment, which simply asks if we follow our values or theirs, misses the richness and the ethical depth of what might all too easily seem like an isolated case of whether it is good for business.

**Approaches Primarily Used:
Virtue, Traditions and Stories.**

Case 18
Operation Reap

The place is the city of *Mbolo*, the sprawling, teeming capital of *Africaria*, and the time is this evening.

Africaria is an African nation that won independence from Britain in 1964. After two years of ineffective attempts at democratic government Africaria became a soft military dictatorship under the leadership of *Gen. John Abraham Oduhga*. Since then President Oduhga has had to foil three *coup* attempts, but today, 30 years later, he still occupies the white monolith on Disraeli Avenue that was once the British Governor's Palace.

In 1966, President Oduhga persuaded *Venus, Ltd.,* a multinational company headquartered in Palermo, Italy, to locate a creosote facility in *Hope Village*, a small community in what was then open countryside about 12 miles from the center of Mbolo. Hope Village was President Oduhga's birthplace, and he wanted to make it a model "community of technological progress" for the new, independent Africaria. From 1966 to 1986 Venus produced creosote and a wide variety of chemical products at its Hope plant. Then the company fell into receivership and sold its facility and 30-acre plot at a bargain price to *Techcellence, Ltd.,* a multinational electronics corporation based in *Gold Beach*, Australia.

Techcellence moved in quickly and began producing a variety of computer parts. From 1986 to 1991 its general manager was *Fred Feckles*, 55. Fred did not really want the assignment, but was finally persuaded to accept. He had five years to go before retirement, was not highly motivated, and complained incessantly about Africarian culture. The operation was not profitable.

When Fred retired in 1991, he was replaced by *Guy Gusher*, who was born in *Outback Canyon,* Western Australia, in 1958. Guy was well regarded, and his appointment as general manager at Mbolo was seen by all as a watershed development in his career.

The transformation that ensued was dramatic. Within two years Guy had the Africarian operation paying off handsomely. Some Techcellencers carped that his success was due to an upturn in international market conditions, but others praised his leadership qualities. Nowadays, Guy is touted more and more frequently as a potential senior officer of the corporation. He does nothing to discourage such talk.

This evening Guy has called a meeting of his senior staff. Purpose: to discuss and garner support for Guy's plan, "Operation Reap," which calls for relocating the Techcellence facility to the new General John Abraham Oduhga National Industrial Park. This well-planned park is close to the Mbolo International Airport and is well served by a new highway. Companies that locate facilities there receive special tax-free import privileges for materials and parts. It is, as Guy announced calmly, "the place for us to be."

The usual staff discussion about logistics, construction costs and the like followed. Guy could see that the discussion was going his way, but that it needed a real sweetener. So he supplied it.

"Look, guys, in addition to all the advantages I've mentioned, we're also going to reap a splendid real estate profit. Now of course, I know that Techcellence is not a real estate company, but what's wrong with making some easy extra money? We bought the Hope site for $300,000 and now the *Marie de Beauclaire Oduhga* Memorial Hospital Foundation is willing to pay us $8 million for it. Mbolo has been growing at a prodigious pace, and what was once open countryside is now urban sprawl. So, naturally land prices have appreciated, and it is now very hard to find a nice open 30-acre site anywhere inside metropolitan Mbolo with the right location for a hospital.

"So, under Operation Reap we sell a property for $8 million that we paid $300,000 for. Then we pay $800,000 to *"Johnnie" Oduhga*, the President's son, who is a legally registered real estate broker. So there's a profit for Techcellence of $8 million minus $1.1 million, or $6.9 million. And mind you, that's tax free — although I have conditionally promised that we will contribute $100,000 to the Building Fund of the Marie de Beauclaire Oduhga Memorial Hospital, which would bring our net profit to $6.8 million. We then pay half a

million for a much better location in the Industrial Park, and another $5 million to build a new facility that will be state-of-the-art. Thus we come out way ahead with a $1.3 million net profit. It's win-win for everybody!"

"Beg your pardon, Mr. Gusher," said a timid reedy voice. It was that of *Diligencia Dorobo*, a Filipina Techcellencer who had arrived three months earlier to serve as environmental affairs specialist.

DD: Did Venus do any environmental appraisals?

GG: No, not as far as I know. Fred Feckles never mentioned anything like that to me. And since I've been here no one from the government has ever bothered me about such matters. I don't think we have to worry.

DD: But Mr. Gusher, I have tested the soil at the Hope site in 18 places, and it is loaded with creosote and several other contaminants that are worse. To clean it up will require removing about three feet of soil from much of the area, and then further detoxification to make really sure the subsoil would be safe for industrial use. However, this would cost only about a million dollars, maybe less.

GG: Well, as long as the President wants his Hospital of Hope as a memorial to his late wife, I think we'll be OK. A million-dollar cleanup would cut our net profit to $300,000, and make Operation Reap harder to sell to the Management Board back in Gold Beach. Besides, both Fred and I have run our own annual environmental audits on pollution, including ground pollution, and Techcellence has come out clean.

DD: I do think that is true, Mr. Gusher. Techcellence itself has been clean. But it is also true that our land is polluted and is unsuitable for a hospital.

GG: Well, all that pollution was done by Venus long before we got here. And besides, it couldn't have been too bad, because you don't see any of our Techcellencers dropping dead around here, do you?

DD: Well, sir, I'm afraid we don't really know that for sure. The fact is that Medical tells me that some of our senior Africarian employees do have anomalous complaints that **could** have been caused by ground pollution.

GG: Well, I don't see why we should be held liable for the sins of our predecessors. And besides, the government never came around and checked up on Venus. No, I think we can go ahead with Operation Reap with a clear conscience. I know that I, for one, can sleep well at night.

Despite this show of bravado, Guy Gusher went home to his apartment feeling strangely uneasy.

Guy thought of his own three kids, whom he had left back in Gold Beach with Mrs. Gusher to be educated — but also, really, because he didn't consider Africaria a very healthy place for kids. But on the other hand, a neat annual bonus, a jump promotion in rank — and he could send them all to the finest private schools in Australia.

What it really came down to, he mused, was this:

- Was Techcellence liable when the Africarian government had never queried it about environmental matters? Clearly not legally. But ethically?

- Was Techcellence ethically liable for environmental damage caused by a predecessor, damage that was legal then and is probably legal now?

- If we have any lingering doubts, wouldn't it be OK to double our corporate contribution to the Marie de Beauclaire Oduhga Memorial Hospital of Hope? After all, Techcellence believes in being a good corporate citizen.

Discussion Questions...

1. Was Techcellence ethically liable for the environmental damage caused by a predecessor company?

2. Does it make any difference that the damage was not illegal during Venus' time and might not be illegal now?

3. Was Techcellence legally or ethically liable, considering that the Africarian government had never asked it about environmental matters?

4. Should Guy inform corporate headquarters in Gold Beach, Memorial Hospital, General Oduhga and his present employees of the contamination problem and suggest ways to clean it up?

5. What should be Techcellence's future role in the socioeconomic development of Africaria?

Commentaries on Case 18

[RTD] What is most striking in this case is the lack of environmental consciousness of the representatives of the organizations involved — Venus, Techcellence and the Memorial Hospital Foundation. Venus, which built and ran a creosote facility, soiled its own nest by dumping creosote and other chemicals on its grounds. Evidently it did not create any special dumping area, since it contaminated even the area on which its plant stood. While it might not have been aware of soil contamination in 1966, it certainly should have been aware of it by the time it sold its facilities to Techcellence in 1986. Even though the property was sold while Venus was in receivership, the company should have notified Techcellence about its contaminated soil. If Venus was so poorly managed that it did not even know that its land was contaminated, it should have known. It was a subsidiary of an Italian multinational that had responsibility for what its Africaria facility did or did not do.

Techcellence is an Australian multinational. That it did not investigate the condition of the land it purchased is at least surprising. More pointedly, if it was unconcerned because it was dealing with a developing country, it can be morally faulted twice: for ignoring its employees' health and for considering its African employees less worthy of respect than its Australian ones. Fred Feckles was a poor manager, and his poor performance included his lack of responsibility in considering the employees' safety — and his own as well. Guy Gusher is a better manager, but evidently never asked about the history of the facility and never thought about or pursued the possibility of soil contamination.

Once Diligencia has reported to Guy that the soil is contaminated (why she did not report this as soon as she discovered the truth is not clear), Guy can and should no longer ignore it. Whether or not he sells the land to the Memorial Hospital Foundation, he is responsible to clean up the contamination. If he does not sell the land, then he should clean it up to protect his own employees. If he does sell the land, then he should clean it up so he can turn over uncontaminated land. This is both ethical and good business. If he did not clean up the land now, Techcellence would be ethically responsible for doing so later and also for any damage done to those who build the hospital, use it or work in it. Since Venus was in receivership, it is doubtful whether Guy could get the Italian parent company to pay all or even part of the cleanup cost, even though he might pursue such a possibility. The fact that Techcellence is ethically required to clean up its land might help Guy sell "Operation Reap" to his staff and to his corporate officers in Australia. Since Techcellence must spend about $1 million for the cleanup, this can be financed from the $8 million it will receive for the land if Techcellence sells it. Otherwise Techcellence will have to pay the same amount from its operating proceeds.

The government of Africaria seems as unconcerned about soil pollution as Venus, Fred Feckles and Guy Gusher. It is clear that whatever antipollution laws might exist in Africaria, they are not enforced. But whatever the reason, no one from the government has bothered Guy — or evidently Venus — about pollution. Even the Hospital Foundation seems unconcerned about the land it is buying, and did not have it tested. The foundation's ignorance or unconcern, as well as the possible absence of any pollution laws, does not affect Techcellence's ethical responsibility. It has the obligation not to harm people, and therefore the obligation to inform the Hospital Foundation about the problem and to clean up the land. Giving an additional $100,000 to the Hospital would not relieve Techcellence of its responsibility for the cleanup. Nor would it be relieved of that responsibility even if the Hospital Foundation said it didn't care about the ground contamination. Since Guy and Techcellence know the potential harm, their responsibility for it remains.

Techcellence and Guy Gusher are still in the enviable position of getting a better location, building a new state-of-the-art facility and reaping a profit of $300,000 after the required cleanup. Guy's problem would be more difficult if the cleanup would result in a loss, but he and Techcellence are ethically required to clean up the land whether or not Techcellence sells it. The fact that Techcellence assigned Diligencia Dorobo to be in charge of environmental affairs shows that at last Techcellence has become environmentally conscious. If Guy decided to ignore the pollution problem and sell the land as-is and without disclosure to the Hospital Foundation, Diligencia has the responsibility, because of her position and knowledge, to inform Techcellence headquarters in Gold Beach, Australia. Should Techcellence's Management Board not take any action to clean up the pollution she would be in a difficult position. She would have to weigh her loyalty and obligations

to Techcellence against her obligation to prevent serious overriding harm to others where she can do so without serious harm to herself. In the absence of more details, it appears that her responsibility to those who would be harmed would require her to inform at least the Hospital Foundation about the soil condition and the dangers it poses.

This analysis has considered only the environmental issue in the case. It has not inquired into whether the $800,000 that will be paid to the President's son, Johnnie, is an appropriate real estate commission or a way for the Foundation to funnel part of its funds to a family member. It has not inquired into any aspect of the purchase price, or into the appropriateness of the special tax privileges or the low land cost for the new plant location. Techcellence should be conscious of these issues, for they have obvious ethical dimensions. But clearly, as the case is presented, the environmental issue is the dominant one.

Approach Primarily Used: Duties.

[WJE] General John Abraham Oduhga has made a true contribution to Africaria by helping to stabilize the country immediately following its attainment of independence. Members of the general's family have also made, and continue to make, their contributions to the country's development. The general's son, Johnnie Oduhga, is involved in real estate. A hospital foundation named in memory of Marie de Beauclaire Oduhga now seeks to provide excellent health care to the citizens of Mbolo.

But questions quickly arise as to how much of this activity is also directly or primarily benefiting the political and financial fortunes of the Oduhga family, as distinct from the Africarian people. Ethically speaking, public officials such as President Oduhga ought to be public servants. Of course, they should be fairly paid for their services. However, the absence of democratic and transparent procedures in Africaria makes it difficult to judge just what fair recompense would be, and whether a public official has received it.

In any country, the government's involvement with business is bound to have problematic aspects. In the United States, for example, such issues have arisen in recent years in some of the activities of the Resolution Trust Corporation. Nevertheless, some such involvement is essential to a healthy economy in any society, since business and government share a common task of seeing that the public is provided with needed goods and services. In the present case, questions quickly arise regarding the $8 million that the Marie de Beauclaire Oduhga Memorial Hospital Foundation is willing to pay Techcellence for a piece of land in Hope Village. It would be useful to know the source of such a large sum. This matter takes on added interest when one considers that Guy Gusher expects Techcellence to contribute $100,000 dollars to the hospital. Also integral to this matter are all the tax-free aspects of the case. On the other hand, if it were to turn out that the funds in question have been accumulated in ways consistent with widely accepted ethical patterns of government and business, then this might be a handsome way indeed to ensure the building of a facility to serve the health and well-being of thousands of Africarians.

The agreement to pay $800,000 to Johnnie Oduhga, the president's son, raises questions. Is this not a rather high fee for the services of a registered real estate broker?

The central ethical issues of this case, however, stem from the fact that the Techcellence electronics plant stands on the site of a former creosote plant. While the former operation has contaminated the soil to the depth of three feet, it seems clear that the Techcellence operation has not in any serious way contributed to further pollution.

Diligencia Dorobo is a trained environmental professional. Until her arrival on the scene, these health questions did not arise. Only she has done the testing of the soil at the Techcellence site. She is firmly of the conviction that a reasonable outlay of money on the part of Techcellence will be good medical, business and environmental ethics. Even though there is the possibility that the contaminants might not be as deleterious as suspected, she believes, for both ethical and business reasons, that Techcellence should not take that risk.

Guy wants to move to the new industrial park not for health but for business reasons. These business reasons are so strong that he does not seriously question the relationship of the law to ethics in Africaria, even though many issues in this area are surely problematic. It is interesting that the ethical unease that Guy eventually comes to feel is triggered by the health, rather than the business, aspects of the case. Diligencia's warning about possible contamination of patients in the new hospital made him feel "strangely uneasy" that night.

Since Guy now knows of the contamination at Techcellence's plant site, he has an ethical obligation to instigate a cleanup procedure to protect his present employees or to alert them to the danger. Does Guy also have an obligation to present this information to the Africarian government or at least to the Memorial Hospital? The answer is surely: yes.

Guy's argument about having no ethical obligation to clean up after Venus' waste carries little validity. Ethically, his actions ought to focus on the future and not dwell on the mistakes of the past. Giving health issues priority over business issues will clearly indicate steps that should be taken to clean up the contamination. At a cost of $1 million the site could be cleaned for Techcellence and for the future hospital.

Given the large sums of money already involved in this transaction, it might be worth negotiating the matter of financing the cleanup with the Africarian government and the Hospital Foundation, one or both of which might come forward with additional funds. If the government, Johnnie Oduhga and the hospital are really interested in the health and well-being of the Africarian people, they might be willing to provide some of the funds needed so the new hospital can truly serve the people of their country.

By cleaning up the hospital site, Techcellence will show that it really has the good of Africaria at heart. Such a highly visible commitment to health, especially regarding the site of a new hospital linked to the Oduhga name, could pay not just ethical rewards but business rewards, and not just in the distant future but in the present. For its part, the Oduhga family, with the financial resources at its command, ought to see this as an opportunity to secure present and future popular respect. And finally, if Techcellence is an ethically responsible corporation, Guy Gusher might well hope that his personal career will not be hurt, and might even be advanced, by a clear and dramatic show of ethical good faith.

Approach Primarily Used: Traditions and Stories.

Case 19
The "Rights of the Monarch"

The Theme

Historically in some parts of Europe a monarch had numerous rights that would seem highly unwarranted by the ethical standards of many people today. Among these rights was intimate access to women in his kingdom, more or less regardless of the wishes of the latter, who were often not consulted in the matter. A similar tradition existed in various other parts of the world.

The Key Question

The key question in this case is: Do such "rights of the monarch" exist vestigially today, in multinational companies? If so, what, if any, action is needed to enforce or change the corporate culture? We illustrate by reference to a corporation called *Cyberex*. Cyberex is a multinational electronics corporation whose corporate culture and ethical aspirations are quite similar to those of Motorola.

The Setting

This case occurred a few years ago, at Cyberex/*Latinia*. Latinia is a country in Spanish-speaking Latin America where Cyberex is well established in a variety of businesses. The immediate scene is the Cyberex/Latinia headquarters, located downtown in the capital city.

The Cast

Maximo, chief of finance for Cyberex/Latinia. Maximo is 36, handsome, suave, smart and highly capable. He is a transpatriate from another Latin American nation, as are several other key managers in this headquarters. He is married, and his wife Miguela recently gave birth to their third child.

Deutero, Maximo's Latinian deputy chief of finance, is 29 and in line to take Maximo's place when the latter moves elsewhere.

Alejandro, chief of human resources, two floors below.

Alicia, personal secretary to Alejandro. Alicia is 24, Latinian, single and attractive.

Mari-Elena, assistant to Maximo until about a year ago, when he abruptly terminated her. Mari-Elena, 27, is another attractive single Latinian.

Wilhelm W. ("Will") Strong, a senior HR manager based at Cyberex headquarters in Shaker Heights, Ohio. Will, 59, is an American. He is widely known as a no-nonsense manager.

Alicia and Mari-Elena are typical of a Cyberex pattern in several countries, in which young single female employees, often of extremely humble origins, seek employment in the corporation as a means of dramatically bettering their station in life. They see Cyberex as an unusual organization that will reward them on the basis of their merit, rather than their family background, personal connections, political orientation or sexual availability.

The Initial Issue

The first inkling of trouble came one day when Deutero phoned Alejandro and asked that they meet for a drink after work. After gulping down his third *tequila*, Deutero summoned his courage: "OK, now let me tell you. Do you know that your secretary is having an affair with my boss?" At that point Deutero was new to his job and full of idealism. He struck Alejandro as being a bit too preachy when he added, "Latinia will never reach its full potential until we can purge ourselves of this kind of *machismo* chauvinism."

Alejandro thanked Deutero and the next day phoned Will Strong in Shaker Heights. The two men agreed that the matter was cause for concern, that nothing could or should be done until definite evidence was available, and that Alejandro should monitor the situation quietly, to see if it were reaching a dangerous point.

Seven months later, that danger point suddenly became all too evident, when the top officer of the business sector in Shaker Heights received a letter from a furious Mari-Elena complaining that Maximo had terminated her because she had refused to come to his house or otherwise meet him off the job.

The Investigation

The top officer ordered Will to conduct an immediate and complete investigation. Will gathered a team of seasoned colleagues and they flew to Latinia to interview all the principals, one by one — systematically, privately, and away from the office:

- First was **Mari-Elena.** "Why," Will asked her, "didn't you first report this matter through normal HR channels?" Her answer was the one he most feared: "Because if I had tried, Alicia would have found a way to block it. Several of us knew she was having an affair with Maximo and that she would do anything to protect him."

- The investigators then questioned **Maximo** several times, and each time he vehemently denied any sexual liaison with Alicia or any sexual advances toward Mari-Elena.

- The focus turned next to **Alicia.** At first, she denied everything. Then, suddenly, she confessed. Yes, Maximo had indeed been taking his monarch's rights. In fact, one Friday morning Maximo had packed his wife off to another country to bear their third child, only that very weekend to enjoy Alicia's intimate companionship at a secluded country resort.

The Immediate Findings

Will concluded that Alicia's confession proved that Maximo had not only taken monarch's rights, but had repeatedly lied about it. Anyone with such character flaws, Will felt, has no business in Cyberex, and especially not in Finance. Should he be terminated?

The Broader Finding

The investigation was thorough, and before long Will found himself concluding, reluctantly, that Maximo was far from the only monarch on the scene. Almost certainly, several other highly placed Cyberexian males were equally guilty. Some of them were Latinian and some were transpatriates from elsewhere in Latin America or from the United States. It was a problem, not just of personal character, but also of cultural "taken-for-granteds," Will reasoned. These powerful males simply took it for granted that such behavior was OK, as long as one was discreet.

It also became clear to Will that members of this small group of powerful males — who often saw each other socially — were quite aware that their own subculture was at odds with the formal Cyberex Culture, with its emphasis on integrity and respect for people. The result: A covert network of "Good Old Boys" had rallied around Maximo and systematically lied to Will and his fellow investigators. (A year later, one of them actually confessed as much to Will **privately** — but swore he would deny it again, if again asked officially.)

Will was also disappointed in Deutero, Maximo's deputy, who had informally reported the Maximo-Alicia liaison seven months before Mari-Elena's letter of complaint had provoked the full-scale investigation. At that time Deutero had been on the job just a month. He had brought a youthful idealism to his assignment and was revolted by the hanky-panky he discovered. By the time the formal investigation occurred, a mere seven months later, Deutero had already bonded with Maximo to the point where he simply refused to answer questions, stating, "I can't answer that, and I must tell you frankly that I am more loyal to my friends than to any organization." Upon hearing this surprising statement, especially from one who actually stood to gain a promotion if Maximo were removed, Will mused to himself, "Wow, personalismo [loyalty to persons rather than principles] in action."

The Sequel

Alicia: Sensing that her usefulness to Cyberex was at an end, she resigned. Cyberex gave her an indemnification payment.

Mari-Elena: She had already found another job. She also received an indemnification payment, as well as the corporation's sincere apologies.

Maximo: We leave to you the decision as to what action, if any, should have been taken.

Other Notable Observations

In the course of his investigation Will also learned some important additional facts:

- Try as they might, Good Old Boys usually will not succeed in being totally discreet. Sooner or later, other employees will find out about an underground liaison.

- Perhaps even more dangerous to morale is the fact that some employees, especially the more cynical or disgruntled among them, will **imagine** that a liaison is taking place, even when in fact it is not.

- Persuasive evidence also indicated that there was **another** Good Old Boys' network operating in Shaker Heights. The members of this network were culturally Anglo-American and formally committed to the Cyberex Culture, but also shared a set of underground understandings that included the premise that once one left Shaker Heights on a sales or marketing trip, it was OK to go after any available woman. However, if anyone from outside the network were ever to inquire, the answer would always be the same: "No, it didn't happen." Saying "Yes, it **did** happen" would not be a practical option, for it would lead to ostracism.

Will mused to himself: "Whoever said that *machismo* is just a Latin phenomenon?"

Discussion Questions...

1. Should Cyberex take action in situations where sexual activity of one form or another strongly influences corporation hiring, firing and promotion policies?

2. Should Cyberex place any formal restraints upon dating and related behavior?

3. Under what circumstances should it be permissible for two willing single Cyberexians of opposite sex working in the same department or facility to date each other? What if they work in different departments or facilities?

4. Under what circumstances should it be permissible for a married Cyberexian to date a willing single Cyberexian?

5. In general, should Cyberex simply accept prevalent local mores in sexual practices, or attempt to encourage more idealistic standards?

Commentaries on Case 19

[RTD] Sexual harassment is unethical, no matter what the culture, because it violates the respect due all people. There are two kinds of sexual harassment: *quid pro quo* sexual harassment and hostile-environment sexual harassment. In the first type, someone, usually senior to the other, suggests, implies, requests or demands some type of sexual favor for which the senior person suggests or states that the junior person will receive something in return. This could be a promotion, a raise, a special perquisite or treatment, a favorable review, or simply the favor of not being terminated. Hostile-environment sexual harassment consists in making some employee uncomfortable through the use of sexually suggestive language, the telling of off-color jokes or stories, the displaying of pictures of nudes, or through other acts that are sexually suggestive or offensive, whether or not directed specifically toward that employee.

The "Rights of the Monarch" case presents both kinds of sexual harassment, but the *quid pro quo* type is especially blatant.

The clearest instance involves Mari-Elena, who was terminated because she refused to go to Maximo's home or to meet him off the job. Despite Maximo's denials, since he was caught in lies about his relation to Alicia, there

is good reason to believe Mari-Elena. In fact Mari-Elena received indemnification from Cyberex, as well as its apologies. This is a blatant case of sexual harassment.

Maximo's affair with Alicia is another instance of *quid pro quo* sexual harassment, even though Alicia did not openly complain. Moreover, this relationship also created a hostile situation in which Mari-Elena, and perhaps many others, did not feel they could use regular HR channels because Alicia was the personal secretary of the chief of human resources and could divert complaints against Maximo and others.

The case raises a number of questions: If Cyberex is serious about changing the "rights of the monarch" attitude within the corporation, what measures can and should it take to do so? What rules, if any, should Cyberex have about office romances, dating between Cyberexians, sexual liaisons and nepotism?

Cyberex must take the issue of sexual harassment and the vestigial "rights of the monarch" attitude seriously wherever it operates. The "rights of the monarch" syndrome is not a cultural peculiarity that should be tolerated or respected. The case makes clear that this is a problem for Cyberex not just in places such as Latinia, but in the United States as well. Clear and explicit guidelines outlining and

forbidding sexual harassment of any sort should be adopted and widely promulgated. Provisions for reporting abuses should also be carefully developed and widely publicized. Finally, the penalty for sexual harassment should be comparable to the penalty for other major infractions of Cyberex standards. At some point clear messages must be sent that Cyberex takes sexual harassment seriously, and that an employee can be terminated for engaging in it. Such rules should cover all unwanted sexual advances and touching, as well as *quid pro quo* propositions and the creation of a hostile environment. Clearly a *quid pro quo* proposition is more serious than the telling of off-color jokes despite complaints about the latter, and the penalty for the former should be greater than the penalty for the latter.

The issue of sexual innuendo, advances or requests that are not unwanted and are mutually desired and encouraged is more difficult and does not necessarily involve lack of respect for persons. Where should a company draw the line? It might take the position that personal relationships of a sexual or romantic type between Cyberexians are not prohibited if they do not adversely affect the work or work situation of the concerned parties or of others, but that those who develop such relationships are liable to suffer the consequences of any complaints should the relationship go sour or should others feel that the relationship harms the work situation in any way. This is a minimalist position and may or may not be put in writing.

Advances, if made by a senior person toward a more junior one, always involve some power differences. Recognizing this, at the other end of the spectrum of possibilities would be a very strict policy that prohibits romantic or sexual relations between Cyberexians in the same department or the same facility. Does this violate the right of Cyberexians to live their lives as they wish when on their own time? It comes very close to doing so, and could result in situations where a couple falls in love and gets married, but feels that they must hide their marriage from the corporation.

In this area of sexual behavior there are many other variations as to what might or might not be allowed. It is usually wise to prohibit anyone from being in a position of direct authority over a spouse, or a member of one's family, or over someone to whom that person has a special close personal relationship. This prevents any conflict of interest as well as any actual or perceived favoritism.

It is the actual, not the perceived, favoritism that is unfair to others and so unethical. But the perception of favoritism where it does not exist can be as damaging to the company and to the morale of other employees as is actual favoritism.

In all these cases, ethical considerations alone do not demand any particular set of rules. What ethics demand is that people be treated with respect, that they not be sexually harassed, and that they all be treated fairly. There are many ways for a company to try to ensure a situation in which this takes place. Whatever the means, the message should be strong and clear, and it should be implemented.

Approach Primarily Used: Duties.

[WJE] Increasingly over the past several years in the United States, attempts have been made to separate public or overt morality from private or covert morality, especially in matters of sexual behavior. Such attempts presume that as long as no one is harmed in an affair, these matters should be left to the free choice and discretion of the parties involved.

In many other cultures, norms for sexual behavior are more overt in many ways. The *machismo* complex found in Latin cultures is but one example of the many structures and patterns of male dominance over women. These patterns are understood privately but are not to be spoken of or acknowledged publicly.

There are understandable, though unethical, reasons why this is so. Ethical practices which benefit all parties involved do not need to be concealed or dismissed. By contrast, unethical schemes require silence to protect the oppressors — so much so that men taking advantage of women might eventually come to think of themselves not as being oppressive, but rather as merely following the patterns of the culture. Public confrontation on these matters might then elicit genuinely felt claims of innocence. And the women so victimized might also come to see themselves not as victims but rather as players in a covert, but well understood

scenario. Such hidden patterns can evolve anywhere at any time and achieve considerable levels of sophistication — as Will Strong discovered among the sales force in the United States.

This tension between public and private is made clear in the fact that Deutero had been the first to raise the matter of Maximo's sexual doings, but not long afterward, refused to cooperate with Will's investigation. Also, Alicia had first denied, then admitted her involvement with Maximo.

Deutero brings into play another line of analysis when he maintains that his friendship with Maximo overrides loyalty to Cyberex. From an ethical perspective, it is important that Deutero and Maximo decide whether they are in business because they are friends, or friends because they are in business.

Can a major company afford, in strictly business terms, to allow and even foster such covert patterns of action? No, and proper policies and practices on the part of a corporation such as Cyberex could also contribute in some measure to the eventual elimination of sexual harassment in the host cultures where Cyberex operates.

Approach Primarily Used: Traditions and Stories.

Case 20
Gender Equity and the
Eye of the Beholder

This case takes place in an Asian nation called *Tairo*. It involves a Taironese married couple who both work for Motorola. The wife is *Mei-Up Paik*, 35, who has been assistant supervisor for Line 3 at the Motorola/Tairo facility for 17 months. The husband is *Woe-Be Paik*, 43, who has been logistics supervisor for all four of the production lines at the facility for several years.

Woe-Be is a graduate engineer and an average performer. He is generally seen as loyal and trustworthy, but not a leader. By contrast, Mei-Up's superiors and the HR staff see her as a likely eventual candidate for a managerial position.

Woe-Be and Mei-Up were married nine years ago. Woe-Be was 34, Mei-Up 26. Mei-Up, by her own designation a "modern woman," had broken tradition by waiting four or five years longer than her parents wished, rejecting several young men whom they had put forward, and finally following her heart to Woe-Be. The romance had started in the Motorola cafeteria. Taironese Motorolan colleagues liked them both, subtly encouraged their friendship, and were delighted when they announced their engagement.

When Mei-Up was promoted 17 months ago, HR staff noticed a certain ambivalence on her part. She finally explained to one of the Taironese HR staff that she was

afraid her salary would be higher than her husband's. However, her reluctance appeared to dissolve when she learned that this was not so, because of her newness in the position.

Still, Mei-Up hesitated. True, her salary would be lower, but if Line 3 were highly productive under her leadership, her **total** income — salary plus bonus — could end up being higher than his.

However, she and Woe-Be talked it over and agreed that she should accept the promotion, and that they would both put **all** their bonus money into a special college fund for their two children, *Yoon-Gee*, 4, and *Hanako*, 2.

That settled the matter. Or did it?

At year end when bonuses were announced, Mei-Up's total salary-plus-bonus income was 40 percent higher than Woe-Be's. She also found in her bonus notification envelope a glowing letter from *Gloria Free* of HR, informing her that she had been selected for the honor of "Motorolan of the Month," based on her performance.

Early the following morning Mei-Up appeared at Gloria's office, visibly disturbed. She begged **not** to be made Motorolan of the Month. Furthermore, tears welling in her eyes, she told Gloria that she wanted to be transferred out of manufacturing and into HR work. Gloria was stunned. "But Mei-Up," she said, "you've broken all records on Line 3. At this rate, your future promotional prospects are very good. Being Motorolan of the Month will help you get there. We need you in manufacturing, Mei-Up, and if you will pardon me for saying it, I think **you** need to be in manufacturing, too. If you shift jobs, given your lack of any HR credential, your total pay will be reduced substantially."

"Yes Ma'am," replied Mei-Up. "I know. But that's what I wish to request."

Gloria felt depressed. "Well, Mei-Up, here is what we'll do. We'll hold off making you Motorolan of the Month. We'll give it to someone else this month, and that way you and I can take a little time to think all this over."

Later that day, Gloria tried to focus her thoughts. "These Taironese," she mused, "go crazy about matters of face — gaining face, losing face." Then a strange thought crossed her mind. Truth to tell, **she** too was afraid of losing face. Yes, she had to admit it; she would lose face if Mei-Up's career did not move forward.

Why? Because at the last three Promotion Board meetings she had championed a promotion for Mei-Up. Three times she had taken a risk, facing down several male Taironese members of the Board who kept insisting, "But she's too young; people won't take her seri-ously" — which, Gloria knew, was really code for "She's a woman." Several times Gloria had caught herself musing: "Those male Taironese know damned well that they can't reveal the **real** reason for their resistance, so to pursue their gender chauvinism, they take refuge in ageism — as if Motorola believed in ageism! Those guys are impossible."

Gloria had deep convictions about the matter. Ever since she had been president of the Women's Career Club back at Manitowoc High School in Wisconsin, she had been determined to level the playing field for women. She and her husband *Ray* began dating at Manitowoc High, and were married while still in college. Their marriage was a fine success, in part because of their deeply shared convictions with respect to gender equity. If anything, Ray Free was more adamant on the subject than Gloria.

Ray and Gloria had both had good careers in Motorola since their 20s, and had also managed to raise two kids in the process. During some of their years at Motorola, Gloria's total compensation had exceeded Ray's but Ray hadn't cared. He was downright accep-tant of it, and it didn't interfere in the least with his being a good husband and father.

That evening back at the apartment, Gloria shared the matter with Ray, now in his ninth month as materials manager of Motorola/Tairo. Ray, who felt deeply committed to Uncompromising Integrity, growled agreement: "Yeah, Glo, you've got it right. I wish Phil [*Phil Fuller*, general manager of Motorola/Tairo] would clean out that whole bunch of male chauvinists, and I think he wants to. But I suppose he can't do it right away. He has to move slowly."

"I also think you did the right thing about the Motorolan of the Month business, Glo," said Ray. "This buys you time to find a real solution to this mess. And I think I have the solution. Why don't you suggest to Phil that Mei-Up get some even more visible credit for her performance?"

Gloria agreed. She went to work. The result: two days later Phil Fuller announced a new problem-solving team to work on Six Sigma quality for the Front End Assembly. Woe-Be, with his logistics experience, was made secretary of the team. Four other Taironese employees, all male, average age 44, were made members. And the team leader? None other than Mei-Up.

Later that day Phil asked Mei-Up to step into his office and closed the door. He smiled benevolently.

"Mei-Up, if your team performs well, I think it has a good chance of being chosen to represent us next January in Schaumburg at the Total Customer Satisfaction Competition. If that happens, your future at Motorola/Tairo will be bright indeed." Mei-Up looked at the floor, and two minutes later politely excused herself, saying that she had to get back to her work station.

Two days later Mei-Up applied for three months unpaid sick leave.

Discussion Questions...

1. What should Gloria do? What, if anything, should she say to Mei-Up? What, if anything, should she say to Woe-Be?

2. Should Mei-Up and Woe-Be have been assigned to the same team (with Mei-Up as team leader and Woe-Be as secretary), knowing that there was already a problem concerning status between them? Should Motorola allow wives and husbands to work together on the same project or in the same department, knowing how marital relationships, tensions and disputes can interfere with work-group morale and productivity?

3. Should the psychology of the relationship between a wife and husband be a factor in considering promotions, honors, bonuses and pay raises? Should Mei-Up's insistence that she did not want to be Motorolan of the Month have resulted in a different response by Motorola?

4. What broader responsibilities does Motorola have when its Key Belief in Uncompromising Integrity clashes with traditional host country values concerning the respective roles of men and women in society, work and marriage? Does Constant Respect for People ever require that Motorola should take into account such host culture values?

5. Should Motorola accept unequal approaches to gender relations, even when doing so interferes with promoting and rewarding the best qualified person for the job? If an excellent woman manager deserves a position in which she will almost certainly find difficulty winning respect from her male colleagues, what steps, if any, should Motorola take to make her well-deserved promotion productive and harmonious?

Commentaries on Case 20

[TD] Gender equity has long been a topic of social concern in Western countries. Indeed it has been emphasized so much in the United States, that Americans can mistake it for a simple issue. In fact, gender equity is a complex set of issues, as the case of Mei-Up makes clear. In the present case, it will help to examine three key issues:

- the definition of gender equity in the workplace;

- the right versus the requirement of gender equity; and

- organizational responses to gender inequity.

It is difficult to define gender equity. Most theorists identify it with a version of meritocracy, an approach to rewarding employees that focuses on merit. A simple version of the principle of meritocracy in the workplace would be: Hire, fire, promote, demote and reward on the basis of a person's performance, and not on the basis of irrelevant criteria, such as race or sex.

If one applies the meritocracy principle to the present case, it seems clear that Mei-Up deserves both a more responsible position and a higher salary than her husband, Woe-Be.

But why is the meritocratic principle to be preferred? Why especially should it be preferred in traditional cultures that assign sharply distinctive roles to men and women in society? The most obvious answer is that meritocracy is appropriate to the workplace (if not to all walks of life) because a business seeks greater productivity, and it follows that people who can perform at higher levels should be placed where they can perform best. This obvious answer is unfortunately not satisfactory, as the following example makes clear:

> Brad and Janet have applied for the managing director job in an investment banking company. Whichever of the two is not made managing director, will be assigned the job of book runner, a position subordinate to that of the managing director. Janet would make a better managing director than Brad. However, because of Brad's difficulty working in a position subordinate to a woman, the greatest productivity would be achieved by making Brad the managing director and making Janet the book runner.

If one were to allow simple overall productivity to define what one means by "meritocracy," then it would follow that Brad should be the managing director and Janet the book runner. Yet this flies in the face of fairness. It follows that one can define gender equity in terms of organizational productivity only up to a point. Fairness is more crucial for the definition of gender equity. This special relevance of fairness has important implications for how one analyzes the case of Mei-Up and Woe-Be.

Because gender equity is primarily an issue of fairness, a corporation such as Motorola, which is clearly committed to gender equity, should be willing to go the extra mile to achieve it. Even apart from the issue of productivity, Motorola cannot allow envious males to sabotage the rights of more productive females. To this extent, Gloria is absolutely right in taking special pains to see that Mei-Up's extraordinary talents are recognized, even if her action shakes up the workforce. Because gender equity is a matter of fairness for Motorola, and because Mei-Up comes from a culture that has not traditionally allowed women equity, special efforts are called for.

But Gloria has a problem, and it is manifested by the same doctrine of fairness that justifies her special efforts. Because gender equity is primarily about fairness, and only secondarily about productivity, Gloria has no right to push Motorolans unfairly to be more productive. Gloria notes that Mei-Up has led Line 3 to record-breaking achievements, and believes that she can accomplish even more in the future. But gender equity simply means that people have a **right** to the positions they are most qualified for; it does not mean that they may be **forced** into such positions. She is failing to interpret correctly or fully accept the signals that Mei-Up is sending about her reluctance to outshine her husband. Forcing Mei-Up to outshine her husband would be unfair. Indeed, it would be no less unfair than **not** allowing Mei-Up the right to outshine her husband, if that were her wish.

How might Gloria have more creatively and sensitively addressed the situation? That is really the key question of the case. The key question is not whether Motorola should embrace uncompromising gender equity, for that decision has already been made and communicated by Motorola time and time again. But uncompromising gender equity is not equivalent to forcing people into positions against their will.

In addition to individual efforts such as Gloria's, organizations such as Motorola can help prepare the way for the Mei-Ups of the future by educating employees about gender equity. By communicating and clarifying for all Mei-Ups and Woe-Bes just how strongly Motorola embraces gender equity in the workplace, the corporation can make it easier for future Mei-Ups to buck tradition and gain deserved recognition. Motorola's organizational responsibility to educate its workforce in the importance of gen-

der equity is especially pronounced when its employees are drawn from certain traditional cultures, such as that of Tairo.

Finally, this commentary would be incomplete without noting that cases such as this one are the **exception,** not the rule. It is far more common for men to assume that women have little interest in advancement, and thereby to unfairly deny them the opportunity. Ironically, Western men are sometimes the worst offenders. Accepting gender equity in their own country, they nonetheless suppose that it is rejected in other cultures — and tolerate discrimination accordingly. It is noteworthy that even in the traditional cultures of Asia, Latin America and Africa, times are changing rapidly and women are successfully assuming roles of great responsibility. Neither the United States nor Germany has ever had a female head of state. But BanglaDesh, India, Israel, Pakistan, Sri Lanka and Turkey have all had female heads of state. The most forward-looking citizens of non-Western countries, including both men and women, eagerly await a future in which women can assume greater and greater responsibility for social and business leadership. Motorola clearly has a stake in that future.

***Approaches Primarily Used:
Rights, Justice and Fairness.***

[WJE] In this many-faceted case two very different ethical value systems are at work, the Anglo-American Midwestern system and the Taironese system. The first is grounded in the solid Midwestern morality that has guided and nourished Motorola from its earliest days and continues to do so. This value system emphasizes a strong work ethic and individual rewards for effort and achievement. Gloria and Ray Free adhere to these values and take pride in the fact that Motorola is committed to a policy of gender-blind promotion. They are pleased and proud to note the advance of women employees in the corporation.

Gloria and Ray could also point to mounting international evidence that they and the Motorola Culture are on the right path. They could, for example, point to the 1995 international congress on women in Beijing, with its powerful commitment to the advancement of the status of women worldwide. They would feel Motorola has good grounds indeed not only for drawing upon its own tradition, but also for aligning itself with this very clear global trend.

Tairo is an altogether different story. Over many centuries this culture has placed the female in what many Westerners would consider a subservient role. When one views this role from the outside, one can easily criticize it. When one attempts to view it strictly from the perspective of the continuity of Taironese culture, one can easily argue that it has been useful and effective in reinforcing certain vital values of that culture, such as the value of the woman as mother and nurturer of the family. Taironese wives are culturally expected to support the roles and advance the reputations of their husbands.

But one must additionally bear in mind that Mei-Up and Woe-Be are also caught up in the Motorola Culture, which is where they spend many hours a day, most days of the week. Even their courtship took place within that corporate culture — namely in the Motorola cafeteria.

In situations such as this it is sometimes possible for a leader to find solutions through the astute use of the time factor. Thus, Gloria has postponed the naming of Mei-Up as Motorolan of the Month. It is vital to bear in mind, though, that the time factor functions best not simply by delaying things, but rather by producing a climate for reflection and growth, so that characters party to a case can more constructively play and develop their roles. Unfortunately, in the present case Gloria has not made astute use of the time factor. While time has allowed her to muse about the chauvinism of the Taironese male staff members, reflection and growth have not occurred. Gloria has not used the time to advance the progress of either Mei-Up or herself.

General Manager Phil Fuller does not handle matters very astutely, either. He seeks to help Woe-Be save face by appointing him to the new Six Sigma problem-solving team. But he gives Woe-Be the role of secretary, which only makes matters worse. Not only is there now still the problem of the wife-husband relationship, but the added one of fitting the proper person to the proper job. Will this appointment be seen by his Taironese colleagues as something of a demotion for the unstated purpose of supporting his wife's role? Gloria was quite right in wanting Mei-Up to remain in manufacturing, where she has strength, rather than moving to Human Resources, where she does not. Woe-Be's strengths should be similarly respected and supported.

In this case Phil, Gloria and Mei-Up have each made definite moves. But there is one character about whom the case reports nothing, and he is really the central character. Now is the time for Woe-Be to make his move. Perhaps he should seek a meeting with Gloria and Phil. If he does not, Gloria and Phil should set up such a meeting. No matter what mechanism is used, ways should be found first to determine Woe-Be's views, and then, if needed, to encourage Woe-Be to reinterpret the situation.

The positive evolution of any culture typically involves moving forward by building upon the best of that culture's past. Some of the best aspects of the Midwestern Anglo-American culture have had to do with respect for the worth and dignity of each individual, highlighted over the past several decades by a trend toward women's liberation. One notes also a deep and serious concern for personal dignity in the Taironese tradition, though in support of a very different cultural value — mutual support for the attainment and maintenance of face.

Ultimately, any ethical solution must be focused on the future. That future, both for Motorola and for the cultures of the world generally, has rather securely built into its scenario the recognition and liberation of women. Neither the Motorola Culture nor Taironese culture can ignore or escape this. So Motorola's action on behalf of Mei-Up is justified. Whatever short-run pain it causes Woe-Be, it places Motorola on the right overall world trend toward a more humane and integrated world culture.

Approach Primarily Used: Traditions and Stories.

Case 21
Purple Toenails

Rose Chaser, 27, grew up in a comfortable home in Muskegon, Michigan. From an early age she had been determined to move ahead into a high professional position. This led her to take a degree in industrial engineering. While in college she decided on a management career, so she promptly earned an M.B.A.

Just before completing her M.B.A. three years ago, Rose met a recruiter from *BatterBest, Ltd.*, a multinational manufacturer of batteries headquartered in Memphis, Tennessee. She was deeply impressed by BatterBest's affirmative policy of gender-blind promotion. When a job offer came, Rose accepted immediately. She threw herself into her management duties at various BatterBest facilities in the United States.

Soon Rose attracted the attention of *Ike Unangst*, 47, vice president of manufacturing. "Rose," Ike said one day, "you are clearly high-potential. BatterBest is in need of an assistant manufacturing manager at its Belostan Facility, and I've taken the liberty of nominating you." Rose was stunned and thrilled. Although she knew little about *Belostan*, a republic of the former USSR, she was sure this new assignment would bring challenge and advancement.

Soon afterwards Rose arrived in *Katnaka*, Belostan's capital. She found Belostan to be bursting with economic activity. Everywhere she turned, she saw the famous Belostanian work ethic in action. And her fellow transpatriate technologists at the *Katnaka Tennis and Swimming Club* had striking tales to tell about how eager the Belostanians were to get a job with BatterBest — **any** job.

Other people Rose met, both Belostanian and foreign, pointed out that Belostan was on a headlong national race against time. Economic growth was desperately needed, because of these factors:

- demographics that would double the national population in 25 years;

- GDP per capita of just $800 per year; and

- 18 percent unemployment.

However, Rose's management training still made her wonder: Why in the world did BatterBest locate a facility here in Belostan — when there are at least three other countries in the region that would be more cost-effective from a logistical and market access standpoint? The problem puzzled her, but she was too busy with her duties as assistant manufacturing manager to give it much further thought.

Among Rose's new duties, she was responsible for the department where the batteries were chemically washed — almost invariably by female employees. Rose soon developed what she felt to be a nice rapport with some of her new Belostanian colleagues, including the four supervisors who reported to her. They were, in order of seniority, *Domingka, Irya, Katrina and Maritza*.

Domingka was a bit cold and distant. But not Irya, who on a personal basis was warm and friendly. However, Rose noticed that in staff meetings Irya always remained silent in the presence of Domingka. Rose gradually figured out that this pattern reflected a desire on Irya's part not to upstage Domingka, who was senior to her in both age and years of service. Domingka was presumed next in line to inherit Rose's job if and when Memphis ever decided to give that job to a Belostanian.

All of Rose's Belostanian colleagues were pleased that she was seriously studying their language and trying to better understand their culture. Every day at lunch she would take 20 minutes to study a new lesson from her text, *Basic Belostanian in 100 Hours*. Rose tried to have lunch with several colleagues each day, so as not to appear to be playing favorites. However, on this day only Irya was present. Rose was working on Chapter 27, "Parts of the Body." She pronounced the names of the various body parts to Irya who, she noticed, looked slightly upset when Rose came to the word for "toenail."

"What's the matter, Irya, didn't I pronounce it right?" asked Rose.

"Your pronunciation is OK," replied Irya, "but there is something else. You might not have noticed because of the kind of shoes we wear here in the plant, but most of our line women have toenails that are shriveled and slightly purple in color, and this is a sign of chemical poisoning. It all makes me so upset. Here

you and I are, committed to equal opportunity for women, building our careers on the backs of our sister employees who are slowly being poisoned."

"That can't be true!" exclaimed Rose.

"Well, I'm afraid it could be," replied Irya, gathering courage, "though I wouldn't dare say so to any of the transpatriates except you. It's the *poisonium chloride* [a fictitious chemical] we use as a solvent on the washing line. You and the other transpats don't change clothes in our women's locker room, but if you did, you would actually see a lot of strange toenails, and you would also hear the Belostanian phrase, *Lebphit*, meaning 'poisoned toenails.' This is not a traditional word in our language, but we use it because it's a lot easier for us to pronounce than '*Angelmeyer's Syndrome*' [a fictitious disease]."

"'Angelmeyer's Syndrome?' What on earth is that?" asked Rose.

"Well, my cousin is a doctor, and he says it's a condition of gradual deterioration caused by ingestion of various chemicals, and it reduces immunity and makes a person more likely to get cancer. But he also says that some of the chemical companies in the United States are arguing that these conclusions are based on incomplete data so I'm not really sure what to believe."

That evening, Rose shuddered as she reflected on just what Angelmeyer's Syndrome might mean.

Momentarily she wondered whether **she** might get the syndrome, then dismissed this as unlikely because she was in the washing-line room only intermittently, not all day like the line women. But yes, she thought, she **had** occasionally noticed ill-formed toenails on women employees who wore sandals while off duty, and especially on those who had worked on the washing line for several years. And yes, the thought **had** vaguely occurred to her that this might be due to the poisonium chloride solvent that was used to wash the batteries. And she also wondered about the protective uniforms the women wore, which had been designed for a different sort of operation involving different chemicals.

Rose found herself searching for ways to deny her suspicions. She felt her conscience easing just a bit as she thought further:

• The toenails might be shriveled just because the Belostanians were genetically different that way. Who knows? But on the other hand, why didn't she ever see sandals-wearing **male** Belostanian employees with shriveled, purple toenails?

• Anyway, employees who were as eager to work as the Belostanians were couldn't really be **that** sick. What a splendid work ethic they have!

Then, abruptly, Rose felt ashamed of herself. That night she had trouble drifting off to sleep.

Two months later Ike Unangst arrived in Katnaka on his quarterly inspection visit. Since Ike was Rose's designated mentor, Rose was naturally eager to let him see how well she was performing. She briefed Ike on her accomplishments, which included the following:

• During the previous quarter she had cut production costs 15 percent, by finding ways to use 20 percent less poisonium chloride and still get the same results.

• She had also reduced waste disposal costs 30 percent by identifying a new dump site for poisonium chloride solvent waste, at the edge of a wetland area just outside of the new *Katnaka Shopping Mall*, which was only 12 kilometers from the BatterBest facility. Previously, the corporation had used the inward-draining desert area at *Arida,* 127 kilometers to the northeast. The new arrangement obviously involved far less transportation cost. It also involved lower disposal cost, because the Katnaka City Development Authority had set extremely low dumping fees as part of a general campaign to attract foreign investment.

Rose was pleased that Ike was so obviously impressed.

The following Friday evening several BatterBest employees gathered for drinks at the Tennis and Swimming Club Bar. Ike was pretty tired and drank a bit too much. Rose took only one drink so she could listen carefully.

Ike was in his mentor mode: "Rose, every profession has its gray side, and for us, it's poisonium chloride. Fortunately for us, the Belostanian government doesn't try to micromanage foreign investors. And thank goodness that Belostan doesn't have a lot of detailed environmental regulations of the type that strangle initiative and enterprise back in the States, with the Environmental Protection Agency on our backs all the time. Of course the Belostanian leadership knows what's going on, but what they want is **development**, and they're not too fussy about details. . . . Yes, Rose, every job has things about it that just aren't too healthy to talk about."

Back home from the club, Rose reflected. It wasn't too healthy for the **employees**, either — young women, some of whom were as deserving and ambitious as Rose herself. Rose ran through the facts in her head:

• We are doing some things here in Belostan that U.S. law would never allow us to do back in the States.

• We are doing other things in Belostan that we **could** do back in the United States, but it would cost a lot more for compliance, and would pose the risk of expensive lawsuits.

• So, we're not in Belostan because of logistics or market access, or even just because of low labor costs; basically, we are here because the Belostanian government looks the other way on pollution.

• The government didn't mention it at the time, but it is now clear that in addition to poisoning our own employees, we are also poisoning the Belostanian public by dumping poisonium chloride waste right near the Katnaka Shopping Mall.

• Of course we **could** switch to *purium chloride* and there would be no health problem, but purium chloride is twice as costly, and this would add 13 percent to what we would have to charge to sell a battery and still make a profit. Then those start-up competitors of ours in *Developia* would easily undersell us, and we could be ruined!

Ike went back to BatterBest headquarters in Memphis and filed what he jokingly called a "rosy" report on his promising understudy. Rose ought to make manager, he thought, about four years younger than most.

Three months later *Zack Zeal* of the Memphis office arrived in Katnaka on a mission to look into any and all health and environmental issues. BatterBest was getting a bad press from an international environmental action group, and part of it had to do with alleged environmental violations in Belostan.

Zack promptly scheduled a private interview with each senior staff person, one by one. As he ushered each of them into a private office, he reassured them that they could speak freely and that whatever they told him would be held in strictest confidence.

Rose's turn came. . . .

Discussion Questions...

1. What should Rose say to Zack in the interview she is about to have?

2. From an ethical point of view, how do you assess Rose's actions during the three months she has been in Belostan?

3. Is it ethically permissible for BatterBest (or any other company) simply to adhere to the local laws governing the disposal of harmful wastes, even if it knows that it is causing harm to people by its action?

4. Does BatterBest have any obligation to change its washing solution from poisonium chloride to purium chloride, given that its competitors use the former, which is cheaper?

5. What is the responsibility of a corporation to reduce risk and harm to its employees, if and when the employees knowingly and willingly accept those risks?

6. Since different countries are at different stages of economic development, and since some of the less developed are not able to both promote development and avoid pollution, who should set ethically acceptable levels of pollution — the government, polluting companies, the people of the country, scientists, environmentalists in other countries, the United Nations or some other group?

Commentaries on Case 21

[RTD] This case raises more issues than can be fully addressed here, and gives less information than we need to resolve some of them.

Rose Chaser is the main figure and neither she nor BatterBest comes off well in this case. Rose is incredibly naive and ethically simplistic for an otherwise bright manager with a potential for rapid advancement. It is only after some time in Belostan that she comes to realize that BatterBest has purposely chosen to open its facility there because it need not worry about legal constraints concerning harm to employees or to the environment, and can operate more cheaply there than elsewhere in the region. Ike Unangst's visit confirms that corporate headquarters knows exactly what it is doing. Since BatterBest's methods of operation in Belostan evidently do not violate Belostanian law, the primary questions one should look at are the ethical rather than the legal obligations concerning harm.

There is a widely accepted moral principle of: "Do no harm." This no-harm principle can be justified in terms of respect for people. Respect for people implies that in general one should not harm them. But at times one might have to harm them if one can help them only by doing so. A doctor may amputate a patient's gangrenous arm — certainly a harm to that person — in order to save that person's life, which is the greater good for the patient. At times harm may be done to some people in order to produce greater good for others, but never in such a way as to violate the rights of the first group. One cannot legitimately kill someone to save six other people to whom a doctor will transplant his heart, each of his kidneys, his liver and each of his lungs. Although the no-harm principle prevents one party from doing harm to another, it is possible and in some cases ethically acceptable for one person to accept harm in order to achieve some greater good for someone else. People may voluntarily donate their kidneys to save someone who would die otherwise. In instances where individuals accept personal harm for the good of themselves, or where they accept it for the good of others, one respects people by requiring their informed consent to the harm.

The same analysis applies collectively to society. A society may accept some harm to itself and to some of its members in order to achieve greater good for itself and for the same or other members, provided that no one's rights are violated. One can help ensure that no one's rights will be violated by requiring the informed consent of those who will be harmed. One can use these two principles in analyzing BatterBest's and Rose's actions regarding BatterBest's employees and the environment.

Let us examine the treatment of employees first. In Belostan BatterBest uses poisonium chloride in its battery-washing process. The case does not explain why the washing line consists "almost invariably of female employees." Is washing of any type considered "women's work" in Belostan, or are only women hired for the washing because it is known to cause harm, or are other factors at work? This issue cannot be resolved on the basis of the limited information the case provides, but is certainly an ethical issue of which Rose should have become almost immediately aware. Rose never looks into this and it is not one of the things over which she loses any sleep. Nonetheless, the issues of sexism and discrimination are present in the case and one can fault Rose's failure to see this.

There are some occupations that are inherently dangerous, such as firefighting or police work or bomb detonation. Those who accept such jobs take risks, and taking such risks is not unethical, provided:

- Those taking them are informed of the risks and their nature and extent.

- Care is taken to eliminate whatever risks possible.

- The good to be achieved by taking the risk outweighs the risk and the harm to the one accepting it.

Since Irya is reluctant to speak openly of the poisoning of the women employees, it is fairly clear that BatterBest does not inform its prospective employees of the risk of harm to which they will be subjected. BatterBest can be faulted for that, even though some companies claim that the data linking poisonium chloride to cancer — and to purple toenails — might be inconclusive. The women on the line know the risks because of the harm they suffer. Can one say that they therefore have implicitly given their consent? This is not the way consent works. It should be asked for and obtained only from persons who have been provided with full information about risks and harms, and it should be obtained **before** exposure to the risk, not after. If the women were fully informed and chose to accept the job despite the information, BatterBest would be slightly less culpable, but not much less, because it also violates the requirement that risks be eliminated as much as possible. BatterBest seems to have taken no steps to eliminate the possible harm to its employees. There is no indication it provides masks, gloves or protective clothing appropriate to the chemicals involved in this operation. Rose, who has cut costs 15 percent by using 20 percent less poisonium chloride, evidently made the cuts not because of her concern about the women but because of her concern about profits. Can

less poisonium chloride be used and still get the job done? If the employees use appropriate masks and protective gloves or clothing, will the risks then be reduced so that they are within a range that a rational, informed person could accept? These are questions to which Rose should have found the answers, and she should then have acted on the answers.

If no mask or protective clothing could be effective, then purium chloride is the available alternative to which Rose and BatterBest should switch. BatterBest might object because this would add 13 percent to the battery's cost, and evidently BatterBest's competitors in Developia use the cheaper poisonium chloride washing solution. But there are two replies to that argument:

- If BatterBest is unethically harming its employees — as it clearly seems to be doing — then it has the obligation to stop such harm, regardless of what its competitors do.

- Zack Zeal has arrived because of the bad press BatterBest is getting about its environmental practices in Belostan. This makes it clear that even if BatterBest is operating within Belostanian law, its actions are subject to global public scrutiny — as are the actions of its competitors. Its practices, because unethical, will not prove profitable in the long run when public opinion turns against it.

A second major area of issues in this case is environmental harm and the subsequent harm to the people of Katnaka. Rose cut disposal costs 30 percent by finding a new dump for the poisonium chloride solvent waste at the edge of a wetland outside the new Katnaka Shopping Mall. As a trained industrial engineer she should have known that a wetland, or anywhere near one, is no place to dump toxic waste, and the fact that it is near a mall only increases the likelihood of harm. She evidently gave the issue of environmental harm no thought, and certainly did no studies of the impact of the waste on the area. On this count she and BatterBest can be ethically faulted. Why it suddenly bothers her after her conversation with Ike is not clear. After all, it was her idea and she claimed credit for it.

But, someone might argue, the local government allows such dumping. Pollution is tolerated less in the United States than in many countries because the United States is a rich and industrially advanced country that can afford pollution control. The trade-off for countries like Belostan is very different. Such countries must weigh the harm of pollution at a certain level against the good that the country will gain from industrial development. They will justifiably be willing to accept more harm from pollution than they would if they were richer, and they do so for the short term so they can become richer. When they become richer, they will lower the levels of allowable pollution.

That argument is valid up to a certain point. Different countries can ethically accept different levels of some pollutants. But no country can ethically ignore the harm that toxic wastes do to its population and allow industry to operate without any pollution restraints. From an ethical point of view, governments are supposed to act for the good of the people they govern. Moreover, those exposed to harm are the ones who should have a say in whether they wish to be so exposed, and they are the ones who should reap the benefit. None of this seems to be true in this instance. It is doubtful that the people of Katnaka have agreed to the dumping of poisonous waste in the wetlands. They are the ones who will suffer. More details are needed before one can ethically fault the government for its lax policies, but on the face of it, since the case says that "the Belostanian government looks the other way on pollution," the government bears some responsibility for the harm that will be done.

Nonetheless, the law is not the only constraint on BatterBest's dumping policy, because ethically it is bound by the no-harm and informed consent principles. So one must con-clude that both Rose and BatterBest are ethically at fault in BatterBest's dumping of poisonium chloride wastes into the wetlands.

It remains to examine Rose's interview with Zack Zeal. If Zack is at all professionally competent he should know, just as Ike knew and just as Rose now knows, that BatterBest purposely located in Belostan because of its lax environmental policies, which BatterBest wanted to exploit for its profit. It is not entirely clear what BatterBest's "alleged environmental violations" in Belostan are, since it is not clear what the laws are, and whether the allegations are legal or ethical in nature. Zack is ethically responsible to report what the corporation is doing in Belostan, and the harm it is causing. If he fails to do so, not only does he act unethically by lying and not fulfilling his responsi-bility, but the environmental groups will eventually show, by uncovering the facts, that his report is inaccu-rate. Rose has the obligation to tell him what she knows about the employees and the facility. Since she chose the new dumping site, she bears responsibility for doing so. If she was not aware of the increased environmental harm she was causing when she made the decision, she should change back to the old dumping site, and so inform Zack. She should also investigate that site and consider whether it is also hazardous and what the alternatives are.

Ike seems to have accepted and bought into BatterBest's unethical approach to environmental pollution and employee harm. Rose seems to be following in his footsteps. She should do what she can to change things, and she might eventually have to leave the corporation if it does not change and if she wishes to preserve whatever ethical integrity she has. She should have learned from this experience to ask a lot more questions and be a great deal more conscious about harm to people and the environment than she has been.

Approaches Primarily Used: Duties, Rights, Consequences.

[RCS] This case is a basic example of what one might call an ethical **crisis,** as opposed to an ethical **dilemma.** In an ethical crisis there is no real question about what ought to be done, only a question whether, given the cost, one is willing to do it. An ethical crisis is a conflict between what is right and what is expedient, whereas an ethical dilemma is a conflict between two or more ethical demands. BatterBest finds itself in a series of ethical crises, beginning with the corporation's decision to locate in Belostan because of its low environmental regulation and culminating in the decision whether to use the safe but more expensive purium chloride in place of the hazardous poisonium chloride. Rose finds herself in an ethical crisis as soon as she realizes that poisonium chloride is having serious consequences for the health of BatterBest's hard-working Belostanian employees. Her crisis involves the question of whether to raise the issue in her interview with Zack Zeal because she is in a position to order the change of chemicals.

BatterBest seems to be on insecure ethical ground from the outset. It is as if the corporation moved to Belostan primarily for the loose environmental regulatory climate, obviously knowing that its industrial process produced intolerable levels of toxicity and a direct danger to its own local employees. True, Belostanian employees display other virtues — their hard work, their ambition and their determination. But Rose becomes quite aware that these virtues by themselves would not have attracted BatterBest. Indeed, these virtues might well have been considered valuable primarily in the light of BatterBest's knowing importation of health hazards. Less dedicated and less desperate employees would probably quit rather than continue to expose themselves to such hazards. Belostanians can be depended on to keep on working even when it has become obvious that they are being poisoned by their work.

One might well distinguish between a responsible company moving to a location where regulation is lighter or looser as a way of saving considerably on compliance procedures and bureaucratic red tape, on the one hand, and an irresponsible company moving to a location where they can knowingly poison the work environment and the local community. The first model is that of a company that prefers self-regulation, that remains aware of and concerned about the environmental effects of its operations, and that might well maintain standards far above those locally mandated, equivalent to what they would maintain at home. Thus, choosing a location on the basis of its easy regulations is not, in itself, unethical. But BatterBest clearly fits the second model. It is a company that chooses a poorly or loosely regulated location because it wants to take advantage of that situation to do what is clearly wrong.

There are several familiar arguments that people use to defend this second position, and no doubt BatterBest executives have used them all. Indeed, the heart of this case is the use of rationalization as a cover for obvious wrongdoing, both on a corporate level and on the part of Rose. Rationalization can take a variety of forms, such as the following:

• First and foremost, one confronts the usual "what about the competition?" and "everyone's doing it" arguments. The first is explicit in Rose's consideration regarding the start-up competitors in Developia while the second is implied. Presumably the competitors would have no such edge if they were not using the same cheap poisonous substances and causing similar damage in Developia. But two wrongs do not make a right, and the added cost and threat of unfair competition are just part of the problem in such ethically charged situations. The goal is to find a way to be responsible and profitable, perhaps by marketing one's responsibility along with the product.

- Then there is the usual cost/benefit argument, but where human lives are at stake, especially the lives of one's own employees, cost/benefit analysis bumps up against other key considerations, notably an employee's right to work in a safe and pollution-free workplace, a community's right to be free from harm and a company's obligation to respect both the environment and the people who work in and around the facility.

- Also, there is the usual argument against "strangling" regulation that has its point and is sure to win a sympathetic business audience. But there is a difference between objecting to the burden of regulatory red tape and refusing to acknowledge and respect the objective of regulation, which is to protect people and the environment.

- And, finally, there is the familiar Third World rationalization: "What they want is **development**," and they will have to accept the risks in return. But Ike is fully aware, as he espouses this bit of corporate rationalization, that the leaders who demand development and the people who take the risks are not the same. Of course, the employees demonstrate that they are willing to take the risk because they stay on the job while knowing its terrible costs

to their health. But the ethical question for BatterBest is whether these people ought to be forced to choose between unsafe employment and poverty. The answer is not subject to mere cost/benefit analysis, or to questions about the competition or the price of the product, and one should beware of dubious arguments about what risks others are willing to take.

Rose is keenly aware of these bad arguments, and she rehearses several of them herself. What is most telling, however, is the way she rationalizes her way into an uncomfortable acquiescence, at least until the critical interview. Her first thought, when she learns about the toxicity of poisonium chloride, is whether or not she herself has been poisoned. She quickly figures out that she is safe, but it is worth noting how easily she forgets how horrible it would be to be one of those victims. She also makes it evident that she had been aware of the possibility that the employees were being poisoned, but she quickly found "ways of denying her suspicions." For example, she considered the outrageous view that Belostanians — at least the females — might be anatomically different. Forgetting about the well-known hard-working temperament of the Belostanians, she rationalizes that they could not be "that sick" if they kept on working, quickly shifting to the contradictory view that they

certainly are amazingly responsible if they can work when they are that sick. To her credit she found a way to use 20 percent less poisonium chloride — though to cut costs, not to reduce toxicity. Nevertheless, she also devised a way (also to cut costs) of substantially increasing the population at risk by finding a dumpsite just outside of town. Rose, in other words, is not merely a passive observer of BatterBest's pollution practices, she is an avid promoter of them.

Approaches Primarily Used: Virtue, Duties.

Case 22
What Price Safety?

This case takes place in 1995 in *Nambu,* an Asian nation with a centuries-old philosophical and ethical tradition emphasizing duty and harmony in all human relationships. In 1969 Motorola formed a joint venture (JV) partnership with a Nambunese multinational company to produce microelectronic products at a new facility in the city of *Anzen*, Nambu. Motorola's ownership share was 60 percent; the local partner company's, 40 percent. Many of the Anzen Facility's key managerial personnel were Motorolans, while the lower-level associates were Nambunese citizens and employees of the partner company.

From its very beginning, the Anzen Facility developed a strong tradition of safety consciousness. Even the most casual visitor to the Anzen plant would notice numerous signs and displays, in both Nambunese and English, urging associates to "Think and Act Safely," "Wear Protective Eyeglasses," "Report Dangerous Situations," etc.

Motorola also had other operations in Nambu. In charge of Human Resources for all these operations, including the Anzen joint venture, was Canadian *Stan Stark*, 47. Stan was based at Motorola headquarters, 300 kilometers north of Anzen. Since first assuming his position five years ago, Stan had made safety one of

his top priorities. He took pride in the fact that during this period he had further reduced the Anzen Facility's already-low rate of accidents and lost workdays.

Sharing in this pride was a Motorolan of Dutch nationality, *Henk Van Dyke*, 38. Henk had been at Anzen for three years, assigned by Motorola to serve as the Human Resources manager for the entire JV facility. He enjoyed working in Nambu, but was somewhat handicapped because he did not speak Nambunese. Henk reported to Stan.

One of the operations at the Anzen Facility was "Final Test Assembly," carried out by three eight-person teams on each daily shift. These team members were all Nambunese employees of the partner company.

The employee relations manager for the Anzen Facility was *Willard Wa*. Willard, an employee of the partner company, was born 54 years ago in a small village in northern Nambu, and had been assigned to the JV partnership since its very first day of operation. Willard reported to Henk.

The manufacturing manager for the Final Test Assembly operation was a Nambunese Motorolan named *Victor Min*, 49, whom Motorola had assigned to the JV partnership for this purpose. To all who knew him, Victor personified a deep dedication to traditional Nambunese cultural values of duty and obedience.

One of the most respected of the Final Test Assembly teams was Team Three, nicknamed the *"Morning Glory"* team. Members of this team were intensely proud of their performance in both productivity and safety, which was among the best in the entire facility. Morning Glory team members viewed this performance as the result not only of exceptional skill, but equally important, of an unusual degree of harmony and cooperation within their team.

When Victor took over management of the Final Test Assembly operation in 1994, he made an effort to get acquainted with everyone under his supervision. He soon felt comfortable with all the Morning Glory team members except one, namely *Tommy Tang*, 31. Tommy had been hired by the partner company only two years earlier, after having spent several years as a mountaineering guide. Compared with most Nambunese, Tommy's values leaned a bit more toward freedom and a bit less toward duty. He hated to wear the protective eyeglasses that all Final Test Assembly associates were required to wear on duty. When his teammates would urge him to put on his safety glasses, he would give a variety of reasons why he couldn't.

On several occasions Victor spotted Tommy in the Final Test Assembly Area **without** his protective eyeglasses. Each time he would counsel Tommy on the need to wear them. The last time he shouted, "Tommy, this is the last time I will see you here without your safety glasses. From now on, you will either wear them or else!"

Then, four weeks later, a terrible event occurred. Victor entered the Final Test Assembly Area and noticed Tommy working closely with his Morning Glory teammates. All of them were wearing their protective eyeglasses **except** Tommy. Suddenly Victor lost control of his temper. He jumped at Tommy and slapped him several times on both sides of the head, screaming, "This will teach you!" Tommy doubled over in pain, holding his ears. Then, despite his pain, he apologized over and over to Victor for not having complied with safety regulations. After two or three minutes of apology, Tommy went to see the facility's nurse.

The other seven Morning Glory members stood in shocked silence. Nothing like this had ever happened before at Anzen. None of them reported the incident. Nonetheless, rumors about it, both accurate and otherwise, spread instantly throughout the entire facility.

That night Victor had trouble sleeping. The following morning he went directly to see Tommy in the Final Test Assembly Area. He noted that Tommy was wearing the required eyeglasses. In the presence of several

Morning Glory team members, Victor apologized and presented Tommy with a red envelope inside of which he had placed a substantial amount of his own money. Tommy accepted the envelope and the apology. The two men then shook hands and parted amicably.

Then, a few days later came some shocking news from the facility's doctor: Tommy had suffered permanent partial loss of his hearing as a result of the slaps he received from Victor. As a matter of standard procedure, the doctor reported this finding to both Stan Stark and Henk Van Dyke.

Stan was stunned. He sat silently for a moment. Then he placed a conference call to Henk and Willard, and questioned them about the incident and the doctor's report. Then Stan decided: "Both of you know that no Motorolan is **ever** allowed to physically assault a fellow associate. Could each of you please investigate this incident, and give me your recommendations within 48 hours."

Willard proceeded immediately to conduct the most thorough investigation he could. The first thing he discovered was that neither Tommy nor any of his teammates wanted to discuss the matter at all. They all felt that their team's harmony would be best served by treating the entire matter as if it had never happened. After all, Victor had apologized; Tommy had accepted the apology; and Tommy was now complying with all safety regulations. So, the only really important thing was to get on with the team's heavy workload.

But Willard persisted. Finally he got some solid facts:

- Several Morning Glory members stated categorically that Victor had never before struck a subordinate or threatened to.

- These team members believed that Victor's outburst of temper was unique, and they considered any repetition unlikely. "Victor has learned his lesson," said one, "and from now on he will handle his stress better. We will help him."

- Victor's personnel file revealed nothing to suggest he was prone to losing his temper or "acting out" violently.

- Tommy, despite his impaired hearing, could still function effectively with his Morning Glory teammates.

Two days later Willard phoned Stan with his recommendations. "Frankly," said Willard, "I think the solution is pretty simple. I recommend that the JV partnership cover all of Tommy's medical costs and then quietly, without any ceremony, make a reasonable indemnification payment to him with our apologies. Beyond that,

I recommend that we do nothing — except, of course, to keep monitoring the situation carefully. In my opinion as a former manufacturing associate, this would be the best solution, because it is now clear to me that the Morning Glory team is functioning well, and continuing to accept Victor's leadership."

A few minutes later, Stan got a call from Henk. "Well," said Henk, "I recommend that we terminate Victor right away. Victor is a Motorolan, and knows very well that he is not supposed to strike an associate. That would be a violation of the basic dignity to which every Motorolan is entitled, and to which I believe all JV partnership employees are also entitled. We cannot allow a Motorolan to **enforce** regulations for our associates' safety by **violating** that safety! That just doesn't make any sense at all. And while we are at it, we should pay Tommy's medical bills and terminate him, too."

Next Stan walked down the hall to consult *Cuthbert Kim*, senior counsel in the Motorola Law Department for Nambu. Stan carefully explained the facts of the case and then asked, "Cuthbert, what's the procedure if I decide to terminate Victor and Tommy?"

"Well, I'm afraid there is no such procedure," replied Cuthbert. "While it is true that under Nambunese law striking a subordinate is grounds for termination, it is **also** true that once an apology has been offered and accepted, the law determines that life can and should go on again, and that termination is not legally justified. So, you **can't** terminate him. And you can't terminate Tommy, either. But of course you could **separate** them from the company, provided you could manage to negotiate buy-out agreements that they would accept."

Stan found this hard to believe, but when he checked with an external Nambunese consulting attorney, he received essentially the same answer.

The next day, Stan asked Cuthbert to do some research and find out how much it would cost to buy the two associates out. Soon Cuthbert came back with the answer: "Since Victor still has about 11 years before he is due to retire from Motorola, he could probably bargain hard. My estimate is that the JV partnership would probably have to pay him about five years' worth of salary plus benefits and fringes. For Tommy, it might be three years' worth, because he is a relatively new employee."

"That's a huge amount of money," gasped Stan. "On the other hand, the behavior that both Victor and Tommy have modeled is certainly not the kind of behavior I want at Anzen. I'll think about it and then let you know my decision."

Discussion Questions...

1. How should Victor have dealt with Tommy's continuing infractions and his refusal to wear appropriate safety eyeglasses?

2. Do Motorola's values and ethics require that Victor and Tommy be separated from their employment? What would be your opinion if Tommy had **not** suffered permanent injury at Victor's hands, even if Victor's behavior had otherwise been just as intemperate and violent?

3. Would any action toward Victor, short of separation, be acceptable? Considering Nambunese law and customs, and given the fact that Victor has already done proper penance, should the JV partnership take its own internal action to further punish him?

4. What should be the decision about Tommy, given (a) that he was indeed violating safety rules, and (b) that he was injured by his man-ager on the job? Is there any justifi-cation for separating Tommy now, after the incident, even if there would have been such justification before the incident?

5. What message would be sent to other associates if both Victor and Tommy were left in their jobs? What if they both were "bought out?" What would be the ethical implications of such a buy-out?

6. If the injuries from the beating were considerably less serious for Tommy than the possible injuries that could have been caused by his not wearing safety glasses, does this justify Victor's behavior? Could one say that less harm was done than might have occurred, and that therefore no further action against Victor is justified? How should the JV partnership deal with a man-ager's loss of temper on the job, when the cause is justified and the frustration is understandable?

Commentaries on Case 22

[WJE] Any instance of an ethical problem in business always occurs in the context of a host culture — in this case, Nambunese. Over many centuries this culture has evolved complex patterns of behavior that depend greatly on respecting and encouraging harmonious interpersonal relationships.

Like members of any culture, the Nambunese people behave from day to day in the modes of their culture almost instinctively, with little reflection on, or understanding of, either the origin or the ultimate validity of those modes. Only occasionally does the culture **itself** become an object of concern — as in this case, in which an unusual incident prompts individuals both inside and outside of the culture to reflect upon those modes. The outsiders in this case are non-Nambunese Motorolans Stan and Henk. The case is further complicated by the fact that the interaction between the Nambunese and Motorola Cultures occurs in the context of a joint venture partnership.

Henk appeals directly to Motorola cultural values, which forbid one employee from striking another. The question then arises whether such an action is also prohibited by Nambunese culture. Here, the reaction of Tommy Tang's seven teammates is of special interest. They are aghast at Victor's action because they have never before encountered such a situation at Anzen. But they seem content with the reconciliation between Victor and Tommy, and understand in terms of their own culture the importance of an apology, and of the acceptance of that apology.

Henk believes that the Motorola standard that forbids such violent action as Victor's should also apply to the JV partnership and so finds grounds to recommend terminating both Victor and Tommy — the former because of the assault, and the latter because of the violation of safety standards. But Henk might **also** want to terminate Tommy just so that no trace of the incident is left to taint the Motorola/Anzen situation. Henk might think that consigning the incident to oblivion would be best for all concerned.

Stan is inclined toward being the guardian of Motorola Culture's ethical values in the administration of the JV partnership. He therefore weighs Henk's advice carefully. However, he learns from Motorola Legal Counsel Cuthbert Kim that **after** the accepted apology, the JV partnership cannot legally terminate the two men. If Stan wishes to separate them, he must negotiate buy-out agreements.

Thus we see the primary values being presented by the two cultures. The Motorola Culture, while it stresses harmonious teamwork, is also concerned with safety. This concern covers both the matter of not wearing the protective eyeglasses, and that of the physical injury done to Tommy. For Stan and Henk, this concern for safety might override the concern for harmony.

The Nambunese culture, by contrast, reverses the priorities of the two concerns. Harmony comes first and safety second — so much so that not only Tommy, but his teammates as well, feel that after the apology the team will function as well as or even better than previously, and that a renewed harmony will help guarantee safety.

The JV partnership can be seen as the **melding** of these two cultures within a corporate entity. Willard Wa understands and applies both cultures, and Stan should follow his advice. Even though Victor had already made a payment to Tommy out of his own personal funds, Willard believes that since Victor is the manufacturing manager of the entire Final Test Assembly operation, the JV partnership **also** should apologize to Tommy and provide a financial indemnification. Willard is also concerned with the safety factor, and evidently hopes that a careful monitoring of the situation will ensure that Tommy will wear the protective eyeglasses. Given the importance of apologetic reciprocity in Nambunese culture, Willard sees a repetition of Victor's violent behavior as highly unlikely.

The most important element of a story line approach to an ethical issue is to encourage all members involved, in an integrated manner, to individually play each of their roles to the best of their ability. Therefore, the JV partnership should not focus on **ending** the case, as Henk suggests and Stan ponders, because such a buy-out would probably violate patterns of Nambunese culture, and so provide no effective discouragement of future violations — while also costing the JV partnership too much money. Rather, Stan and Henk should concentrate on providing the kind of **harmony** that will allow the interaction to continue. Such a solution would allow for the continued development, enhanced by diverse points of view, that can often produce ethical advances by keeping everyone involved focused on the future and not on the past. Such an effort would provide the best context for answering questions about possible future safety problems and personal conflicts. The more the JV partnership can operate truly as a melding of both the Motorola and the Nambunese cultures, the greater the likelihood that it will function harmoniously and productively. The more each culture stubbornly tries to go its own way, the less chance there will be for the development of cooperative ethics in the JV partnership operation.

Approach Primarily Used: Traditions and Stories.

[TD] Two factors make what would otherwise be a straightforward, "no-brainer" decision in the United States to terminate Victor Min a far more difficult decision in Nambu.

• First, Nambunese culture embodies starkly different ethical values regarding employee termination and dispute resolution — and a hallmark of a successful corporate ethics program is to respect the values of other cultures. Indeed, in the present case, the Nambunese emphasis on personal restitution, and on the group's willingness to help facilitate a long-term solution, reflect underlying values that members of almost any culture would respect. We all respect individuals who admit their mistakes and attempt to make up for them, and we also respect groups that display forgiveness and facilitate long-term success.

• Second, the company at which Victor's behavior occurred is a joint venture, not a wholly owned Motorola subsidiary. What might be Motorola's sovereign authority in a 100 percent owned subsidiary, is reduced by the 40 percent ownership of the Nambunese partner company.

Nonetheless, difficult as these two factors make the decision, only one right answer appears to exist for the most critical issue: Victor must be separated. To understand why, we must examine a key concept used by ethicists called "moral free space."

"Moral free space" refers to the phenomenon in which two cultures hold different — even directly conflicting — positions concerning a given area of behavior, and yet ethicists find it impossible to declare that one culture's position is morally superior to the other. For example, it appears impossible to show that one country's interpretation of when insider trading is wrong is morally superior to another country's interpretation. Rather, what is important is that **each** country defines the concept of insider trading clearly for participants in **its** markets. Most ethicists take the general position that each country is entitled to exercise its own moral free space — within limits.

But "within limits" is a key phrase. For example, no ethicist could plausibly argue that the practices of child labor slavery (children sold into ongoing, enforced labor by their parents) and enforced child prostitution are morally acceptable — **even** if those practices are generally accepted within a given country's culture or subculture. So the obvious question that arises for a

company such as Motorola is: How to establish the limits on the moral free space of a given host culture?

Two answers to this question are necessary: the first is procedural and the second is substantive. The procedural answer involves:

- an appropriate institutionalized **mechanism** for incorporating different cultural input into the analysis of an ethical issue; and

- appropriate **procedures** to define the limits on moral free space.

Two examples will illustrate how procedures can be instituted:

- In Mexico in 1996, Motorola began developing host-country teams consisting of local managers to help interpret the application of the Motorola Code of Conduct and other Motorola ethical values. In 1997 this initiative, called the Motorola Ethics Renewal Process (MERP), was expanded to a number of other countries, with the hope that eventually Motorolans around the world will be able to make use of host-country as well as centralized interpretations of ethical norms.

- Another example is Texas Instruments, a company that in 1995 won an award for having the best overall ethical program. For years this company has utilized a global committee, consisting of representatives from all major global regions, in interpreting its ethical responsibilities.

In the present case, Stan Stark's first move should be to use such a Nambunese committee to interpret the ethical question of how to handle Victor against the background of Nambunese culture. The committee will know better than he about the significance of the personal gift that Victor gave to Tommy, about how seriously to take Team Three's assertion that the group is functioning smoothly again, etc. The recommendations of this committee should be submitted both to Stan and to an ethics committee at Motorola's headquarters (which usually would choose not to intervene).

Now to the second, **substantive** question: What action should Stan take, after he studies the report of the Nambunese ethics committee? On the basis of the limited facts presented in the case, it is difficult to see how Stan's decision could be anything other than to separate Victor. However, **how** Victor is separated (for example, with what buy-out terms), and **how** Tommy is handled, can be significantly influenced by the ethics committee's recommendations. But to fail to separate Victor would be to abuse the limits of "moral free space," for two reasons:

- Though moral free space is important, business ethicists agree that it should be limited by fundamental **international** values, such as human rights.

- Moral free space must also be limited by the fundamental **ground rules** that a company develops for interpreting ethical issues. Companies should frame these rules in a way that tolerates a certain amount of moral free space — but once framed, they cannot be waived. Indeed, if a corporation finds that it cannot engage in a joint venture without sacrificing its fundamental principles, then it must refuse the joint venture opportunity, or if already in it, drop out.

In the present instance, both a fundamental international human right and a fundamental Motorola ground rule limit the ability of Stan Stark to excuse Victor through the concept of moral free space.

- One of the most widely accepted fundamental international rights is "the right to physical security." By indiscriminately striking Tommy, Victor violated Tommy's right to physical security.

- Furthermore, by striking Tommy, Victor violated a fundamental Motorola ground rule, one that applies to **all** Motorola operations, even those conducted through a joint venture.

In a purely pragmatic sense, the situation is made easier by the fact that Motorola owns the majority of the joint venture and that Victor is a Motorola employee who was assigned to the joint venture. But even without these facts, the ethics of the case strongly suggest separation as the proper solution.

As a precaution against ethnocentrism, we should now ask: Would such a solution be an affront to Nambunese values? Hardly. To illustrate, let us take a "reverse example," as follows:

- A Nambunese company engages with an American company in a joint venture located in the United States.

- The Nambunese company is majority owner.

- The Nambunese company assigns one of its **American** employees to the joint venture.

- This American employee engages in an action that violates a U.S. law and a fundamental international right, which is also a fundamental ground rule of the Nambunese company.

In such an instance, it seems unlikely that Americans would view the termination of the American employee as an affront to U.S. culture. Indeed, they would **expect** the employee to be terminated.

No culture is perfect, and cases are bound to arise where multinational companies must take a stand for some values over others. For example, research into Japanese safety practices has shown that Japanese workers will sometimes lie about a serious injury they suffered on the job, claiming that it happened at home. They do this in an effort to save face for an error they regard as their own fault — even though they know that this will make them ineligible for compensation from the company. It is noteworthy that both American companies operating in Japan, and some Japanese companies, have taken stands **against** this practice. They have argued that the purpose of compensation insurance is not to assign "fault," but to compensate workers who — even though they might have erred personally — undertook risks on behalf of the company, and might now be otherwise unable to support themselves and their families.

Unlike Victor, Tommy should **not** be separated, but compensated. All compensation to Tommy should come from the company, not from Victor, and Tommy should be required to pay back to Victor the money that Victor passed to him in the red envelope. Clearly Tommy erred by failing repeatedly to wear his protective eyeglasses. However, it is true that the joint venture **also** erred by not warning him in a systematic fashion, so that he could have been punished according to a structured, accelerating series of sanctions, which eventually could have culminated in termination if he persistently failed to respond to warnings. Since we do not know how such a systematic warning system would have affected Tommy's behavior, termination would not be justified.

Approaches Primarily Used: Rights, Traditions and Stories.

Case 23
Phony Phones

Capricornia is a nation in the Southern Hemisphere, rich in natural resources. It has a small and very wealthy upper class, a small middle class, and a vast working class, most of whose members live in poverty. Capricornia is industrializing rapidly, but the process has been messy, and the country has more than a bit of a "Wild West" atmosphere.

Corruption has long been institutionalized. This means, among other things, that Capricornian government officials who refuse to go along with their colleagues in corrupt practices often end up being **penalized** in matters of promotion and benefits. This pattern is especially noticeable in Capricornia's Bureau of Customs, with its army of underpaid customs collectors.

Three months ago, however, a historic event occurred. An economist named *Ernesto Prohonesto* was elected President of the Republic on a "clean government" reform platform, promising to abolish corruption. He wears the presidential sash proudly and speaks in reassuring rhetorical phrases. However, careful Prohonesto-watchers note that beneath the rhetoric he is clearly making haste slowly. He knows that too many influential people in the electorate (including many of his supporters) want him to go hard on "the other guy's" corruption — but easy on their own.

When *CelluLux, Inc.* began marketing in Capricornia some years ago, it knew that corruption existed in the Capricornian Bureau of Customs, yet reasoned as follows:

- The corporation could still do business in Capricornia because that kind of corruption would not affect CelluLux or its products.

- There was ample evidence that a rising middle class was finding corruption **impractical** in the modern global business context — quite apart from how they might feel about it ethically. Sooner or later, CelluLux thought, this disgust would find political expression.

And, in the election of Ernesto Prohonesto, it did.

But there was another problem. Capricornia is a proud and nationalistic country, and for some while has pursued what most experts would consider to be an extremist policy of "import substitution." Some years ago, in order to protect its "infant industries" (some of which did not then exist, and even now do not exist), it began exacting import duties of 35 percent on telecommunication products. This is a staggering rate when compared with the 10 percent tariff in nearby *Temperacia*. The Temperacian rate is low enough so that local importers seldom bother to cheat on their tariff payments.

Capricornia's 35 percent rate, by contrast, is nothing less than an open invitation to cheat. President Prohonesto would like gradually to reorient the nation to an "export-friendly" policy, and bring the tariff rate down. However, he must proceed carefully, because:

- Even though the tariff is often evaded, it still produces sizable revenue that Capricornia urgently needs to support development projects in education, health and transportation.

- Prohonesto is currently leading an ambitious national fiscal belt-tightening program, and it would be politically impractical to drastically cut this source of government revenue.

CelluLuxers in Capricornia have for some years been vaguely aware of hanky-panky in the Customs Bureau — but they have avoided all direct involvement. Some of them, frankly, have not **wanted** to know the details of how the system actually works.

Suddenly, the situation changes dramatically. *Jason Litigio*, an accountant in CelluLux/Capricornia's Accounts Payable, has been terminated for improper conduct, and is having great difficulty finding another job. Desperate, Jason is threatening to become a whistle-blower by exposing a number of corrupt practices and implicating CelluLux. He threatens to supply documents regarding two cases to the Anti-Corruption Bureau, which could involve CelluLux in expensive and embarrassing litigation in the Capricornian court system — an institution not known for moving swiftly. The cases are as follows:

- Case 1: *Josue Evadro*. Evadro is a prominent Capricornian businessman who routinely orders large numbers of CelluLux cellular phones from Davenport, Iowa. He specifies that the invoice should be sent to him in Capricornia, but that the **goods** be shipped **not** to Capricornia — but to his "partner" in Miami (where the legal claim of CelluLux ownership ends). In Miami, Josue's "partner" repackages the phones three to a box, with labels reading:

CONTENTS:
ONE CELLULUX CELLULAR TELEPHONE
FRAGILE — HANDLE WITH CARE
PLEASE EXPEDITE

Why, whistle-blower Jason wants to know, has CelluLux never questioned Evadro's strange practice of having CelluLux send the invoice to a Capricornian address, but having the product sent to a U.S. location?

- Case 2: *Jaime Escribaro*. Escribaro uses a different practice. He, too, is billed in Capricornia and receives his consignments in Miami. However, instead of switching contents, he switches evaluations, attaching to each box a phony invoice that shows the value of the phones to be less than a third of the amount he actually paid.

Now the issue is joined. CelluLux/Capricornia must make a decision between fighting and stalling.

- If the decision is to **fight,** CelluLux would go out of its way to identify corrupt behavior, and report the facts (quietly if possible) to the Anti-Corruption Bureau, with the hope of helping reduce such behavior in the future. At the same time, CelluLux would advise customers, such as Evadro and Escribaro, that they must take delivery of their shipments in Capricornia, not Miami.

- If the decision is to **stall,** CelluLux would find a way to persuade Jason to muffle his whistle, and avoid the possibility of endless official hearings and substantial legal costs.

Lights are burning late tonight at CelluLux/Capricornia headquarters, and lots of sweet Capricornian coffee is being consumed, as the leadership debates what to do. They must decide quickly, because Jason has set a deadline of next Thursday — and no one doubts the mischief that this disgruntled ex-CelluLuxer could cause.

The discussion continues for hours. Gradually, transpatriate *Grant Graves* emerges as spokesman for the **"Let's fight"** position. Grant grew up in Cloquet, Minnesota, and has spent his entire career with CelluLux.

Grant is adamant that CelluLux must fight, and gives his reasons:

- It is the ethical thing to do.

- Though we value diversity, let's face it: CelluLux is basically an American corporation. As Americans, we have a duty to carry the mantle of world leadership. Americans value the rule of law. One doesn't support the law by allowing it to be violated.

- The corporation has formally and legally agreed in writing to abide by the laws of Capricornia.

- As a good corporate citizen, CelluLux should encourage the orderly collection of taxes, which provide urgently needed revenue for many development projects.

- People highly respect the name "CelluLux" and expect **more** from us than from others. Therefore we have a special duty to do the ethical thing, and a special need to be **seen** doing it.

- In the future there will be other whistle-blowers, and other Evadros and Escribaros. Sooner or later, shipping packets will be opened, and questions will be asked about why mislabelled shipments bear the CelluLux logo, or why mispriced shipments bear our papers.

- If we set an example, other multinationals will follow. We can foster this process by conferring quietly with our main multinational competitors in Capricornia, and taking the lead in developing a joint stance on corruption in the Bureau of Customs. After all, such collective and concerted action by foreign companies can often be a powerful strategy for bringing about legal and ethical change.

• President Prohonesto rode to power because of genuine public indignation against corruption. This indignation is definitely going to lead to reform sooner or later, so Cellulux should position itself on the leading edge of this wave of change.

Meanwhile, as midnight approaches, Capricornian CelluLuxer *Pedro Compromiso* emerges as an equally passionate spokesman for the **"Let's stall"** position. Pedro grew up in Frontera Province, the "wild west" corner of Capricornia where folks have a saying, "If a law doesn't have legs, why run from it?" Pedro's loyalty to the corporation is intense, partly because it treats him honestly and rewards him on his merits, whereas he believes most Capricornian companies would not.

Nonetheless, Pedro is for stalling, and gives his reasons:

• As a CelluLuxer, I am not proud of this kind of minor corruption, but as a Capricornian I must admit that it is institutionalized in my country. After a glass of rum or two, every one of my Capricornian business friends will admit that he does it, and some of them will even brag about it. That's the way things work here.

• Why risk inadvertently stumbling into a situation where Capricornian authorities might perceive us as guilty of collusion?

• Why tilt the playing field to our competitors' advantage? Some of them we can trust — but the others, never! Don't be naive!

• The 35 percent tariff is an extreme form of nationalism, dating back to an earlier period in which Capricornian policy makers worshiped the idea of import substitution. That policy failed miserably, and people know it. The 35 percent tariff has got to be lowered or it will choke off development in my country. Meanwhile, although I might not approve of these tariff dodgers, I've got to admit that they are succeeding in getting cellular phones into my country at affordable prices, and into the remote areas where telecommunication is urgently needed for development. In a way, those people are not scoundrels at all, but heroes resisting an arbitrary, arrogant government.

• The best thing for CelluLux is to just sit tight and allow others to evade this mistaken policy until enough people see that it doesn't work. Then the Parliament will change the law.

Around 2:00 AM the leadership finally agreed on what to do. . . .

Discussion Questions...

1. Should CelluLux representatives negotiate directly with Jason Litigio? Why or why not? Is talking to Jason the same as giving in to blackmail? Is compromise with an unethical troublemaker itself unethical? Should the corporation consider giving Jason his job back?

2. Now that CelluLux clearly knows about the tax-evasive smuggling that is being committed by two of its customers, Josue Evadro and Jaime Escribaro, should the corporation refuse to deliver phones to them other than at their Capricornia billing address? Should it cease doing any business at all with them?

3. Does CelluLux (or any company) have a responsibility to know what its customers are doing with its products? What is the extent of that responsibility?

4. Would fighting a potential scandal — which would, of course, trigger and broadcast the scandal — be ethically the most proper course for CelluLux, as Grant Graves argues? Would it be the most prudent course of action? What do you think would be the effect of such an action on Capricornian corruption and Capricornian tariff policy?

5. How should CelluLux deal with the present tariff scheme in Capricornia?

Commentaries on Case 23

[RCS] This case raises a number of difficult questions. The specific problem is how an ethical corporation, protective of its good reputation, deals with a scoundrel, for Jason Litigio is certainly nothing less. The more general problem is how CelluLux should deal with corruption in other countries, especially where corruption has been institutionalized. This case is complicated by the fact that the new president of Capricornia has been elected on a "clean government" platform, and gives at least lip service to serious reform. A further question is how CelluLux should deal with an absurd tariff scheme, such as the one in this host country, since breaking the law of the land — even if it is a stupid and self-destructive law — is not an ethical option. In one sense, then, CelluLux must make a straightforward business decision: Is it worth selling cellular phones in Capricornia, given the 35 percent markup in costs? Once it has made that decision, cheating or evading the tariff is not an acceptable option.

What is not clear in this case is the seriousness of Jason's accusations or the extent of the potential damage that he could bring about. It is also not clear that CelluLux is responsible for someone else's repackaging, shipping or reselling of its products, nor is there anything odd about billing an order to one address and shipping it to another. What Josue Evadro and Jaime Escribaro do with their CelluLux phones is not primarily CelluLux's responsibility. CelluLux has only a qualified obligation to know or find out what its customers do with their orders. (If the product concerned were military hardware, the ethical obligations would be urgent.) This case makes it seem as if, prior to Jason's threat, CelluLux had had no knowledge (nor any way of knowing) about the two tariff evaders' activities. Furthermore, it is by no means obvious that these two cases, even if acknowledged by CelluLux, would bring about the expense and embarrassment Jason anticipates. Nor is it clear how "swiftly" the Capricornian Anti-Corruption Bureau would move in such an event — given its obvious potential to raise the issue of tariffs in the most embarrassing way.

The problem with dealing with scoundrels is that it is virtually impossible to stay entirely clean oneself, whether one resists, or fights, or tries to ignore them. In Texas, there is an old saying: "Don't get in a fight with a pig. The pig will enjoy it, and you'll just get filthy." It is by no means clear in this case that "fighting" will be an expression of CelluLux's integrity, nor will it save CelluLux's reputation. More likely, it will damage both. "Stalling," on the other hand, might take many forms. If it is a matter of tolerating and even encouraging corruption, that is out

of the question. If, on the other hand, it is a matter of "making a deal" with Jason, that is, in itself, not unethical. What complicates that option is the fact that it is tantamount to giving in to blackmail. It is not clearly unethical to give in to blackmail (assuming that one did nothing wrong in the first place), but it is obviously undesirable for any number of reasons (including the practical reason that the blackmailer can always repeat and escalate his threat). It is not clear what sort of "stalling" — as opposed to outright litigation — is recommended. Much will turn on this important question of options.

Nor is it entirely clear what Jason wants. A job, one presumes. With CelluLux again? Or with CelluLux's help? That, one might think, is in itself no big deal. At least, it wouldn't be, if it were not presented in the context of blackmail. The circumstances of his dismissal for "improper conduct" are not described. Was Jason himself guilty of a crime? (Frivolous but effective "wrongful dismissal suits" are probably not as common in Capricornia as they are in the United States.) Can Jason be persuaded to drop his threat with a counterthreat, namely, to expose his own lack of credibility and possibly provide potentially damaging evidence against him? Would this be ethical? "Hardball" behavior sometimes invites a hardball response, and so long as any allegation CelluLux would raise against Jason sticks to the facts and (unlike Jason himself) stays within the bounds of fair and decent behavior, that might become an ethical option by default. (It is the very nature of a moral dilemma that whatever one decides to do, it is always less than optimal.)

But countering Jason with a fight or a threat is already giving up too much. The choice between fighting and stalling would seem to be an unimaginative range of alternatives. A third approach would simply be to talk to Jason. See what he wants. Perhaps a "good faith" effort to help him find a job will be all that is necessary to resolve this otherwise extremely unpleasant case — it being understood that such an effort would be based on empathy, and not to be construed as a "reward" or "payoff." Perhaps he can be convinced that his litigious behavior would only be self-destructive in the end (as such things usually are). Get a broader range of options, then see what further action might be necessary.

And as for the tariff and the corruption it causes, CelluLux should help and encourage President Prohonesto in his efforts toward economic and political reform.

Approaches Primarily Used: Duties, Justice and Fairness, Consequences.

[TD] The case of the "Phony Phones" has all the markings of reality. The dilemma it raises, or ones like it, happen every day around the world to tens of thousands of companies. Both managers and academic theorists have been baffled at the phenomenon where host country rules are irrational, where local businesses have learned to avoid the irrational rules, and where external suppliers become unwitting partners in illegality. Furthermore, when the illegality is winked at, and when no one threatens to blow the whistle, the practice usually continues quietly.

What raises the issue to the surface in "Phony Phones" is that the illegality may no longer be winked at (witness Prohonesto's rise to power), and that someone has threatened to blow the whistle (Jason Litigio).

The first lesson of this case is obvious. A deep, nagging difficulty like that of the "phony phones" should be confronted before it heats to the boiling point. When there is more time, and less pressure, the number of options open to the corporation expands dramatically.

It helps next to separate the particular issues in the case. Each has its own logic, and its own set of practical difficulties. There are four key issues, namely:

1. How responsible is CelluLux for the actions of a second party (that is, Evadro and Escribaro)?

2. How active must CelluLux be in discovering misbehavior on the part of other companies?

3. How should CelluLux treat threats by employees to blow the whistle?

4. What course of action should CelluLux take?

The answers to questions 1–3 will determine the proper answer to question 4. The first three questions should be examined in turn:

1. How responsible is CelluLux for the actions of a second party (that is, Evadro and Escribaro)?

This is the question that some business ethicists have referred to as the issue of "secondary agency." The moral standards that apply for secondary agency are lower than for primary agency. One never holds others responsible for the same standards to which one holds oneself as a condition of doing business with them. The dry cleaning shop one uses might or might not live up to one's standards of charity. But while one may seek out an alternate, more charitable, dry cleaner, one is not morally required to do so. This is not only moral common sense, it is also articulated in the principles of global agreements. For example, the Caux Roundtable Principles for conducting international business specify rigorous standards of conduct for a multinational corporation concerning its own behavior, but impose much less responsibility upon that corporation for the behavior of companies with which it does business. (pp. 7–8, *Principles for Business*, 1994, published by the Caux Round Table, 1156 15th St., NW, Suite 910, Washington DC 20005-1704). The Caux principles are transcultural, developed by business people around the world. They are rooted in two basic ethical ideals: *kyosei* and human dignity. The Japanese concept of *kyosei* means living and working together for the common good — enabling cooperation and mutual prosperity to coexist with fair competition. The more Western "human dignity" refers to the intrinsic value of each person (Caux, page 2).

It does not follow, however, that "anything goes" in the area of secondary agency. Two situations usually require one either to break off business relations with a customer or supplier, or to refrain from engaging in business relations in the first place:

A. When the customer is a systematic violator of fundamental rights.

B. When one has reason to know that the customer is systematically breaking legal and/or ethical principles in a way that **requires** one's implicit or explicit cooperation.

"B" seems to apply in the present instance. Even if CelluLux was unaware of these illegal activities previously, Jason's threat to blow the whistle has now brought them to the corporation's attention. Of course, CelluLux should speak to Evadro and Escribaro, as well as using other means to verify the facts of their activity. If the facts prove true, the corporation is obliged to break off doing business with both customers. (As long-term evaders of the rules, however, Evadro and Escribaro might covertly hire third parties to order and handle billing for orders in Miami.)

2. How active must CelluLux be in discovering misbehavior on the part of other companies?

Is it ever acceptable for a company to refrain from investigating a suspected instance of unethical or illegal behavior on the part of another company with which it does business? And is it ever acceptable for a company to refrain from disclosing to officials an instance of lawbreaking it suspects? The answer to these questions is "yes." Companies are not police authorities, nor are they moral guardians of the ethical behavior of other companies. Not only do they have far less responsibility for the ethical and legal behavior of other companies than for their own, they are not equipped or authorized to serve as enforcers of behavior.

It follows from this that until Jason spoke out against the activities of Evadro and Escribaro, CelluLux might have committed no errors. The corporation might have had faint suspicions of untoward practices, but no clear evidence of wrongdoing. Only in a situation where CelluLux has good reason to believe illegal activity is occurring, is it ethically required to seek confirmation or denial. Note that short of a full-scale investigation with authorization to search critical records (authorization that a private company cannot possess), CelluLux might be unable either to confirm or deny illegality on the part of the customer. In this instance, CelluLux might wish to follow the example of many other companies, namely, to ask their large customers — and especially ones they have reason to suspect of illegal activities — to sign a document declaring that the goods they receive from CelluLux are not being illegally smuggled into another country.

3. How should CelluLux treat threats by employees to blow the whistle?

Any company's responsibilities change dramatically when an employee threatens to disclose wrongdoing. CelluLux, following Jason's claims, has potential information that it lacked before, and might have responsibilities to follow up on that information and change customer practices accordingly (see

No. 2 above). Still further, CelluLux should follow the general rule of taking all whistle-blowing attempts seriously, and investigating them carefully.

The present case, however, adds a fact of enormous ethical significance, namely that Jason was terminated for improper conduct, and is effectively blackmailing the corporation with the threat of whistle-blowing. It follows from this that in addition to carefully checking his claims, CelluLux must absolutely refuse to give in to blackmail. Whatever else it does, CelluLux must not reward Jason for his blatantly unethical threat. Had Jason threatened to blow the whistle while still an employee at CelluLux, the situation would be different.

4. What course of action should CelluLux take?

The analysis offered in answering the preceding three questions makes this answer obvious. Prior to Jason's assertions, the ethical situation was markedly different — especially if CelluLux was relatively ignorant of the illegal activities of Evadro and Escribaro. After Jason's assertions, CelluLux must:

- Refuse to compensate Jason in any manner.

- Seek to confirm or deny the charges of illegality on the part of Evadro and Escribaro.

- In the event they are unable to confirm or deny the charges, require Escribaro and Evadro to sign a statement declaring that they are not smuggling CelluLux goods into any country.

- Defend its actions through the judicial process in the event Jason makes good on his threat.

One last question to ask is, "Should CelluLux use the opportunity afforded by Jason Litigio's whistle-blowing to promote reform of business practices in Capricornia?" Unfortunately, we do not have enough facts to answer this question decisively. Such efforts are usually far more successful when carried out in cooperation with other companies, and in instances where a company's own self-interest is not directly at stake. Neither condition is present in this case. Nonetheless, the reform of background institutions in host countries is the only complete solution to questions such as those raised by "Phony Phones." If CelluLux is not part of the solution — either through this opportunity or another — it will be part of the problem.

Approach Primarily Used: Rights.

Case 24
A Tale of Two Cities

This tale involves two very different cities in the state of *Orefornia* in the western part of the United States:

- The city of *Mt. Airworth*. Elevation: 3,500 feet. Population: 12,000. Median cost of a house: $201,000.

- The city of *Downwind*. Elevation: 700 feet. Population: 4,500. Median cost of a house: $59,000. Downwind is located 17 miles southwest of Mt. Airworth.

Our story involves a corporation called *ChipperMax*, a major manufacturer of semiconductors.

Since the 1970s ChipperMax has had a highly profitable facility on the southwestern edge of the city of Mt. Airworth. One factor in the 500-employee facility's success is Mt. Airworth's extremely high quality of life. This enables the corporation to attract and retain highly talented R&D and manufacturing associates. Mt. Airworth offers wonderful outdoor recreation and other amenities. It has remarkably clean air and water. It is "a great place to raise kids."

Downwind is a very different sort of place. The town received its descriptive name from miners who came to the area during the 1876 Gold and Silver Rush. Those early arrivals were impressed by the year-round strong prevailing winds that sweep down from the mountains to the northeast. Downwind is thus literally downwind from Mt. Airworth, and any air pollution generated in Mt. Airworth is bound to affect the quality of life in Downwind.

Downwind is not nearly as upscale a community as Mt. Airworth, but it does have its attractions. For one thing, the town has an abundance of ethnic restaurants, reflecting its mixed immigrant population: Indonesian, Cambodian, Hmong, Vietnamese, Mexican and Salvadorean. ChipperMaxers from Mt. Airworth often drive to Downwind for delicious food. And Downwind restaurants are also wonderfully inexpensive, in part because many of their employees are undocumented immigrants who fear deportation and are hardly likely to complain openly about their low wages.

Since the late '70s ChipperMax/Mt. Airworth has been dependent on a prime supplier in Downwind, the *Achilles Supply Co*. Achilles employs about 400 workers. Many of them are recently arrived immigrants.

Achilles is a strange organization. Profits have zigzagged up and down from year to year. Management has been spotty and a bit unpredictable. From time to time ChipperMax/Mt. Airworth has seriously considered shifting to another supplier. But it has never done so, partly because some of the items that Achilles supplies are so heavy and bulky that it would cost considerably more to source them from farther away. Rather than abandon Achilles, ChipperMax decided to loan their supplier a highly capable technical adviser. He is veteran engineer *Horatio "Ace" Hurlihan*, 54. Ace's assignment was to help Achilles improve its assembly process and product quality, and to explore other ways for ChipperMax to help keep Achilles viable and profitable.

The person responsible for assigning Ace to Achilles is ChipperMax/Mt. Airworth's general manager since three years ago. She is *Blanche Taylor*, 51. Blanche's career is a remarkable success story. She is one of the first minority women ever to be elevated to such a high post in operations. Blanche joined ChipperMax 27 years ago, just after graduating from college, and has been at the Mt. Airworth facility for the past 20. When she first entered ChipperMax, she recognized the corporation as a good employer. Even so, she did not dream that the day would ever come when a minority female would be promoted beyond the lower rungs of middle management. And yet — because she performed well and showed a deep understanding of her business — the impossible has happened. Blanche holds a position of real authority. ChipperMax has provided her with business and financial goals and broad operational guidelines, but otherwise has left her free to shape her budget as she chooses.

The Achilles facility is located in the *Downwind Industrial Progress Park* on the northeastern edge of the city. The park was established by the Downwind Industrial Progress Foundation, a quasi-public organization chartered by the City Council in 1976. The Foundation's purpose is to promote the creation of semiskilled family-wage jobs for Downwind's large population of citizens with limited formal education.

The Progress Park was the brainchild of *Burleigh Braxton Slemp III*, a fourth-generation Downwinder and major player in local politics and real estate. Slemp once told a gathering of notables that "our

Downwind Industrial Progress Park represents the kind of government-private sector cooperation for which Orefornia is justly famous."

Achilles was the first major company to locate in Progress Park. Slemp regarded Achilles as a "magnet" enterprise that would attract other suppliers for ChipperMax — and in fact things did work out that way to some extent.

However, in 1996 there came a shock. Progress Park became the object of a scathing attack by a local environmental organization called the "Bold Research, Education and Truth House" (BREATH). BREATH took the case to court. BREATH told Judge *Maria Martinez* that Progress Park was nothing but a mockery of the ideal of public-private cooperation, designed to make windfall profits for a few landholders and promoters. BREATH spokesperson *Grace Gasper* virtually shouted to the court that it made no sense to locate Progress Park on the northeast side of town. "Your Honor," she said, "the location of this park is senseless and inhumane. Even a child can understand that future generations of Downwinders will be breathing dirty air every day of their lives."

BREATH even offered to purchase some marginal farmland to the **southwest** of Downwind and sell it at cost to the City, for use as an industrial site. "That way," explained Grace, "the wind will carry our industrial air pollution southwest onto Paiute Desert, where practically no one lives."

Burleigh Slemp, speaking for the Downwind Industrial Progress Foundation, roared his opposition. "Your Honor, requiring the relocation of Progress Park like that would be grossly unreasonable and unfair. We created Progress Park for the benefit of the community, well before any of this environmental legislation was ever enacted. The companies that have located there have done so in good faith. If you were to order them to move, most of them would go out of business."

Judge Martinez finally ruled as follows:

• Factories already established in Progress Park, such as Achilles, could remain there and continue operation as long as they did so in an otherwise lawful manner.

• No new polluting factories could be sited there.

Strangely enough, in her early years as a ChipperMaxer at Mt. Airworth, Blanche Taylor chose not to live in that community. Instead, every day she commuted 17 miles each way from a modest bungalow in Downwind. She shared that home with her widowed mother, *Mary Martha Taylor*. That way, the two women could keep their expenses down, and finance several family members through college. Besides, Blanche, being a minority American herself, felt more comfortable in culturally diverse Downwind.

Only after Blanche became general manager at Mt. Airworth did she move there. There were three reasons for her move:

• She could now afford it.

• She wanted to live closer to work and reduce travel time.

• Most importantly, Mary Martha, aged 81, had emphysema and the air pollution in Downwind sometimes made her seriously short-winded.

Ace Hurlihan was not long in submitting his report to Blanche. His central recommendation, to both Achilles and ChipperMax, was that ChipperMax should sell some of its "pollution rights" to Achilles. This would be possible, he explained, under the terms of the U.S. Clean Air Act as amended in 1991, which under some circumstances permits a "clean" company that produces less air pollution than the amount it is allowed, to sell its unused pollution rights to a "dirty" company that produces more pollution than it is allowed — provided that the resulting **total** pollution rate in that airshed would still remain within legally allowed limits. Such pollution rights could be used in Downwind (though not in airsheds already at their limits, such as those of Chicago or Phoenix). The federal and Orefornia authorities are known to be especially inclined to allow sales of pollution rights in cases where it can be demonstrated that the heavily polluting company — in this case Achilles — would probably otherwise go bankrupt or at least need to terminate a significant number of employees.

Ace explained the situation to his boss: "Blanche, this arrangement would be a natural one. You see, Achilles has more capacity than it is allowed to use. If it weren't for those pollution laws, they could put all three of their production lines to work two shifts a day — rather than two lines working only one shift a day. This would increase their daily air pollution by an estimated average of 37 percent. However, with more production and today's favorable market, the profit potential would go up dramatically. That would be good for Achilles of course, but also good for ChipperMax. It would assure us of having a stable and solvent supplier — rather than having to worry about whether Achilles will even be in business a year or two from now. Not only that, but ChipperMax gets the $500,000 per year that Achilles will pay us for the pollution rights. It's a 'win-win' situation — right?"

Blanche thanked Ace for his work and promised a decision within two weeks. Then she considered the issues:

- First of all, we **ourselves** are clean. No one has even hinted that ChipperMax/Mt. Airworth has ever polluted the local airshed.

- The deal would be legal. And profitable. And it would be doing a favor for a loyal supplier. So why shouldn't I go ahead with it?

- It would also be attractive from a cost recovery standpoint. After all, ChipperMax/Mt. Airworth is clean **because** through the years we have spent $3 million to install scrubbers. The pollution rights sale would really be a sort of "amortization" of our investment over six years. And why **shouldn't** we be compensated for being good corporate citizens?

- A $500,000 annual windfall would be great for my profit-and-loss statement. It would free up enough funds to permit me to assign several bright young ChipperMaxers to full-time R&D work on innovations. One of these innovations would be a project to cut down on ChipperMax's water pollution. Our water pollution rate is already low, but I want to reduce it still further.

- But there is one deeply troubling question that just won't go away. Is it really ethical in the first place to pass a law that allows companies to "sell" the right to dirty the air that people breathe? After all, **without** such a law, the air would certainly be cleaner for us all. As far as people's health goes, the optimum amount of air pollution equals the **minimum** amount — especially for older people like Mom, who have really awful respiratory diseases.

- And what about environmental justice? Is it an accident that the people who will be most affected if we sell pollution rights to Achilles will be minority Americans like myself?

- And of course there is the public relations aspect. As soon as BREATH finds out about this — watch out! Grace Gasper will scream for a public hearing, and she is a powerful orator.

Finally, late in the evening of the thirteenth day, Blanche made up her mind.

The following morning she phoned Ace and gave him her decision. . . .

Discussion Questions...

1. What should Blanche's decision be:

• To sell the pollution rights to Achilles, greatly increasing the latter's production but also increasing pollution in Downwind? or

• To refrain from such a sale and try to improve productivity and dependability at Achilles in some other way?

2. How could ChipperMax force the issue with Achilles, both to improve the latter's dependability **and** to cut down on their pollution, but without selling them "pollution rights"?

3. Should a corporation like ChipperMax be rewarded (or expect to be rewarded) for being an environmentally good corporate citizen?

4. Should Progress Park be forced to move to the Southwest edge of Downwind, thus protecting the citizens of that city? Could ChipperMax help in any way to encourage this solution to the problem?

5. Should there be laws that allow the sale of pollution rights from one company to another, or should there be absolute levels of tolerance, adjusted by factory?

Commentaries on Case 24

[TD] Blanche Taylor must decide whether to sell pollution rights from the Mt. Airworth ChipperMax facility to Achilles. She definitely should NOT sell them. In order to understand why not, it will help to examine both:

• The rationale for laws creating a market in pollution rights; and

• The moral rights that are at stake in pollution controversies.

Blanche might at first be tempted to sell ChipperMax's pollution rights, since doing so would be consistent with a legally authorized government program designed to lower overall pollution. In fact, the concept of a market in pollution rights is fundamentally sound. It relies on the greater efficiency that can be gained by distributing pollution control costs. Consider the following (oversimplified) hypothetical example. Plant A and Plant B are located in the same airshed. Each plant pollutes at a rate of 1,000 tons of sulfur dioxide per year, for a total of 2,000 tons annually. Government tests have shown that 2,000 tons of sulfur dioxide per year creates hazardous pollution levels. The government therefore demands that A and B lower their total combined tonnage to 1,000 tons per year or less. Yet, because the production processes at Plant A are different from those at Plant B, Plant A can take advan-

tage of a new, high-technology "air scrubber" that will cost $100 per ton to eliminate sulfur dioxide. Plant B, on the other hand, has a different production process and cannot take advantage of the new technology, so it must acquire an old-fashioned, less efficient air scrubber that will remove sulfur dioxide at a rate of $200 per ton.

Consider the following two options:

• Option 1: The government could force both A and B **each** to lower their annual emissions by 500 tons apiece.

• Option 2: The government could force A and B to lower their emissions so that the **total** emissions of sulfur dioxide for this airshed will be reduced by 1,000 tons — allowing either to purchase pollution rights from the other in order to make this happen.

Under Option 1, the required reduction can only be achieved at a cost to A of $100 X 500 = $50,000; and to B of $200 X 500 = $100,000, for a total cost of $150,000.

Under Option 2, if A sells pollution rights to B at a cost of $150 per ton, and B purchases enough rights to satisfy its pollution requirement, the required **total** reduction is achieved at the following costs:

• Plant A pays $100 X 1,000 tons to eliminate the entire 1,000 tons of pollution that are required to be

eliminated, for a scrubbing cost of $100,000. However, Plant A receives from Plant B $150 X 500 = $75,000. So, Plant A's net cost for compliance with the law is only $100,000−$75,000 = $25,000. Thus, Plant A comes out ahead by $100,000−$25,000 = **$75,000.**

• Plant B complies with the law at a cost of $150 X 500 = $75,000. Thus, Plant B comes out ahead by $150,000−$75,000 = **$75,000.**

• In short, Plant A and Plant B each come out ahead by $75,000, for a joint total saving of $150,000. This saving can be applied to other developmental needs of each company — to the benefit of the stakeholders in each company, and, ultimately, the community.

Clearly Option 2 is superior. It allows both companies to save a substantial amount of money while at the same time resulting in exactly the same reduction of total pollution. Option 2 has the further advantage that it could even be arranged both to save money and to clean up more pollution.

Selling pollution rights makes sense because it takes into account the relative technological efficiencies of various means of eliminating pollution. In situations where society wants total air quality to remain below specified levels, for a given airshed, it makes sense to utilize these relative efficiencies in pollution control.

Notice, however, that the rationale for selling pollution rights rests on the assumption that air pollution disseminates more or less **evenly** into the atmosphere. For example, the pollution that comes from the exhausts of 10,000 cars is more or less evenly distributed over any given city.

Unfortunately, this assumption cannot be made here. The Downwind Industrial Progress Park is located upwind from a residential area, and the more pollution it generates, the more the residents will suffer. Indeed, this direct pollution effect is clearly what Judge Martinez had in mind when she ruled not to allow new polluting factories to be located in Progress Park. There is no justification for pollution credit sales in this case, because residents would not be as well off with a market in pollution credits, as without such a market. Since Achilles' air pollution does not disseminate evenly into the atmosphere, residents of the Downwind airshed would suffer directly if such a market in pollution credits were allowed.

It is, then, an unintended consequence of the existing law that pollution credits sold by ChipperMax to Achilles would adversely affect the citizens of Downwind. Therefore, ChipperMax has a responsibility **not** to take advantage of this law to do something that is unethical, namely, harm Downwinders.

Finally, it must be noted that in the long term, ChipperMax would not benefit from taking advantage of this quirk in the pollution laws. The public outcry could be sufficiently loud that it would cause harm to the morale of ChipperMax's employees, to its public reputation, and to the standard of treatment accorded ChipperMax by the government authorities.

Approach Primarily Used: Rights.

[RCS] This case raises issues that go far beyond the capacities and policies of any one company, and beyond the ability of any one individual to resolve. There are at least three issues:

- Questions about justice — for example, those stemming from the divide between the rich and the poor, the advantaged and the disadvantaged — and about what considerations the one group owes to the other.

- Questions about the role of law in maintaining the delicate balance between the protection of the environment and the promotion of human productivity and prosperity (including profitability).

- Questions about the adequacy and extent of any environmental-industrial policies, to which quick answers, whether "as clean as possible without regard to cost," or "darn the environment, full speed ahead," are simply unacceptable.

Mt. Airworth and Downwind represent pairs of cities that can be found everywhere in the world. Those who live in places like Mt. Airworth are generally those who prosper on the profitability of industry, who run the industry and provide its managerial and executive class. Those who live in places like Downwind generally work for wages, and while they might depend on the profitability of the company as far as their jobs are concerned, they are not directly concerned with profits. The former can afford better housing, a better environment, and the advantages of an upscale lifestyle. The latter get what they can. Almost everywhere in the United States and around the world, there are differences between those who are (more or less) "on top" and those who are not. It is not surprising that this "up-down" metaphor often manifests itself literally, as in this case, in geographical location. But the metaphor extends far beyond the circulation of polluted air. One need not be a critic of capitalism to be concerned about the fairness of such situations, and feel the obligation not to add further disadvantages.

That is the ultimate concern in considering this case. On the surface, it concerns the environment. But, on a deeper level, it raises questions about obligations and justice, as Blanche Taylor reveals in her thoughts about the situation. The plain and simple fact is that those who are most adversely affected by pollution tend to be those who lack the financial or political power to protect themselves. Thus the case also involves not only this particular law (whose merits are clearly debatable) but the nature of law as such. The purpose of law is to provide justice by rendering everyone equal, by eliminating the advantages of the wealthy and the powerful and protecting those who cannot easily protect themselves. It does this by providing guidelines, rules and sanctions.

Of course, everyone knows that laws are imperfect instruments of justice, and that full equality under the law is hard to come by. But this presents a question about the "spirit" versus the "letter" of the law. The spirit of environmental protection laws is to promote as clean an environment as possible while making room for industry, progress and prosperity. The idea behind environmental protection laws is not "protection for the privileged" but "protection for everyone." This alone is good enough reason to question the "right" to sell pollution privileges. Any such arrangement is bound to work to the detriment of those who are least capable of protecting themselves.

The letter of the law, on the other hand, is full of compromises. What bothers Blanche Taylor, as a good ChipperMaxer, is the danger to her corporation's integrity in the face of the compromises allowed by law. What Ace Hurlihan has recommended is perfectly legal, and advantageous to ChipperMax, but it goes against the spirit of ChipperMax's previous environmental measures. This spirit continues to be demonstrated in Blanche's plans to further reduce ChipperMax's water pollution. Blanche feels the tension between the aim of the law, namely to reduce pollution — and the compromises required to make the law workable, namely to reduce the overall amount of pollution by providing an incentive to "clean up their act" for companies that can afford to do so.

One of the most interesting personal aspects of the case is the often unappreciated role of minority progress in improving the sensitivity of companies. Usually, minority hiring and promotion are discussed in the controversial context of "affirmative action," "equal opportunity," and the unfairness of discrimination of any kind to all parties involved. Blanche knows first-hand the disadvantages of those who are without power, and now that she is in a position of power, she is sensitive to the plight of people like her mother, and how they are affected by seemingly distant corporate decisions. One can imagine how the same case might look to a manager who has never left Mt. Airworth for even a brief visit to Downwind, who has never experienced the pollution firsthand. All of the benefits of the sale would be evident, but the costs to others would be hidden. For Blanche Taylor, there are no hidden costs.

On a much larger scale, however, the issue of justice forces one to rethink the point of the law itself. Granted, its purpose is to limit pollution, but is this the most effective and fairest way? From an industrial point of view, the law rewards companies like ChipperMax for minimizing their pollution. For companies like Achilles, that cannot afford to cut pollution, the law allows a loophole, a way around environmental regulation. They can buy the right to pollute. Isn't this a form of corruption? True, it is permitted by law, but there can be laws that encourage corruption, as well as laws against corruption. What is legal is not always what is right. Why should a company be allowed to buy the right to do what everyone agrees is in itself wrong? On the other hand, what other options does a company that produces pollution but is limited in its finances or technology have?

Approaches Primarily Used: Justice and Fairness, Consequences, Ideals.

Chapter Five:
Key Conclusions

In working together to produce this book we have developed seven key conclusions that we believe are worth sharing briefly here:

1. Motorola justly prides itself on its ethical track record. Its lapses have been few and far between. Yet the cases in this volume are based on reality, and they show how such lapses can have embarrassing and occasionally serious consequences for Motorola or similar corporations.

2. There is no reason for Motorolans in the future to have to endure the distress that cases like these have caused their predecessors. By discussing the cases and reading the commentaries, Motorolans can better learn how to keep similar cases from arising — and how to deal with them directly if they do arise. It is preferable to ask questions early, and to take action promptly when confronted with any hint of a compromising situation. We hope this book will reassure all Motorolans that they are encouraged to raise and voice ethical issues and to seek the guidance of others at any appropriate level in the corporation.

3. It is essential that Motorolans appreciate and understand the different cultures in which they operate, but this does not necessarily mean that everything they find in a host culture is ethically acceptable, even if tolerated in that culture.

4. Motorola's Key Beliefs of Constant Respect for People and Uncompromising Integrity are crucial to its success. Throughout this book instances have arisen in which the pursuit of Uncompromising Integrity has clashed, or seemed to clash, with the pursuit of Constant Respect for People. We have therefore made a special effort to help Motorolans to find ways to meet two simultaneous needs:

• The need to effectively communicate these two Key Beliefs to people who have grown up in a wide variety of host cultures around the world.

• The need to harmonize Constant Respect for People with Uncompromising Integrity in the context of particular host cultures and situations.

5. We urge Motorola University, and all other training organizations in the various Motorola businesses, to emphasize the importance of organized group discussions of the cases in this book. Participants in an organized discussion group will usually see and raise a variety of issues and considerations, even in cases that appear simple and straightforward. Moreover, after all the reasons are stated, and all the views expressed, a consensus usually emerges on the major issues. For example, the four ethicists in this volume give a variety of reasons why bribery is wrong. But their reasons are all compatible and all the commentators finally agree in their judgment on that issue — a judgment that coincides with Motorola's own stance on bribery. Ethical standards, such as those contained in Motorola's Code of Conduct or TCS Card, can be defended from many different positions and from positions that come from many different cultures.

6. It is of course essential that Motorola make a profit, stay on the cutting edge of technology and remain a leader in its chosen fields. Yet we would note that not only are being successful and being ethical not incompatible, but that acting ethically is an essential and indeed defining feature of Motorola as a human organization, and one of the key reasons why Motorola is an organization worth working for. Moreover, even though acting ethically in a given situation might reduce profits in the short run, in the long run it is good for profits — while acting unethically in pursuit of a short-term gain

is often extremely costly in the long run. In short, ethical behavior gives competitive advantage to a global business.

7. The existence of this volume is evidence of Motorola's commitment to ethical behavior. That commitment is real, just as Paul Galvin's was real. For Motorola to maintain and further develop its reputation as an ethical corporation as it moves into the third millennium, the corporation and its employees must act ethically, and be so perceived by people in the different host cultures in which it finds itself now or in the future. This is a challenge to which all Motorolans can and must rise.

We wish Motorola every success in meeting that challenge.

Afterword

Glenn A. Gienko

*Executive Vice President and
Motorola Director, Human Resources*

This is a vital book, designed to keep Motorola a great place to work. By facilitating transcultural dialogue about how to make sound and effective ethical decisions in Motorola's growing global environment, it will help validate and strengthen our Key Beliefs in Constant Respect for People and Uncompromising Integrity, upon which our very future depends.

As our corporation nears its seventieth anniversary, we Motorolans can take justified pride in our ethical standards, which have been essential to our business success. However, pride in our past must not lull us into complacency about our future. We cannot simply assume that the future will imitate the past, for never before in human history has the past been as poor a predictor of the future, as it is today. Complacency is indeed our greatest enemy, and alertness our greatest ally.

Years ago, it was much easier to achieve consensus on corporate ethical issues. Motorolans then knew each other better because we were far fewer in number and virtually all of us came from the United States. By relying on well-understood Midwestern American norms of behavior, we were able to steer an ethical course that gained widespread public approval.

Today, ethical issues are vastly more complex. We are now a corporation of global reach. Every year we hire thousands of new Motorolans, from widely divergent cultural backgrounds. Today, a Motorolan might be assigned to work actively, via the new information technology, with another Motorolan located thousands of miles away, and hailing from a very different cultural background. This new kind of global virtual teaming requires trust, and trust must be built on a solid ethical foundation.

Today, our customers, too, are vastly more diverse. New customers come to Motorola every day from every corner of the world. Our challenge is to welcome these customers, and to understand and respect their cultural traditions, without sacrificing our core ethical values. With each new culture Motorola encounters, we must appropriately define and demonstrate the meaning of Constant Respect for People and Uncompromising Integrity.

To achieve our potential in the new global marketplace, we must also attract the most talented employees. We must be a premier employer in all ways, including ethically. When I consider my own career with Motorola, now of more than 20 years, I am certain that our Key Beliefs are what has helped bond me to this extraordinary company. As a parent and member of my community, I am proud to tell people I work for Motorola.

As an officer of the company, I know that ethics are not just a management matter, but **everyone's** responsibility. Difficult ethical challenges occur in all facets of our lives every day, and each of us must rise to meet those challenges. The key to Motorola's future success, and to its ability to contribute to the well-being of the world, lies in an honest and vigorous process of continuing ethical **renewal.** This book has been and will be used as a resource in a new Motorola Ethics Renewal Process (MERP), with which I am associated.

MERP was established in 1995 by the Motorola Management Board. Its purpose is to confront ethical problems openly and systematically in the very spirit found in the cases and commentaries presented in this book. MERP seminars are being conducted worldwide wherever Motorola operates, with participation by managers and employees from corporate and sector headquarters, and from the various host countries. These seminars are intended to create an atmosphere of **trust,** and to promote a full and free sharing of ethical issues, both real and potential. For example, seminar facilitators invite participants to discuss honestly any issues that might keep them awake at night, or that they perceive may make Motorola less competitive. Through such honesty, participants learn from each other and conclude that our strong values are in fact a competitive advantage for Motorola.

In MERP seminars, Motorola's Code of Conduct is presented not as an engraved stone tablet, but as an **expression** of the corporation's Key Beliefs in Constant Respect for People and Uncompromising Integrity. The Code is seen as a document that is subject to reasoned and systematic adaptation to local cultural conditions. Such adaptations must, however, be based on solid cultural understanding, and be made knowingly — as in the example of local gift-giving and -receiving traditions described on page 232 of this book. We must, in short, exercise caution not to be ethnocentric, but also not to unknowingly compromise the essence of our Key Beliefs.

As its name implies, MERP is a process and not a program or an event. With leadership from Motorolans at the highest levels, our goal is to **empower** Motorolans at **all** levels to take responsibility and be accountable for ethics, and to make dialogues about ethics and values as common as discussions about quality, cycle time or customer satisfaction. To be effective, however, those so empowered must be educated. MERP is a prime means for pursuing that educational goal, and this book is one of MERP's tools. I urge all Motorolans to read this book, and all managers to use it in providing day-to-day leadership for effective value-based ethical decision making. By such efforts, we will produce globally valid ethical standards that all Motorolans will be proud to live by.

I also commend this book to our friends (including vendors, partners and competitors) in global technology and business, and to scholars and students everywhere.

Schaumburg, Illinois
January 1998

Recommended Readings in Business Ethics

In this book we have kept our definitions and presentations as concise as possible, and resisted the temptation to go into detail. In fact, though, ethics is a complex field. For those readers who care to further explore business ethics, the following books might prove useful. A number of them are by authors of this volume, so that if their commentaries have sparked the interest of some readers, they can see what those authors have to say elsewhere.

Beauchamp, Tom L. and Norman E. Bowie, Eds.

1997 *Ethical Theory and Business. Fifth edition.* Prentice-Hall, Upper Saddle River, NJ. ISBN 0-13-398520-2. A widely used anthology covering many of the basic issues in business ethics.

De George, Richard T.

1993 *Competing with Integrity in International Business.* Oxford University Press, New York, NY. ISBN 0-19-508226-5. A survey of issues in international business. It focuses on ethical strategies for multinationals wishing to conduct business ethically in less developed countries, in countries with corrupt environments and in countries with economies in transition.

1995 *Business Ethics.* 4th edition. Prentice-Hall, Upper Saddle River, NJ. ISBN 0-02-328020-4. Provides systematic, comprehensive coverage of the field. It explains techniques of moral reasoning, examines the justice of economic systems, and explores the wide variety of business ethics issues from product safety to workers' rights and from downsizing to information technology, both within the U.S. framework and in the international arena.

Donaldson, Thomas

1989 *The Ethics of International Business.* Oxford University Press, New York, NY. ISBN 0-19-505874-7. This book offers broad theoretical frameworks for dealing with dilemmas in global business ethics. Issues that receive special attention in the book include conflicts between home and host country norms, doing business in countries with systematic human rights abuses and hazardous technology abroad.

1995 *Case Studies in Business Ethics,* co-edited with Al Gini. Fourth edition. Prentice-Hall, Upper Saddle River, NJ. ISBN 0-13-382433-0. A collection of case studies set in both domestic and international contexts. The length of the cases varies from less than a page to 20 pages. Topics include employee-employer relations, downsizing, gender discrimination, mixed cultural contexts and the environment.

Ellos, William J.

1990 *Ethical Practice in Clinical Medicine*. Routledge, London and New York. ISBN 0-415-05070-7. Although this is a case-study text on medical ethics, it outlines a detailed approach to virtue and ethical skill that is applicable to problem solving in business matters.

1994 *Narrative Ethics*. Avebury, Aldershot, England and Brookfield, VT. ISBN 1-85628-623-1. This book outlines an ethical approach that emphasizes creativity to construct freshly productive scenarios for advancing beyond case resolution toward growth and development.

Solomon, Robert C.

1992 *Ethics and Excellence: Cooperation and Integrity in Business*. Oxford University Press, New York, NY. ISBN 0-19-506430-5. A vision of business ethics that focuses on personal and corporate character, on the nature of cooperation and the importance of virtues and integrity in business.

1994 *The New World of Business: Ethics and Free Enterprise in the Global 1990s*. Rowman & Littlefield, Lanham, MD. ISBN 0-8226-3030-3. A general account of business life at the end of the century, a consideration of its history, and the images through which we think about business. Special emphasis on business ethics, social responsibility and justice.

Toffler, Barbara Ley

1986 *Tough Choices: Managers Talk Ethics*. John Wiley & Sons, New York, NY. ISBN 0-471-83022-4. Interviews with managers about ethical issues, followed by commentary.

Trevino, Linda and Katherine Nelson

1995 *Managing Business Ethics*. John Wiley & Sons, New York, NY. ISBN 0-471-598-488. An introductory text dealing with ethical dilemmas faced by the individual, the manager and the organization. Includes discussion of philosophical and psychological factors of decision making and corporate culture and brief advice from executives.

Readers might wish to consult the following journals, the first more for the general reader, and the latter two more academic:

- *Business Ethics: The Magazine of Socially Responsible Business* (52 S. 10th St., No. 110, Minneapolis, MN 55403-2001).

- *Business Ethics Quarterly: The Journal of the Society for Business Ethics* (Society for Business Ethics, c/o Prof. Ronald Duska, The American College, 270 S. Bryn Mawr Ave., Bryn Mawr PA 19019).

- *Journal of Business Ethics* (Kluwer Academic Publishers Group, P.O. Box 358, Accord Station, Hingham, MA 02018-0358).

Appendix One: The Motorola Code of Conduct

December, 1997

The most recent version of the Motorola Code of Conduct covers many of the more formally codified aspects of Motorola's ethics, aspects that are often related to or governed by law. To some extent it can be regarded as the formal core of Motorola ethics. However, in the Motorola Culture, like any, there is always a broad distinction between explicit law and implicit custom. Some issues are bound to arise that are not covered by any formal code – or if they are, only partially. Thus, many of the ethical issues raised in the 24 cases in this book are outside the scope of Motorola's Code of Conduct.

This is not to say that the Motorola Code of Conduct is unimportant; on the contrary, it is very important. Moreover, it is a document that, by its very nature, is subject to revision through time. As you read this code, therefore, you might ask yourself whether there are **other** issues – perhaps including some that are raised by the cases in this book – that **also** should be covered in subsequent versions of the Code of Conduct.

This success of Motorola depends on the judgement of each and every Motorolan. Every day, in dealing with the people around us, we make decisions that determine our future. While business conditions change constantly, we adhere to a principle that never changes – uncompromising integrity.

Integrity is the centerpiece of the Motorola Code of Conduct. Ethical behavior requires familiarity with the Code, combined with common sense and respect for people. Taken together, these elements are essential for sound judgement – the ability to know the right thing to do.

I hope you will read this carefully. I think you will find it a practical guide in dealing with the ethical issues we face as a dynamic, growing corporation.

Christopher B. Galvin
Chief Executive Officer

Table of Contents

Policy

Policy

Since its inception, the keystone of Motorola's business success has been integrity with respect to its dealings with customers, suppliers and governments. The highest order of ethical conduct has and continues to be the very foundation of our enterprise. These qualities have been instilled and transmitted throughout the Company.

The following statement of business philosophy and objectives applies to all components of our Company. It is intended to be read and applied as part of and supplementary to our already widely disseminated statements on the subject of business ethics and standards of conduct set forth in our For Which We Stand document.

This Code of Conduct provides firm, uncompromising standards for each of us in our dealings with agents, customers, suppliers, political entities and others. The Code re-emphasizes and provides further guidance regarding policies which have been an integral part of Motorola's business philosophy from the beginning.

Adherence to this Code is the responsibility of each employee of Motorola and a condition of continued employment. It will be administered uniformly throughout the Company and independent of the practices of other companies. Adherence to the Code will continue to be the subject of management attention, periodic audits of our Internal Audit Department and reviews by the Business Ethics Compliance Committee.

The terms "Motorola" and "Company" as used in this Code of Conduct include Motorola, Inc. and all of its affiliated companies.

A. Improper Use of Company Funds & Assets

Section 1. The funds and assets of Motorola shall not be used, directly or indirectly, for illegal payments of any kind.

Example: The payment of a bribe to a public official or the kickback of funds to an employee of a customer would be in direct violation of this section of the Code.

Section 2. The funds and assets of Motorola shall not be used, directly or indirectly, for payments, gifts or gratuities of any kind, whether legal or illegal, which directly inure to the personal benefit of any agent or employee of any entity with which Motorola does business, with the following exception:

1. Unless prohibited by the policy of the customer, Motorola may give as social amenities to customers and employees of non-government customers normal sales promotional items bearing the Company's name or items of insignificant value such as flowers and candy.

Under no circumstances may the payment of a gratuity or fee (or gift of any kind) be made to a government employee whether in recognition of efficient service or otherwise.

Section 3. The funds and assets of Motorola shall not be used, directly or indirectly, for political contributions, whether legal or illegal. The term "political contributions" is used in its broadest sense and includes local, state or national fund-raising dinners, banquets, raffles or any funds or gifts (including the free or discounted use of property or services) which could be routed, directly or indirectly, to a political candidate, party, committee or organization.

Example: The foregoing prohibition of political contributions would be violated if a manager directed any employees to work for a political candidate or party or used company funds to reimburse employees for political contributions made with their private funds.

This section is not intended to limit or otherwise restrict: (1) the personal political activities of

Motorola employees, or (2) the right of Motorola employees to make personal contributions to any Motorola political action committee.

Section 4. Motorola shall not enter into any agreements with dealers, distributors, agents or consultants:

1. which are not in compliance with the applicable laws of the United States and with the laws of any other country that may be involved; or

2. which provide for a commission rate or fee that is not reasonable and commensurate with the functions or services to be rendered.

Example: It would be a violation of this section of the Code to provide a sales agent with a commission on sales of Motorola products which the Motorola employee knows is intended to be used in part as a kickback to employees of the customer. (See the relevant Corporate Financial Practice for further guidance regarding these matters.)

Section 5. The funds and assets of Motorola must be properly and accurately recorded on the books and records of the Company in accordance with generally accepted accounting principles and practices and no false or artificial entries shall be made in the books, records or accounts of the Company. No payment made on behalf of Motorola shall be approved or made with the intention or under-

standing that any part of such payment is to be used for any purpose other than that described by the documents supporting the payment.

Example: It would be a violation of this section of the Code of Conduct to purposefully issue an invoice or other document which inaccurately reflects a transaction.

B. *Customer/Supplier/ Government Relationships*

Section 1. Information disclosed by a customer to a Motorola employee and clearly identified verbally or in writing as sensitive, private or confidential shall be protected from disclosure to unauthorized persons inside and outside the Company to the same extent as Motorola sensitive, private or confidential information is protected, except where such information was already known to Motorola, is available from other sources, or is generally known outside the Motorola or customer organizations.

Example (a): A customer makes Motorola aware of a confidential project for which he is contemplating use of Motorola products. He asks Motorola to hold the discussion in confidence. His request will be honored. The information will not be disclosed within the Company to persons without a reasonable need to know in order to serve the best interests of that customer. Nor will the information be disclosed to any persons outside the Company except where required to comply with a law or regulation.

Example (b): Motorola's price and delivery quotation to a customer will not be disclosed to Motorolans without a need to know and never outside the Company unless the information has been released by the customer or supplier or is required to be released by law or regulation.

Section 2. Employees of Motorola will respect the laws, customs and traditions of each country in which they operate, but will, at the same time, engage in no act or course of conduct which, even if legal, customary and accepted in any such country, could be deemed to be in violation of the accepted business ethics of Motorola or the laws of the United States relating to business ethics.

Section 3. Employees of Motorola shall not accept payments or gifts (other than advertising novelties or other items of nominal value), including any favors which might be regarded as placing the employee under some obligation to a third party dealing or desiring to deal with Motorola, provided, however, in rare circumstances, where the refusal to accept a gift (other than gifts of nominal value referred to above) may be impossible without injuring the legitimate

business interests of Motorola, such gifts may be accepted so long as the gift inures to the benefit of Motorola and will not inure to the benefit of the Motorola employee.

Example (a): Included within the scope of this prohibition is the acceptance by Motorolans of presents from suppliers at Christmas as well as the acceptance by Motorolans of money, property or services (e.g. free trips) from business associates.

Example (b): A Motorolan traveling on Motorola business may accept the courtesy of free lodging in a customer facility so long as properly noted on the Motorolan's travel expense records.

Example (c): Suppliers win Motorola business on the basis of product or service suitability, price, delivery and quality. **There is no other basis.** Attempts to influence procurement decisions by offers of any compensation, commission, kickback, paid vacation, special discount on a product or service, entertainment or any form of gift or gratuity must be firmly rejected by all Motorolans.

Section 4. Motorola may, unless otherwise prohibited, pay the transportation and lodging expenses, incurred by customers, agents or suppliers, prospective or otherwise, in connection with a visit to a Motorola facility or product installation for any reasonable business purpose, including on-site

examination of equipment, the participation in a training session or contract negotiations with Motorola, but (except for ground transportation provided by an accompanying Motorolan) only in such cases where prior to any such visit:

1. the written approval for the payment of such expenses has been obtained from both the office of the division general manager and the general counsel and whenever practicable, the senior management of the traveler has been informed of the payment of such expenses by Motorola, or

2. Motorola is obligated by contract to pay such expenses and the obligation is specifically delineated.

All such expenses must be accounted for in accordance with standard travel procedures. General accounts, such as sales promotion, should not be charged for travel expenses. Payment of such expenses by Motorola may only be made if they are not otherwise prohibited. For example, payment of such expenses by Motorola could be prohibited in a particular situation by applicable law or regulation, by a contract, or by the policy of the customer, agent or supplier.

Section 5. Motorola will not employ any individuals known to be related, by blood, marriage or adoption (except relationships more remote than first cousin), to any person having influence over the purchasing decisions of any private or public entity to which Motorola sells any of its products, unless such employment is first disclosed to and approved in writing by (i) the senior management of such private or public entity; and (ii) the general manager of the Motorola group/division involved.

C. *Conflict of Interest*

Section 1. Secondary Employment

1. A Motorola employee shall not:

- be employed by any other firm or person, including self-employment, if such firm or person is a competitor or supplier of Motorola, or

- be employed by any other firm or person, excluding self-employment, if such firm or person is a customer of Motorola, or

- engage in any activity where the skill and knowledge the employee develops or applies in the employee's Motorola position is transferred or applied to such activity in derogation of the present or prospective business interests of Motorola.

2. A Motorola employee shall not have any relationship with any other business enterprise which might affect the employee's independence of judgment in transactions between Motorola and the other business enterprise or otherwise conflicts with the proper performance of the employee's duties at Motorola.

3. A Motorola employee may not accept any appointment to membership of the Board of Directors, standing committee, or similar body of any outside company, organization, or government agency (other than charitable, educational, fraternal, political, community or religious organizations or similar groups) without first receiving the prior approval of Motorola's Chief Executive Officer, whether or not a possible conflict of interest might result from the acceptance of any such appointment.

Section 2. Personal Financial Interest

1. Supplier-Customer Relationships. A Motorola employee may not have any interest in any supplier or customer of Motorola which interest could in any respect compromise the employee's loyalty to Motorola.

2. Competitor Relationships. A Motorola employee may not have any interest in another enterprise which might appear to adversely affect the employee's judgment regarding the employee's job or loyalty to Motorola. The proper application of criteria concerning the effect of a specific interest on an employee's judgment and loyalty will vary somewhat with the circumstances of each employee,
but generally, the greater the job responsibility of the employee within Motorola, the higher the employee's duties are in these regards. Careful consideration must be given by all employees to investments in enterprises similar to Motorola. For instance, investments in companies primarily engaged in semiconductor manufacturing and major competitors in wireless communications equipment manufacture should be avoided. Other limitations may arise from investments in companies whose business is similar to the Motorola employee's group or sector organization and even more so regarding investments which are similar to the employee's day-to-day responsibilities.

In case of a remote or relatively minor business similarity which does not adversely affect one's judgment or loyalty, an employee may find that there is no conflict in owning interests:

1. in a company, the shares of stock of which are publicly held and traded on a national securities exchange or automated quotation system; and

2. where the amount of stock owned by the employee is (a) less than one one-hundredth of one percent of the class outstanding, and (b) less than 5 percent of the employee's net worth.

3. Interest of Associates. The interest of a Motorola employee's associate in a supplier, customer or competitor of Motorola may create a conflict-of-interest depending upon the facts and circumstances of the particular case.

"Associate" for purposes of this policy statement shall mean:

1. any relative of a Motorola employee, any person living in the employee's household or to whom the employee furnishes support or any person having a personal relationship, similar to the above, with a Motorola employee;

2. any business in which the employee has a financial interest, any creditor or debtor of the Motorola employee, or any other person benefits to whom could reasonably be expected to relieve the Motorola employee of some obligation or obtain for the employee some personal advantage or gain; or

3. any trust or estate administered by such persons or in which they have a financial interest as a beneficiary.

4. Business Involvement with Associates. A Motorola employee may not cause or influence Motorola to do business with any business in which the employee or an associate is interested. If an instance occurs where it is impor-

tantly to Motorola's advantage to enter into such a transaction, the proposed situation shall be submitted in writing to, and receive prior written approval of, Motorola's General Counsel before any commitment is made. Such approval will not be granted unless it can be ascertained that the terms of the transaction are to be determined by competitive bidding or are established by law, or are determined under other conditions which clearly establish an arm's length fairness of terms.

Section 3. Inside Information

1. A Motorola employee may not buy or sell, or recommend to others to buy or sell, any security or other interest in property based on knowledge derived from such person's employment. Employees should avoid transactions in the area of real estate which Motorola may be considering buying or selling or has decided to buy or sell.

2. A Motorola employee may not disclose confidential Motorola information to any person other than in the proper discharge of the employee's Motorola duties.

D. Operating Procedures

Section 1. If at any time a Motorola employee (or a subordinate or an associate of a Motorola employee) has engaged, or is about to engage in any activity covered by the Code of Conduct, the employee should promptly make all facts known to Motorola's Senior Vice President and General Counsel who will:

- Give advice to employees concerning the Code of Conduct;

- Make factual investigations where indicated;

- Determine whether the facts give rise to a violation of the Code of Conduct and advise the Chief Executive Office of each violation, and recommend the remedial action to be taken; and

- Consider exceptions from the Code of Conduct on a case by case basis.

Section 2. Motorola's Senior Vice President and General Counsel will cause the Code of Conduct to be circulated periodically to each officer, director and certain other employees.

Section 3. In all substantive matters relating to the administration of this Code of Conduct, the Senior Vice President and General Counsel shall confer with the Business Ethics Compliance Committee.

Supplemental Guidelines for Government Contracting to the Motorola Code of Conduct

(Amended March 10, 1997)

Purpose and Scope

Motorola recognizes that conducting business with public institutions imposes a special trust, and a corresponding need for special knowledge concerning government requirements. The purpose of these Supplemental Guidelines is to emphasize the ethical and legal standards Motorola employees, agents or representatives ("Motorolans") must maintain in all aspects of conducting business, either directly or indirectly, with the "Government," which includes both (i) state, territorial, and local governments, including public agencies and institutions, and (ii) the United States Government, and universities, foreign governments and other institutions that receive United States Government grants, financing or contracts.

These Supplemental Guidelines contain a statement of our commitment to compliance in public contracting. Examples of ethical standards as they apply to a select number of activities necessary to conduct business with the Government also are included. These Guidelines have the same force and effect as Motorola's Code of Conduct. They apply to all Motorola sectors or groups which market or sell, either directly or indirectly, Motorola products or services to the Government. Thus, these Guidelines refer to both prime contracts and subcontracts as "Government contracts."

Commitment to Compliance

All Motorolans engaged in any aspect of a transaction with the Government shall adhere to all applicable laws, regulations and contract requirements governing the transaction. Each Motorolan involved in such activities shall become knowledgeable of all relevant laws, regulations, or contract requirements.

Guidelines

When applicable, specific attention should be given to the following areas of special concern in Government contracting:

A. Classified Materials

Motorolans must strictly adhere to relevant law, Motorola policy and contract requirements pertaining to the use, dissemination, handling, and control of classified material furnished to Motorola for its use in the performance of U.S. Government contracts. In particular, Motorolans must comply with the Defense Industrial Security Program (and similar civilian agency programs).

All Motorolans having access to or responsibility for classified material are expected to be familiar with appropriate regulations and Motorola policy supplementing relevant security regulations. Any suspected violation of Motorola policy, federal law or regulations, and any loss, compromise or suspected compromise of classified information, shall immediately be reported to the local Motorola Security Officer for appropriate action.

B. Contract Testing, Inspection and Performance Requirements

Contracts are to be entered into and performed in good faith. Motorolans should be aware of and adhere to all contract testing, inspection and performance requirements. Only Motorola products which strictly meet those requirements should be provided to the Government, absent specific prior WRITTEN approval from an authorized Government official allowing Motorola to furnish products deviating from the contractual requirements. Motorolans must neither provide the Government something different than what is required, nor fail to adhere scrupulously to inspection and testing requirements.

C. Billing, Invoicing and Charging Practices

When billing or invoicing Government customers, Motorolans shall adhere strictly to all contract and regulatory requirements governing the preparation and presentation of such bills. Motorolans are prohibited from charging or billing to contracts costs that are not permitted under the applicable contract terms, regulations and cost principles and standards. Both direct and indirect costs which are to be charged to Government contracts must be accurately and consistently recorded in accordance with regulatory guidance as supplemented by Motorola policy. Regardless of contract type, invoices and claims for payment or statements related to such claims must be accurately and honestly made.

Motorolans have the responsibility to know and understand how their time and other charges are to be charged or otherwise accounted for. Intentional or reckless mischarging of costs in connection with Government contracts is strictly prohibited. Careless mischarging is also a serious matter, subject to discipline. Each employee's time must be charged according to the work actually performed, and on no other basis.

D. Contract Certifications

Each Motorolan responsible for the preparation or submission of a proposal, bid, claim or other representation related to a Government contract shall know and strictly comply with all applicable certification requirements. No certification in connection with a Government contract shall be made without making a good faith inquiry as to the underlying facts. Each Motorolan is individually responsible for the accuracy of data supporting each certification affecting Government contracts. This includes not only Motorolans who actually sign certifications but also those who provide information relating to certifications.

Particular attention should be paid to certifications related to the accuracy, currentness, and completeness of cost or pricing data when required by the contract. In such cases, it is Motorola policy to disclose to the Government or prime contractor all data which a reasonable buyer or seller would believe might significantly affect price.

E. Statements, Communications and Representations

Each Motorolan shall take care to ensure that all statements, communications, and representations to Government representatives are accurate and up to date. This includes compilations of existing documents and files that are made available for Government review. Misleading omissions, as well as inaccuracies, must be avoided.

Special care must be taken with representations concerning most favored customer pricing, discount data and other information supporting a Multiple Award Schedule contract or exemptions from requirements to submit cost or pricing data.

F. Gratuities and Kickbacks

As a general rule, no Motorolan should give, offer or promise anything of value to any Government official in a position to influence any Governmental decision with respect to Motorola. If, however, applicable law or regulations permit a particular Government official to receive items of a nominal value, such items may be tendered by an employee with the express prior WRITTEN approval of the employee's department manager or in strict compliance with formal WRITTEN policy of a Group or

Sector; for nonemployees (such as a consultant) the cognizant Motorola manager must provide express prior WRITTEN approval. Under such circumstances tendering of items of nominal value does not constitute a gratuity. No Motorolan, however, may give, offer, or promise anything of value (nominal or otherwise) in an attempt to influence the outcome of any Governmental decision on the behalf of Motorola.

No Motorolan may give, offer, or promise anything of value (e.g., entertainment, meals, or gifts) to any Government contractor or subcontractor or their employees for the purpose of improperly obtaining or receiving favorable treatment in connection with a Government subcontract. Nor shall any Motorolan solicit or accept anything of value from any Government contractor or subcontractor or their employees for such purpose. Additionally, Motorolans must report to their supervisors and to the Law Department all offers or solicitations of this nature.

G. Conflicts of Interest and Procurement Integrity

No prospective employment discussions shall be held with any U.S. Government employee until the Motorolan making contact with the prospective employee has reminded the prospective employee that they must comply with all relevant recusal laws and regulations and provide Motorola with copies of necessary recusal statements and approvals.

In addition, several federal laws and regulations place limitations on the ability of current and former U.S. Government officials to engage in business with the U.S. Government, either as employees or consultants of U.S. Government contractors. Motorolans seeking to hire or retain as a consultant former U.S. Government employees should consult with the Human Resources Department or the Law Department concerning these limitations. All Motorolans formerly employed by the U.S. Government shall be aware of and strictly comply with any restrictions which apply to them. Motorola's Human Resources Department will advise Motorola employees as requested concerning issues related to potential conflicts of interest.

Federal law also restricts the solicitation, disclosure and use of non-public U.S. Government information, including source selection and proprietary data. Motorolans are required to be aware of and comply with all restrictions and other requirements pertaining to such data.

Inquiry and Reporting Procedure

Any Motorolan who has questions regarding these Supplemental Guidelines or who has observed or suspects a violation of them, the Motorola Code of Conduct, or any other law or regulation should immediately contact his or her supervisor, the Law Department, or the Motorola Hotline. You may choose to be anonymous except where indicated. How to contact the Motorola Hotline:

By phone within U.S./Canada: 1-800-5-ETHICS

By phone outside U.S./Canada: +1-602-441-5757

By mail:
Motorola Hotline
P.O. Box 10551
Scottsdale, AZ USA 85271-0551

By E-mail (NOT anonymous): ETHICS

By Internet
(NOT anonymous):
Ethics@mot.com

See Also:

- *A Guidebook for Motorola Leaders*

- Relationships (Intents and Operating Practices)

- Joining Motorola (Intents and Operating Practices)

- Protection of Company Assets and People (Intents and Operating Practices)

Appendix Two: Motorola/Japan Gift-Giving and -Receiving Policy

A. Gift Giving

1. Corporation Funds
Corporation funds shall not be used, directly or indirectly, for illegal payments of any kind, or gifts other than those stipulated in this NML Gift Giving Policy.

2. Individual Funds
Individual funds of NML employees shall not be used, directly or indirectly, for illegal payments or for matters which cause a conflict of interest with NML.

3. Pre-Approvals
A commitment or a payment of a gift which falls within the relevant section of the NML Gift Giving Guidelines [see below] must have prior written approval of the general manager in charge of the relevant function, and the Finance Department.

4. [Extraordinary Situations]
In the event a situation arises where a gift in excess of the Guidelines is required, prior written approval must be obtained from the general manager in charge of the relevant function, the Finance Department, the Law Department, and the President.

B. Prohibited Gifts

1. The funds and assets of NML shall not be used, directly or indirectly, under any circumstances for:

a. An illegal payment. Examples: a bribe to a public official, or a kickback of funds to an employee of a customer.

b. Gifts which are used for the personal benefit of any person who works for a company with whom NML does business, except sales promotional items which bear the company's name or logo, or except as provided in the Guidelines.

c. Political contributions. The term "political contributions" is used in its broadest sense and includes local, regional, or national fund-raising dinners, banquets, raffles, or any funds or gifts (including the free or discounted use of property or services) which could be routed, directly or indirectly, to a political candidate, party, committee, or organization. This is not intended to limit or otherwise restrict (1) the personal political activities of NML employees, or (2) the right of NML employees to make personal contributions to any Motorola political action committee.

d. On-going gift giving.

e. In no event shall Motorolans use corporation funds for gifts to be given as part of an entertainment expense related to gambling or gaming of any sort.

2. Gifts from subordinates should not be accepted by any Motorola employee.

C. NML-Special Exemptions
The following special exemptions to the Motorola Code of Conduct are provided to NML to accord with Japanese custom:

1. Two gift seasons
In lieu of seasonal gifts (*O-seibo* and *O-chugen*) [the two main annual gift seasons], NML will make an appropriate gift to charity on behalf of our customers [rather than to a customer company itself, or one of its agents].

2. Gifts from vendors
Receiving gifts from vendors or business associates is not permitted, unless to refuse or return the gift would disrupt the business relationship, and provided that the gift, if accepted, is used for the benefit of the corporation and not the individual. In principle, all gifts should be returned to the sender with a copy of Form Letter A

[politely informing the giver that the gift is being returned], signed by the recipient. In exceptional cases when the gift must be accepted, the recipient should send a copy of Form Letter B [politely requesting that the giver refrain from such giving in the future].

3. [Gifts of minimal value]

Giving gifts of minimal value, preferably Motorola promotional items, as part of an entertainment expense is normally acceptable on the condition that the entire transaction has been pre-approved by the general manager in charge.

D. Limitation on Gifts to the Government

1. Gifts to government officials may violate Japanese and U.S. laws as well as violating the Motorola Code of Conduct. When a ceremonial gift is required, a preference should be given to Motorola promotional items. All gifts to government officials must be approved in advance by the general manager in charge, and the Law Department.

2. Any gift in any amount given at any time to a governmental official for the express purpose of obtaining favorable treatment is illegal. Any gift so tainted cannot be offered or given under any circumstances by any NML employee, directly or indirectly.

E. Plant/Installation Tours

NML may pay the transportation and lodging expenses incurred by customers or suppliers to a Motorola facility or product installation for any reasonable business purpose.

1. In such a case, written prior approval of the President and the Law Department must be obtained.

2. Also, the senior management of a traveler of a customer or supplier must be informed of the payment of these expenses by NML.

3. NML may also undertake reasonable accompanying entertainment expenses.

F. Code of Conduct Advisory Committee

A Code of Conduct Advisory Committee has been formed in order to assure full compliance with and equitable enforcement of this procedure in light of the special circumstances which apply in Japan. The Committee consists of [several top-level officials of NML]. After consideration by this Committee, issues concerning the Code will be determined according to normal corporate procedure.

The above policy is buttressed by "NML Gift Giving Guidelines" indicating in explicit detail the limits of the cultural adjustments NML is prepared to allow. The following are excerpts from these Guidelines, slightly abridged.

Policy

NML may provide congratulatory and consolatory gifts to business-related parties as appropriate in accordance with these Guidelines.

Since gift giving on such occasions is an expression of our business relationship with the recipient company and not an individual relationship, the gift should be made in the name of NML and should be accomplished in a timely and appropriate manner.

Congratulatory and consolatory events must be reported immediately in writing to the employee's supervisor and the Personnel Department.

Pre-Approvals

A commitment or a payment of a gift which falls within the relevant section of the Guidelines set forth below must have the prior written approval of the general manager in charge of the relevant function, and the Finance Department. Use Form A. In the event a situation arises where a gift in excess of the guideline is required, the prior approval must be obtained from the general manager in charge of the relevant function, the Finance Department, and the Law Department.

Business-Related Parties [Eligible to Receive Gifts]

The business-related parties [covered in these Guidelines] include customers, suppliers, consultants, etc., who provide significant contributions to our business operation and/or have a close and long-standing business relationship with us.

Business-Related Persons [Eligible to Receive Gifts]

The following persons are eligible to receive gifts under these Guidelines:

- a company's Chairman or President.

- a Department Manager who is in charge of NML business.

- a Deputy Department Manager or Section Manager who is in charge of NML business.

- a Supervisor or lower who is in charge of NML business (subject to prior written approvals of the employee's Section Manager and above in this case).

[Value of Gifts]

[In the chart below, the value of the gift is determined either by:

- the value of the transactions per month, in millions of yen, between the company in question, and NML, or

- the length of time that the recipient of the gift has had a close business relationship with NML; or both.]

[The left-hand column of the chart indicates the appropriate recipient of the gift — whether a company or one of its parts, or an individual. The gift values are expressed in thousands of yen. As of this writing, 1,000 yen equals about eleven U.S. dollars. Thus, even the maximum gift of 100,000 yen would be the equivalent of less than US $1,000.]

Category of Recipients	Category A	Category B	Category C
Transactions per month	20 mil yen or more	10–20 mil yen	Less than 10 mil yen
Length of time connected with NML	20 years or more	10–20 years	5–10 years

[Allowable amounts in thousands of Yen]

Wedding

	Category A	Category B	Category C
Chairman/President			
Principal	70–50	50–30	30–10
Child	50–30	30–20	20–10
Other person in charge of NML business	Send a congratulatory telegram in the department manager's name on behalf Provide a gift (e.g. a gift coupon of 10 K yen or less) at discretion of the department manager in charge.		

Longevity

	Category A	Category B	Category C
Chairman/Pres.	70–50	50–30	30–20
Conferment of Rank or Decoration			
Chairman/Pres.	70–50	50–30	30–20
Other directors in charge	50–30	30–20	20–10

Sickness or Injury (Flowers/Fruits) Equivalent to:

	Category A	Category B	Category C
Chairman/Pres.	10–5	5	5
Other directors in charge	5	3	3
Accident or Casualty			
Company facility	100–50	70–30	30–10

New Office/Plant Construction	Category A	Category B	Category C
Company facility	70–50	50–30	30–20
Opening Ceremony			
Sales Office/Branch	70–50	50–30	30–20

Foundation Anniversary (10 years or more)	Category A	Category B	Category C
Reception	70–50	50–30	30–10
New Chairman/President			
Chairman\Pres.	50–30	30–10	10

Retirement Relocation (Memorial Gifts or Cash)	Category A	Category B	Category C
Chairman/Pres.	20–10	20–10	10
Officer or Dept Mgr in charge	10	10	5

Condolence

	Category A	Category B	Category C
Chairman/Pres.			
Principal	100–70	70–50	50–30
Spouse/Child/Parent	70–30	50–30	30–10
Dept Mgr and above in charge of NML business			
Principal	50–30	30–20	20–10
Spouse/Child/Parent	30–20	20–10	10
Deputy Dept Mgr or Section Mgr in charge of NML business			
Principal	30–20	20–10	10
Spouse/Child	10	10	10
Parent	10	—	—
Other person in charge of NML business			
Principal	20–10	20–10	10
Spouse/Child	10	10	10
Parent	10	—	—

Appendix Three:
Preliminary Case Guide for Facilitators

This appendix provides a Preliminary Guide to the 24 cases in this book, to help the facilitator or instructor **tentatively** identify the cases that would or would not be most appropriate to meet the educational and organizational needs of a particular learning audi-ence. We have kept the Guide as brief as possible. In reading the chart below, please keep in mind that the "Summary" of a case does not do justice to its complexity or nuances. Similarly, the listing of a case's "Major Topics" does not do justice to the number of sub-topics that are covered — in the case itself, and especially in the commentaries that follow it. We urge you to **read** all the cases in the book as general preparation, and then to carefully **study** the cases that you assign to a particular learning group.

Case	Title	Setting	Summary	Major Topics
1	"Uncompromising Integrity" and Egregian Justice	Non-Western Nation.	Employee steals Company property of minor value and manager reports employee to police, who then execute employee summarily.	Differing cultural and legal standards regarding fair punishment for a crime. Respect for individual dignity.
2	The Phantom Air Ticket	Eastern Europe.	Employee purchases two coach air tickets at same price as one (allowed) business ticket so wife can accompany him on business trip. HR Manager approves.	Falsification of documents. Employee's life balance.
3	"Nurturing" A Deal	Developing Nation.	Long-time customer's Purchasing VP strongly hints that Company could sub-stantially increase business — and beat out competitors — if it provided "gifts" of about 8% of sale price.	Differing cultural standards regarding gifts, bribery, kickbacks. U.S. Foreign Corrupt Practices Act.
4	Profits and People	United States.	Manager of Company Task Force con-cludes that positions of three Task Force members should be eliminated, and that a U.S. plant should be closed and moved overseas.	Right-sizing that shifts production out of country. Fairness. Respect for individual dignity. Employee loyalty.

Case	Title	Setting	Summary	Major Topics
5	Friendship or Mutual Bribery?	Western Europe.	Business relationship between fellow employees becomes close personal relationship between families. Favors provided or implied might stretch ethical boundaries.	Gifts. Entertainment. Conflict of interest.
6	Constant Respect for — Human Rights?	Asia.	Host country is governed by authoritarian military junta which purchases large amounts of Company telecomm products to monitor and tyrannize its people.	Human rights. Relations with repressive governments. Social responsibility.
7	When Is Information "Proprietary"?	Western Industrial Nation.	Company researcher with adjunct professorship at local university accidentally discovers proprietary information of competitor in university computer lab, copies information, and shares it within Company.	Proprietary information. University relations. Research issues.
8	"Hardship" and the Eye of the Beholder	United States and Developing Nation.	Manager and family from developing nation have difficulty adjusting to life without servants in the United States; want Company to pay for servants.	Differing cultural standards regarding total compensation, especially fringe benefits related to long-established lifestyles.
9	Personal Luxury or Family Loyalty?	Developing Nation.	Manager newly assigned to his poor homeland submits inflated receipts for housing (up to maximum Company will pay) so he can subsidize education of his very poor siblings.	Falsification of documents. Company housing policy. Respect for individual dignity.
10	Performance Bonuses: How to Allocate?	Asia.	Manager implements new performance bonus — paying an equal dollar amount to each employee regardless of seniority — based on performance of business unit.	Differing cultural standards regarding fairness in compensation. Group versus individual rewards.
11	The Golf Clubs That Would Not Disappear	Asia.	Transpatriate manager is loaned expensive set of golf clubs by local distributor for Company — for two years.	Gifts. Bribery. Differing cultural standards regarding gifts as rapport enhancers versus ethical infractions.

Case	Title	Setting	Summary	Major Topics
12	Are Training Budgets Geographically Equitable?	Latin America.	Poor training is a factor in industrial accident. Transpatriate manager investigates and discovers that Company provides employees with a less adequate training budget for professional development in this host country, than in industrial host countries.	Access to training, and allocation of training budget, for professional development. Fair treatment regardless of host country.
13	Rupert's "Royal" Gift	United States, Asia.	Intellectual Property Manager buys counterfeit watches overseas, gives them as gifts to fellow employees without disclosing that they are fake.	Gifts. Intellectual property and patent infringement. Deception. Personal character.
14	Facing Face	Asia.	Manager suggests helping terminated employee save face by hinting that he might be rehired in future.	Performance reviews. Maintaining "face." Respect for individual dignity. Deception.
15	Just When Is a "Tip" **Only** "To Insure Promptness"?	Nation of Former Soviet Union.	Employee gives "tip" to guard at embassy to expedite visa process.	Tips. Bribery. U.S. Foreign Corrupt Practices Act. Acting ethically even when not legally required.
16	Paying "Respect for People" in a Red Envelope	Asia.	After a fire, host country employees collect money for local fire brigade, partly in fear that brigade would otherwise destroy production line.	Cultural differences regarding the rewarding of people who perform public services. Tips. Bribery. Extortion.
17	Is Motorola Its Agent's Ethical Keeper?	Non-Western Nation.	Freight-forwarding fees escalate dramatically, prompting investigation by new transpatriate manager. Story in international newspaper names Company's freight agent as guilty of bribery, and Company as ignorant or worse.	U.S. Foreign Corrupt Practices Act. Bribery. Extent to which Company is responsible for ethics of its agent.
18	Operation Reap	Africa.	Plan to sell Company land at attractive price as site for new hospital is complicated by learning that previous owner polluted the site.	Environmental responsibility. Government relations. Acting ethically even when not legally required.

Case	Title	Setting	Summary	Major Topics
19	The "Rights of the Monarch"	Latin America.	Male senior manager had affairs with local female employees; terminated one who did not go along. Investigation reveals few employees willing to discuss, and probably similar patterns in the United States.	Differing cultural standards regarding gender equity. Sexual harassment. Respect for individual dignity. Personal loyalty.
20	Gender Equity and the Eye of the Beholder	Asia.	Husband and wife both work in same Company facility. Wife recently received more money, recognition and opportunity than husband. Uncomfortable, she requests transfer to lower-paying position in different department.	Fairness in compensation. Gender equity. Maintaining "face." Respect for individual dignity.
21	Purple Toenails	Nation of Former Soviet Union.	Toxic chemical in manufacturing process harming many female employees, and toxic waste threatening local populace.	Differing cultural and legal standards regarding workplace safety. Gender equity. Environmental responsibility.
22	What Price Safety?	Asia.	Supervisor strikes and seriously injures employee who repeatedly ignores safety rules and warnings.	Differing cultural and legal standards regarding safety, workplace violence, team harmony, and employer's right to terminate an employee.
23	Phony Phones	Latin America.	Ex-employee threatens to publicly disclose that certain large customers are illegally avoiding tariffs into this traditionally corrupt, but fast-changing host country.	Extent to which Company is responsible for ethics of its customer. Falsifying documents. Whistleblowers. Extortion. Government relations.
24	A Tale of Two Cities	United States	Company has opportunity to sell its pollution rights for substantial sum to nearby supplier, but the probable result would be dirtier air for thousands of poor residents.	Environmental responsibility. Supplier relations. Community relations. Social equity.

About the Authors

RS Moorthy is Director of Research and Strategic Capabilities, Global Leadership and Organizational Development, at Motorola, where he addresses strategic global business issues in the areas of business ethics, corporate social responsibilities, socio-economic systems, technology and culture, global leadership development, global diversity, knowledge management and organizational change processes. He contributes to organization consulting intervention, research-based applied knowledge and educational resources for the corporation, and manages the Motorola Ethics Renewal Process (MERP) initiative, which is now being successfully implemented worldwide. Moorthy has been a Motorolan for 21 years, the first 10 of which he spent in manufacturing operations at Motorola/Penang in his native Malaysia, and at Plantation, Florida. He then became Training Manager at Motorola/Penang, where he worked with the University of Malaya in establishing off-campus graduate degree engineering programs, and co-founded the Penang Skills Development Center — both firsts in Malaysia. In recognition of these contributions, the Governor of Penang conferred upon Moorthy the title of *Pingat Jaya Masyarakat*. In 1989 Moorthy joined Motorola University, and in 1991 founded its Center for Culture and Technology, with the mission of promoting transcultural competence among Motorolans worldwide, offering programs of education, training, research, consultation, future visioning and publications. Moorthy has published a number of articles in professional journals, and is senior coauthor of *Visions of the Iridium Era* (Motorola University Press, Fall 1998).

Richard T. De George is Director of the International Center for Ethics in Business, and University Distinguished Professor of Philosophy, Business Administration, and Russian and East European Studies at the University of Kansas. He studied for a year in Paris and a year in Belgium and received his Ph.D. from Yale University. He then spent a year doing postdoctoral work in Switzerland and the Soviet Union. Professor De George has been a research fellow at Yale University, Columbia University, Stanford University and the Hoover Institution. He is the author of more than 150 articles, and the author or editor of 17 books, including *Ethics, Free Enterprise, and Public Policy* (Oxford University Press 1978); *Business Ethics* (Prentice-Hall), now in its fourth edition (1995), and also available in

Japanese; and *Competing with Integrity in International Business* (Oxford University Press 1993). He has served as a consultant on business ethics for a number of companies, and has been the president of several academic organizations, including the American Philosophical Association, the Society of Business Ethics and the International Society of Business, Economics and Ethics. He was recently featured in *Business Ethics: A European Review.* Professor De George has lectured or consulted in 26 countries on five continents; he was one of three Americans to negotiate a U.S.-U.S.S.R. official exchange; and in 1996, with Bill Gates and Nelson Mandela, received an honorary doctorate from the Netherlands Business School for his pioneering work in business ethics.

Thomas Donaldson is the Mark O. Winkelman Professor of Business Ethics at the Wharton School of the University of Pennsylvania, Philadelphia, where he teaches and writes in his specialty, international business ethics. From 1990 to 1996 he was the John F. Connelly Professor of Business Ethics in the School of Business, Georgetown University, Washington, D.C. There he was voted Distinguished Teacher of the Year by MBA students and Distinguished Researcher of the Year by business school faculty members. He has authored or edited many books, including *Ethics in International Business* (Oxford University Press 1989) and *Corporations and Morality* (Prentice-Hall 1982). The latter book has been translated into Korean and is being translated into Japanese. His article on managing international business ethics,

"Values in Tension: Ethics Away from Home" was published in the *Harvard Business Review* (September-October 1996). Professor Donaldson serves on the International Committee at the Wharton School, and is a member of the editorial board for *Jing Ji Lun Li Jan Jiu Cong Shu* (Ethical Economy: Studies in the Ethics, Culture, and Philosophy of the Economy), a Chinese-language book series. He has also written on issues of ethics and international politics, and is a board member of the Carnegie Council on Ethics and International Affairs. He has lectured and consulted to many domestic and foreign multinational corporations, including AT&T, IBM, Bankers Trust, Walt Disney and the Western Mining Company of Australia as well as The World Bank.

William J. Ellos, S.J., until recently held the Charles Miller Professorship, teaching professional ethics at Saint Mary's University in San Antonio, Texas. He has also taught at Marquette University, St. Louis University, the Gregorian University in Rome, Gonzaga University, and Loyola University in Chicago, and lectured at the Catholic University of Nijmegen, the Instituto Scientifico Ospedale San Raffaele in Milan, Beijing University, Beijing Normal University, and the University of Chicago. Prof. Ellos is a fellow of the MacLean Center for Clinical Medical Ethics at the University of Chicago, and an associate of Saint Edmund's College in the University of Cambridge. He is author of two books and numerous articles on ethical practice. During 1997 he was involved in programs of lecturing, consultation and fac-

ulty development in professional ethics, which included five weeks of faculty development work at the Bowater School of Management and Marketing at Deakin University in Melbourne. Currently he is co-developing a course in corporate business ethics for the University of Zurich, and is collaborating in development work with the Center for Economics and Business in Prague and the Chamber of Commerce and Industry of the Russian Federation in Moscow. His 1998 plans call for teaching in the Institute of Management and Labour Studies in Jamshedpur, and working with the business school of Reitaku University in Tokyo, the Chinese Academy of Social Sciences in Beijing, and the Ateneo de Manila. Professor Ellos works in seven languages.

Robert C. Solomon is currently Quincy Lee Centennial Professor of Philosophy and Management at the University of Texas at Austin. He is the author or editor of nearly 30 books, among them *Above the Bottom Line* (Harcourt Brace Jovanovich 1981, 2nd ed., 1993); *It's Good Business* (Atheneum 1985); and *Ethics and Excellence* (Oxford University Press 1992). His latest book, *New World of Business: Ethics and Free Enterprise in the Global Nineties,* (Rowman and Littlefield 1994), was named "one of the best books of the year" by *Choice* magazine. Professor Solomon is also the author of *The Passions* (Doubleday 1976) and *About Love* (Simon and Schuster 1988), as well as numerous books on European philosophy. He and his wife, Kathleen M. Higgins, have written *A Short History of Philosophy* (Oxford 1996), which includes extensive chapters on non-Western thought and religion. They have also edited two books on world philosophy, including chapters on Japanese, Chinese, Arabic, Persian, Latin American and African philosophy. Professor Solomon has done ethics programs for Chemical Bank in New York, AT&T, IBM, Conoco Oil, Southwestern Bell and other Fortune 500 companies, as well as programs in Europe, East Asia, Australia, New Zealand and Latin America. He has taught at Princeton, UCLA and Harvard, and has been visiting professor at several overseas universities, including nine years at the University of Auckland. Professor Solomon is working with the former Finance Minister of Chile on an extensive consulting and writing project in Mexico, on the subject of trust in business.

Robert B. Textor is Professor of Anthropology, Emeritus, at Stanford University, and Courtesy Professor of International Studies at the University of Oregon. At Stanford he was also Professor of Education, and this led to his service as President of the Council on Anthropology and Education, the largest organization of its kind in the world. He also taught for several years in Stanford's Science Technology and Society Program. Professor Textor has studied four Asian languages and done fieldwork for nine years in Asia, at both urban and village levels. He has also worked for two years in Europe. His research interests include development, education, high technology, values, religion, sustainability and the preservation of cultural identity. For the past 20 years he has approached these areas partly from a "futures visioning" perspective, and has taken

leadership in developing rigorous methodologies for doing so. Among his numerous books are *The Middle Path for the Future of Thailand: Technology in Harmony with Culture and Environment* (as methodological and editorial collaborator with Dr. Sippanondha Ketudat), in Thai and English (East-West Center Press 1990); and *Austria 2005: Projected Sociocultural Effects of the Microelectronic Revolution* (with others) in German and English (Vienna, Verlag Orac 1984). For the past seven years Professor Textor has been a consultant to Motorola, working primarily in transcultural competence education, technology and development, telecommunications and culture change, and strategic visioning/forecasting.